Bill Campbell
The Voice of
Philadelphia Sports

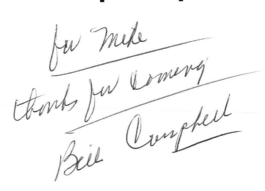

For Mike

thanks for coming

Bill Campbell

Mike:
I hope you enjoy
the inspiration!

Sam Carchidi

Also by Sam Carchidi
Miracle in the Making: The Adam Taliaferro Story

"This isn't meant as a putdown to anybody in today's market, but there's only one Bill Campbell. Maybe because I grew up in the radio age and he left such an impression. I can still hear him now, 'Van Brocklin, looking, looking, LOOKING....' He put the game in your mind with a vivid description. Nobody compares to him."

— Harry Donahue, KYW sportscaster

"Bill was great doing the Phillies and 76ers, but I've never heard a broadcast as exciting as the Eagles' championship in 1960. His calls have stayed with me forever."

— Rich Wescott, baseball author

"When I was a kid, I thought of Bill Campbell as The Voice of Philadelphia Sports — probably because he was. So the fact that I later became a regular guest on his radio show was one of the great thrills of my whole career. Talking baseball with Bill Campbell? I should have paid HIM to do that."

— Jayson Stark, ESPN

"Soupy always spoke the truth. If something controversial happened, he never avoided it."

— Tom Brookshier, former Eagle and ex-broadcaster

"Some of my most pleasant memories of covering the Phillies revolve around Bill Campbell singing at the Beachcomber Restaurant in Clearwater Beach."

— Stan Hochman, Philadelphia Daily News columnist

"For almost three quarters of a century, Bill Campbell's familiar resonant, measured voice has come into our homes, as welcome as a visit from a favorite uncle. If it was a momentous sports event involving a Philadelphia team, chances are he was the one broadcasting it. Generations have grown up listening to Bill and have come to put their trust in him — a higher compliment a journalist cannot hope for."
— Bill Lyon, former Philadelphia Inquirer columnist

"He didn't hold a vendetta against me at all…for what had happened; he was always so nice to me over the years and I'll never forget that."
— Phillies broadcaster Harry Kalas

"He's meticulous in his preparation; he's the ultimate professional — with a great voice.'
— Jack Scheuer, Associated Press sportswriter

"In my youth, Bill Campbell brought me vision in the dark, through a transitor radio that lay under my pillow long after bedtime. That vision soon morphed into lesson, both about the games and life. When I think of Bill Campbell now, I think of fairness and eloquence and a professional bar that few broadcasters will ever reach."
— Anthony Gargano, WIP talk-show host.

Bill Campbell

The Voice of
Philadelphia Sports

By Sam Carchidi
Foreward by Ray Didinger

Middle Atlantic Press
Moorestown, NJ

To "Jersey Jo" — as The Dutchman called her —
with all my love and gratitude.

— Bill Campbell

To JoAnn, Sara and Sammy — you make my life beautiful.
Also, to my dad. I once promised that you would be a part of
my next book's dedication. You may not be here now,
but I feel your inspiration every day.

— Sam Carchidi

TABLE OF CONTENTS

Wherever you walked — through the rowhouse streets of South Philadelphia, past the apartment buildings in Center City, on the beaches at the Jersey Shore — Bill Campbell walked with you. His voice was everywhere. It was the warm, comforting thread that connected the seasons.

Basketball in the winter, baseball in the spring and summer, football in the fall. Bill talked us through all of it. Game by game, month by month, generation after generation. It didn't matter if it was Norm Van Brocklin fading back, Jim Bunning winding up, or Wilt Chamberlain driving for the basket, we were gathered around the radio, waiting for Bill to tell us what happened. With his words, he painted every picture and captured every emotion.

I remember sitting with my father at the kitchen table, listening to Bill call an Eagles exhibition game. It was a sultry August night, but when Timmy Brown fielded a punt and Bill's voice began to rise — "He breaks a tackle, he's in the clear" — my arms were covered with goosebumps. I knew it was just an exhibition game, no big deal, but Bill's voice crackling over our radio — "he's at the 30, the 20, they won't catch him" — told me otherwise.

Bill was more than a play-by-play announcer; he was a story-teller who set the scene and brought it to life. When he described a Richie Allen home run, you could see it. It didn't matter if you were sitting on your front steps, riding in your car, or walking down the boardwalk with a transistor radio pressed to your ear, you felt like you were in a box seat at 21st and Lehigh, watching the ball as it disappeared into the North Philadelphia night.

When the Phillies were on the West Coast, I would slip my Philco radio under the pillow and listen to the game. Somewhere around the third or fourth inning, I would usually doze off only to be jolted awake by the sound of Bill's voice: "Long drive, deep right field. It could be...it IS... home run, Johnny Callison." Then I'd fall asleep again, this time with a smile on my face.

There was an intimacy to those broadcasts that does not exist today. With the 24-hour sports networks, there are so many games and so many voices, they all run together. With almost every game now on television, the old-fashioned radio call, with its rich detail and graceful imagery, has become a lost art. When Bill described a double play turned on a warm summer evening, it was like poetry. He did not have any gimmicks or catch phrases. He didn't need them. He had his voice and his words and that was enough.

He had a way of calling a game that made you feel like he was talking directly to you. Maybe it was his Philadelphia roots and the ease with which he drew upon that history, dropping in references to Connie Mack, Joe Fulks, and Bert Bell. Maybe it was the homeboy passion he brought to his broadcasts. He may have been in the press box, but his heart was in the bleachers with the rest of us. At least that was how it sounded.

When Chuck Bednarik tackled Jim Taylor to win the 1960 NFL championship, Bill's words — "the Eagles are the world champions" — felt like our words. And four years later, when the Phillies blew the pennant, Bill kept the painful vigil with us. It is impossible to imagine him calling games in another town. His talent could have taken him anywhere, but it would not have been the same, working in New York, Chicago, or St. Louis. He is Philadelphia. He wouldn't have it any other way and neither would we.

Merrill Reese, now in his 30th consecutive season as the voice of the Eagles, grew up idolizing Bill Campbell. He brought a radio to the games at Franklin Field so he could listen to Bill's broadcasts as he watched the action unfold. When you hear Merrill call a game today, many of his trademarks — setting the formation on every play, providing a vivid picture for the listener — are things he learned from the man they call "The Dean."

Bill's gift for the language was evident in his writing. Several Philadelphia sports columnists contributed stories to the 1960 championship game program, but the best piece in the magazine was Bill's profile of Eagles general manager Vince McNally, who was known as the Gray Ghost. Here is a sample:

"Vince and I have spent a great deal of time doing the same things together from one end of this big country to the other. We have worried together, fretted together, have even prayed together on occasion, and all the while we have chain-smoked a heck of a lot of cigarettes. Actually, what qualifies me to write about Vince is that all of the cigarettes he has lighted for the last 11 years have been mine, so I do have quite an investment in him."

He concluded, "On this day at Franklin Field, they're going to play the biggest game of his life and the guys down there on the field would be the first ones to tell you that they'd be watching it on television if it hadn't been for the Old Gray Ghost. What do you think the Ghost sent me for Christmas? A carton of cigarettes. All this success must be going to his head."

Much has changed in Philadelphia over the past seven decades. Teams moved, franchises changed hands, stadiums were leveled and others were built in their place. Through it all, Bill Campbell has been a constant. Today when he does a KYW radio commentary, whether he is reminiscing about Del Ennis or critiquing Allen Iverson, I sit up and pay attention. His is a voice to be heeded — and cherished.

— *Ray Didinger*

INTRODUCTION

Clarity sometimes arrives from the most unexpected sources.

In this case, it arrived from a long-lost friend, who, through an e-mail, unintentionally made me realize why I wanted to write a book on Bill Campbell.

In the 1960s, Freddy Massa was one of my grammar-school classmates when I grew up in Haddon Heights, New Jersey, a Norman Rockwell, tree-lined suburb about seven miles from Philadelphia. I moved out of the town when I was 12 and had only talked to Freddy a few times in the last 30-plus years, but he contacted me from his California home when he stumbled upon a question-and-answer sports website that I write for *The Philadelphia Inquirer.*

We e-mailed each other, caught up on things, and I mentioned that I was writing a book on Bill Campbell, who announced Phillies and Eagles games during our formative years in the '60s.

And that's when I had my moment of clarity.

When I mentioned Bill Campbell's name, Massa unknowingly sent back a powerful statement:

"His voice," he said, "is tattooed to our souls."

How elegant. How poetic. How true.

I can still hear that excited voice describing Richie Allen homers as they orbited out of old Connie Mack Stadium. "That's a ROOOOOF-TOP job!" he'd proclaim, or "What a TITANIC shot by Allen!"

For people in my generation, hearing Bill Campbell's voice brings us back to a simpler and kinder time, a slower-paced era when most families had stay-at-home moms and a much stronger connection with their neighbors. This was before malls, before computers, before the Internet, before 24/7 news coverage. Most families had one car and one black-and-white TV that carried basically three channels.

Back then, radio was king and, as a result, we developed a precious bond with the announcers of our sports teams.

As a broadcaster, Bill Campbell thrived in those innocent days.

Seven decades later, in a materialistic world where everyone seems to be in a hurry, he is still thriving, still one of the most respected broadcasters in the industry, still a voice of reason in a mostly chaotic Philadelphia sports scene.

How has Campbell remained at the top of his profession for all these years? I mean, this is a man who has been around the Philadelphia sports scene so long that he has done radio interviews with Connie Mack.

Repeat: Connie Mack.

As I started this book, one of my missions was to unravel the secret behind Campbell's lasting power. When WIP radio's Paul Jolovitz asked callers to name the "Mount Rushmore" figures of Philadelphia sports, Bill was near the top of the list, along with icons like Mike Schmidt, Wilt Chamberlain, and Bobby Clarke. Why was he just as popular today as he was in the 1940s?

Campbell, by the way, had to be coaxed into writing the book. His wife and daughter did the coaxing. They knew Bill had priceless stories that no one else could tell. Who else has been around Philadelphia sports personalities from Connie Mack to Gene Mauch to Charlie Manuel, from Buck Shaw to Dick Vermeil to Andy Reid, from Eddie Gottlieb to Irv Kosloff to Ed Snider? Who else has been around virtually every baseball, football, basketball and hockey player who has played in this city during the last seven decades?

Being a modest sort, Bill was reluctant to talk about his success. At one point, he proclaimed, "If at any time you think there's not enough material for a book, we can stop and there will be no hard feelings."

The material was endless. There were lots of highs — his fairy-tale marriage, his rise to fame — and a few lows. There was reverence when he talked about a woman he never knew, his mother. There was bitterness as he recounted the very public firing by the Phillies. Through it all, he never ran out of stories. Never was he at a loss for words when he discussed the sports personalities who came in and out of his life — and in and out of yours.

But in order to find out what Bill has meant to generations of Philadelphians, I went to the people who supplied a unique perspective — the radio and TV listeners. They're the ones who took Bill into their homes and, like a favorite uncle, didn't want him to leave.

They're the ones who listened to the wonderment in Bill's scratchy voice as he described Chamberlain's 100-point game in 1962, and the Eagles' dramatic world championship win over the Green Bay Packers in 1960; they're the ones who suffered with Bill as he announced the Phillies' games during their infamous 1964 collapse, or when his voice tried to mask the pain during the 76ers' 9-73 season in 1972-73.

They're the ones whose day was brightened by his no-nonsense KYW radio commentaries that — whether he criticized Donovan McNabb's reluctance to run, or questioned Terrell Owens' character — always seemed to get to the heart of the matter.

They're the ones who have that voice — oh, that magical, friendly, honest voice — tattooed to their souls.

— Sam Carchidi

CHAPTER ONE

"Oh, Baby!"

As he sat in a nonsmoking booth at Ponzio's Restaurant in Cherry Hill, New Jersey, on this sticky summer morning, Bill Campbell, once a two-pack-a-day puffer, was continually interrupted from his breakfast.

He didn't mind. The veteran sports broadcaster, his mood matching his cheery burgundy pants, enjoyed pushing aside his bacon-and-egg omelet as other diners approached.

"Congratulations, Bill!" said one man in his 30s. "You deserve it."

"Bill Campbell, you're a Hall of Famer!" said another diner, a casually dressed man who looked to be in his 40s. "It should have happened a long time ago."

"Pardon my interruption," said a 60-something man who wore a suit and tie, "but I just had to tell you how happy I am for you."

"You're kind," Campbell said in that distinctive voice that makes you feel comfortable, makes you feel home. "Very, very kind."

Campbell was being congratulated for being named to the Basketball Hall of Fame. The announcement came a few days earlier, and the reaction of Ponzio's diners showed just how much Campbell has meant to listeners over the last seven decades. Black and white, young and old, working stiffs and white-collar executives, Bill Campbell had touched them all, and the basketball award was just an excuse for them to thank "The Dean" or "Soupy" for being a small part of their lives.

Maybe "small part" isn't accurate. After all, how many people have been a part of our lives for such a long period of time?

Let's put it this way: If you are a Philadelphia sports fan and are between the ages of 10 and 90, you have probably listened to Bill Campbell. Older fans have heard him since the 1940s; he has been the voice of the Eagles, Warriors, Phillies, and 76ers, and, in addition to announcing Big 5 basketball games and Penn (back when Penn was more popular than the Eagles), Temple, and Penn State football, he was one of the pioneers of the TV sportscast that appeared on the nightly news.

Younger fans aren't familiar with that side of him. Some know him as the guy that comic Joe Conklin used to hysterically imitate when he worked for all-sports WIP radio ("Oh, baby!" and Campbell's other signature lines became a part of his sometimes-risque routine.) Conklin's impersonation was so true-to-life that at a Philadelphia Sportswriters' banquet one year, a teenage fan asked Campbell for his autograph. After he signed it, the fan looked at the signature and was dumbfounded. And a bit disappointed. "Oh, I thought you were Joe Conklin," he said.

Others know Campbell for the talk show he did from 1987 to 1992 on WIP — he gave the station credibility, said the station's star, Angelo Cataldi — and his heartfelt sports commentaries on KYW Newsradio.

He is as Philadelphian as Tastykakes, the Liberty Bell, and booing.

When you look at the hundreds of highlights during Campbell's career, two stand out: his description of Wilt Chamberlain's 100-point performance in a 1962 game that Campbell said "seemed like a farce at the time," and the Eagles' 17-13 upset victory over Green Bay in the 1960 NFL championship game at Franklin Field. Campbell calls that game his most memorable broadcasting event. Ever.

In the Chamberlain game, Campbell was at his best. His rat-tat-tat, machine-gun style painted a picture that percolated with drama. Listen to it today and you can envision the 7-foot-1 Chamberlain, his shiny white short-shorts barely covering his backside, his white socks nearly climbing to his knees, as he relentlessly fought to reach triple-digits against the New York Knicks:

"Let's see if they foul somebody quick. Rodgers throws long to Chamberlain. He's got it. He's trying to go up. He SHOOTS. No good. The rebound Luckenbill. Back to Chamberlain. He shoots, up. NO GOOD! In and out. The rebound Luckenbill. Back to Ruklick. Into Chamberlain..."

As for the Eagles broadcast in the 1960 championship, the legend and stature of that game grows with each season in which the Birds fail to win the Super Bowl. As the 2006 season approached, the 1960 title was the last time the Eagles could be called NFL champions.

Listening to Campbell broadcast the final play of the 1960 championship game, you feel as if you're sitting on one of those skinny wooden benches at Franklin Field:

"I wish you could be here to see 67,000 people standing. STAND-ING! What an ELECTRIFYING finish to a great game and a great season. Starr is over the ball. This will be it! Starr's back to throw. He takes time. He throws over the middle. It's caught at the 15. Running hard...."

Campbell did Eagles games until the end of the 1964 season, but nothing compared to the euphoria that surrounded the 1960 team. It was a season that, from Campbell's perspective, was made even more special because of his close friendship with The Dutchman, Norm Van Brocklin, the club's veteran quarterback.

Bill and his wife, Jo, became so attached to Van Brocklin that their daughter, Chris, called him "Uncle Dutch."

Said Jo Campbell, who married Bill after a romance that began when they worked for WIP radio in the 1940s, "Dutch had the bluest eyes. Bluer than Paul Newman's."

Bill Campbell and Van Brocklin, a man who had a reputation for his gruff nature and his General Patton presence, were inseparable. When they weren't golfing or watching game films, they were socializing at each other's homes. They lived near each other in Delaware County, Pennsylvania.

The Dutchman was the brother that Bill Campbell never had.

A few years later, Campbell would find another "brother," one of his Phillies broadcast partners, Richie "Whitey" Ashburn.

Ashburn, the one-time Phillies star center fielder, was a country boy from Tilden, Nebraska. Campbell grew up in Philadelphia. Ashburn was a man of few words, a man who spoke softly and slowly. Campbell was a storyteller with rapid-fire delivery. Ashburn, whose dry humor became as famous as his throw that helped the 1950 Whiz Kids win the National League pennant, could captivate audiences with "inside" stories on his playing days. Campbell wowed listeners with his knowledge and his unmatched preparation.

The men were very different, but baseball was their common ground. Both respected the game, loved the game. That love was transparent in the wonderful dialogue they shared with listeners during games.

It was like sitting at a corner bar, or on a South Philly stoop, next to two guys who were having a good-natured debate:

"Pitchers aren't worth a darn, Bill, when you compare them to the guys who are in the everyday grind. All they do is work a couple of times a week."

"But Whitey, they're the most important players in the game."

"C'mon, Soupy. They're the worst athletes around. They can't hit, can't bunt, can't run, can't field their positions. You can't name me three pitchers in the world who can field their positions; they don't even know what base to throw to."

"Whitey, don't you think you're exaggerating?"

"All they do is throw the hell out of the ball. And if God didn't give them a big strong arm, they'd be out on the bread line."

Latter-day listeners would recall the magical chemistry that Ashburn and Harry Kalas displayed in the broadcast booth. That chemistry was started by Campbell and Ashburn. "Their personalities," said Herbie Ashburn, the wife of Rich, who died suddenly in 1997, "just blended together."

"Dad always attributed a lot of his success to Bill because Bill guided him," said Richard Ashburn, Whitey's son. "Bill nurtured him."

———•———

Bill Campbell was in his glory when he did baseball. By the time he got the Phillies job in 1963, he was a veteran of the Philadelphia sports scene. He had done the Eagles and the Philadelphia Warriors. He had done Penn football and Big 5 basketball and nightly TV and radio sportscasts.

None came close to his affection for baseball. It was the sport that conjured sweet memories of his father because the two had attended countless games together since their first trip to Shibe Park in 1929. Campbell liked the rhythm of the sport, liked the slow pace. He liked baseball so much that he took a $10,000 pay cut to take the Phillies job in 1963: WCAU had been paying him $25,000 to be its sports director; the Phillies gave him $15,000.

In the next years, Bill's salary rose, and so did his appreciation for the game. By Saam was the veteran in the cramped, smoke-filled booth but, to many listeners and to many in the industry, it was Bill Campbell who was the club's No. 1 announcer. Saam was the consummate pro and a man who would one day receive a broadcaster's award at the Hall of Fame in Cooperstown. It was Saam who taught Campbell about the art of being prepared, and it was Saam whose friendly, easy-going Texan manner made him such a broadcasting icon. But Saam was more scripted that Campbell; he was a nuts-and-bolts guy who was more comfortable with batting averages than discussing the personalities behind the averages. Campbell was comfortable in both areas. He was a conversationalist, and he and Ashburn had a way of humanizing the players and giving the listeners more than the ball-strike count, the score, the play-by-play.

Bill Campbell (left) conducts an interview with Phillies manager Ben Chapman (circa 1946).

This was an era when announcers were identified with their teams. Saam was the longtime broadcaster with the Phillies who, once upon a time, announced Philadelphia A's games. There was Mel Allen with the New York Yankees, Bob Prince with the Pittsburgh Pirates, Curt Gowdy with the Boston Red Sox, Vin Scully with the Los Angeles Dodgers, Jack Buck with the St. Louis Cardinals, Jack Brickhouse with the Chicago Cubs, Ernie Harwell with the Detroit Tigers. The list went on and on.

Many of them would one day be headed to the Baseball Hall of Fame. It seemed only natural to think that Bill Campbell would join them.

That's what made the post-season 1970 developments so puzzling.

In a move that created a firestorm of controversy, Bill Campbell was fired by the floundering Phillies, a club that had managed to draw only a little over 700,000 fans to home games that year. The Phillies insisted that one of their beer sponsors was behind the decision. They also acknowledged that they were trying to create a new image that coincided with their move from Connie Mack Stadium to Veterans Stadium: new digs, new uniforms, new announcer.

As if a new announcer would transform them from perennial losers to pennant winners.

Nearly four decades later, Campbell and his family are still pained by Bill Giles' decision.

Campbell's daughter, Chris, remembers the firing and seeing her dad cry for just the second time in her life.

How would Campbell pick up the pieces? Why did he have to pick up the pieces? Was it just because Giles, then finishing his first year as a Phillies executive, wanted to hire his old Houston buddy, Harry Kalas?

In 1970, Bill Campbell's career was at a crossroad.

He could have faded into the background, could have lost his connection with Philadelphia's rabid sports fans.

Perhaps the reason that didn't happened can be found in Campbell's background.

Bill Campbell was used to being a fighter, used to facing adversity.

Decades earlier, as a youngster, he had to endure much more trying situations. His mother died when she delivered him and his father kept it a secret from Bill (then known as Billy) for 11 years. Bill Campbell was left with emotional baggage that few have had to overcome. He lived with his father for a while before moving in with aunts and then back with his sports-minded dad. His dad remarried, but eventually became separated, an unheard-of development in the 1930s.

During his childhood, Bill Campbell moved from home to home and changed schools six times. From that unstable environment rose the most lasting voice in the history of Philadelphia radio.

Somehow.

"By all rights," said Bill's loving and devoted wife, Jo, "he should have been a criminal."

Instead, he became a Philadelphia treasure.

CHAPTER TWO

A Tragic Beginning

Losing your mother in childbirth, psychologists say, can leave emotional scars that are nearly impossible to overcome.

It is understandable, then, that Bill Campbell doesn't like to talk about his loss.

He knows little about his birth mom, the former Nan Muldoon, except for the stories he has heard from his adoring aunts over the years.

For Bill's dad — William Thomas Campbell Sr. — it was difficult to talk about the woman who died after delivering "Billy" on September 7, 1923.

Nan (Muldoon) Campbell died while giving birth to Bill in 1923

Bill Campbell Sr. was a traveling paintbrush salesman whose job took him up and down the East Coast. The lifestyle was no place for an infant, so young Bill spent the first few years of his life being raised by different aunts.

Bill Campbell Sr. loved his son, protected him, took him to ball games and prize fights, sent him to the best private schools until he couldn't afford them anymore.

But there was a sadness that seemed to permeate the elder Campbell. His own mother had died while giving birth to him in 1896. Twenty-seven years later, his wife suffered the same fate while delivering their son, Billy.

Though Bill Sr. was friendly and accommodating on the outside, the deaths left him bitter and empty. As Bill Campbell looks back on it, he can understand his dad's feelings.

"In all fairness to my father, he got a bad break," he said. "His wife dies in delivering his first child — me. He was married less than a year when I was born. I don't think, as I look back on it now, that he ever really got over it. You know, it was a tough blow. Just imagine if that happened to you."

Bill's Aunt Mae gave him a chilling picture of how much his mother's death had affected his father. "She told me that at the funeral, he was so overcome with grief that he picked her body out of the casket," Bill said.

Some of Bill Sr.'s bitterness disappeared when he fell in love with Margaret Graham, his second wife. They met at a chorale group they had joined and they were married in 1925, when Bill was a toddler. In a few years, Bill had two sisters, Polly and Julie.

Bill was nearly three years older than Polly — a devilish girl who, to the disbelief of her brother, later became a nun — and four years older than Julie.

Margaret, Bill's new mom, was in the first graduating class at Immaculata College (1925). Bill Sr. dropped out of St. Joseph's Prep after three years.

"I think he always resented the fact that my mother had a college education and he didn't," Julie said. "He would kind of make fun of that. But there wasn't much fun in it for him and I do think that was an issue."

Margaret started to drift apart from her husband, but their young children didn't notice. They were too busy being kids, too busy having fun with their friends.

Jimmy O'Malley was one of those friends. He and Bill had a bond: baseball. Whether they were playing it or sneaking into Shibe Park to watch their beloved Philadelphia Athletics, baseball was at the center of their universe. The A's were their favorite team, but they would also venture over to Baker Bowl to watch the lowly Phillies. Baker Bowl had a short outfield porch, and homers would fly out of the stadium during batting practice. If you retrieved a ball and showed it at the gate, you were allowed into the game for free.

"I lived at the ballpark when I was in grammar school," Campbell said. "School would get out around 2:30 and the games started at 3, so that's where we went."

Going to A's games with Jimmy was an event, especially when it was a holiday doubleheader. When the A's were home on Memorial Day, the Fourth of July, or Labor Day, Bill and Jimmy were usually there.

"They had separate admissions for the holiday doubleheaders," Bill said. "They'd play the morning game at 10 o'clock and the second game didn't start until about 3."

The pace of the games was much different in those days. There was no styling for the TV cameras. No long delays for commercials.

"The games would be over in two hours," Bill said. "If it went more than two hours, it was an exceptionally long game. With Lefty Grove and those guys pitching, you'd finish in an hour and 30 minutes, maybe 1:40 or 1:50."

Bill and Jimmy were maybe seven or eight years old. They'd pay 50 cents to watch the first game, then would hide in the ball park for several hours so they didn't have to pay admission to the nightcap.

They'd hide in the nooks and crannies of the ballpark; they'd pack jelly sandwiches and eat them while they were curled up in bathroom stalls, their feet up in the air so they wouldn't be detected by the ballpark police.

"There was this one security guard we'd always see around the ballpark and I think he knew what we were doing," Campbell said. "He'd say, 'I'm gonna get you guys today.' But he'd never find us. We always got away with it and we were very proud of the fact that we never got caught."

He laughed at the sweet memory.

"If we ever got caught, it would have broken our record," he said. "We couldn't let that happen."

In one of those holiday doubleheaders, he remembers the great Lefty Grove — a man who would finish with exactly 300 victories and be inducted into the Hall of Fame — winning a morning game against the Yankees.

"A guy named George Earnshaw pitched in the afternoon; he was a right-hander from Swarthmore College and he pitched a good game, but going into the late innings he got into trouble and Mr. Mack had somebody warm up in the bullpen," Campbell said.

Mr. Mack, of course, was Connie Mack, the legendary A's manager and a man whom Campbell would one day interview. And revere. On this particular day, Campbell and his young friend were staring at the pitcher that Mack had asked to warmup.

"It's Lefty Grove!" Jimmy O'Malley yelled.

"It can't be?! He just pitched nine innings in the first game!" Bill said.

But Jimmy was right. It was Grove. And it was an ending that Bill Campbell would never forget.

"He came in," he said, "and struck out Babe Ruth in a tough situation."

The ending was sweeter than the jelly sandwiches.

———•———

Growing up in the Logan section of Philadelphia, Bill was a typical boy who seemed to spend more time on makeshift baseball fields than he did at his North Philly home.

"He wasn't a hang-around-the-house type kid," said his sister, Julie. "Nobody was back then. He always had groups of boyfriends all over the area. There was a big park not too far from us and he'd always be playing ball."

When he wasn't playing ball, he was watching it. He especially liked watching his Uncle Brick play football for St. Joseph's Prep in

Philadelphia. Everyone called him "Brick" because of his red hair, but his given name was William, and he was the younger brother of Bill's mother, Margaret.

"He used to collect college football pennants — Penn, Notre Dame, all the teams — and he gave them to me after he went into the seminary when he graduated from St. Joe's Prep," Campbell said. "I was five or six years old at the time and I really looked up to him. Brick is one of the people who got me interested in sports."

Like Brick, Bill was pleasant and nice to be around.

"Everybody liked him," Julie said. "They'd say, 'Oh, you're Bill's sister,'" she said. "After that, I got a certain amount of acceptance."

For a while, the Campbells were the all-American family. Bill, who was then nine years old, and his two sisters had lots of friends and life was good. Bill tolerated his pesky younger sisters, even taught them how to dance. Margaret seemed content to run the house, make standard meals — Bill loved her sauerkraut — and read her books. Bill Sr. was doing well for himself as a paintbrush salesman.

But fallout from the Depression hit. Hard. Bill Sr. lost his job. Strapped financially, the Campbells moved from their home on the 5200 block of North 15th Street to the home of Margaret's parents. The move was only a block, to another part of Logan, but looking back on it, Bill Sr. and his wife grew miles apart.

For Bill Campbell Sr., living with his in-laws created tension. It was tough enough that he was always searching for work. It was made even tougher because of the constant meddling of his mother-in-law.

Within two years, the marriage was over. This was the 1930s, when separations were almost unthinkable, almost scandalous — especially to a Catholic family like the Campbells.

Bill was 11 at the time. Polly was eight, Julie seven. Their bond would be placed in jeopardy.

Bill doesn't remember the specifics surrounding the day his mom and dad separated. Julie does. She remembers returning from school with Polly, and their parents telling them to find Bill and bring him home. Bill was playing ball in the park when Julie and her sister delivered the message.

"Mom and Dad want you home," said Julie, unaware of why the request had been made.

"OK. I'll be there."

Bill got home before the girls. When he arrived, his father instructed him to get into the car with his suitcase. They were moving, leaving his mother and two sisters behind.

For years, Julie felt guilty about prying Bill loose from his ball-game and telling him to go home.

"I thought, 'If we hadn't found him that day, he might still be living home and maybe he wouldn't have left,' " she said. "I haunted myself with that. Isn't that stupid?"

There was never any question as to how the children would be divided. Bill was not related by blood to the woman he called Mom. He would live with his birth father. His sisters would live with their birthmother.

Bill, then in sixth grade, and his dad moved into an apartment that was several subway stops from the rest of the family. It was painful being separated from his sisters and the only mom he had ever known.

Fact is, he thought Margaret *was* his biological mom. There was no reason to think any differently.

After the family split up, Bill's dad divulged a long-kept secret: He sat down his son and told him about Nan and her tragic death when she delivered him. "I could not believe it," Bill said. "I was in shock. I wasn't any good for weeks after he told me. At first, I didn't believe it, but it came from my father, so it had to be true. After that, I guess I adjusted. There was nothing I could do."

Still, he would lie in bed at night and wonder what Nan was like.

"All this time," he said, "I thought Margaret was my birth mother."

Right around the same time, there was more upheaval in Bill's life. And it happened because of an accident inside a Catholic church, of all places.

As part of their chores, the Holy Child altar boys, including Bill, were cleaning the religious statues in the church. Poor Frank McQuaide was on a ladder when his dust cloth got caught on the back of a Blessed Virgin Mary's head. "The statue had to be six feet tall. All marble, and it came down right on top of him," Campbell said.

An ambulance rushed the youngster to the hospital, and it wasn't until several hours later that Bill learned his friend's fate.

"We knew he was badly hurt, but we didn't know what happened," Campbell said. "My father went to confession that night and the priest told him that Frank had died."

Bill Sr. came home and gently broke the news to his son.

———

Margaret Graham and Bill Campbell Sr. seemed like a mismatch. Margaret was quiet and an avid reader. Bill Sr. was personable and a great storyteller — traits that his son would inherit.

"He was a very outgoing guy and he had an absolutely marvelous singing voice," Bill said. "He sang in all the parish shows and minstrels. His greatest hero, besides those in sports, was Enrico Caruso. He had Caruso records and he played them all the time. My dad sang at our wedding and he performed at a lot of places. I remember when we were kids, he would be singing while he was shaving upstairs, and if he hit a note that wasn't right, he would run all the way down the steps to the piano and hit the right key, and then run back upstairs and continue the song."

Bill Sr. sang in the local Irish minstrels.

"There are songs that I hear today and they remind me of my father," Bill said.

His voice filled with pride as, in a quiet tone, he broke into a tender rendition of "The Rose of Tralee", a famous Irish ballad:

*"The pale blue moon was rising above the green mountain,
the sun was declining beneath the blue sea..."*

After his parents separated, Bill would stay in contact with his mother and sisters, but the family was deeply divided. The parents weren't friendly with each other and it put a strain on their children. The girls sided with their mom; Bill sided with his dad. Bill and his sisters felt awkward when their friends and classmates would discuss their family situations. Their friends had normal families, with a Mom and a Dad making the rules. Bill felt motherless, his sisters felt fatherless.

"It bothered all of us," Julie said. "At that time, I didn't know one of my friends whose parents were separated. You just didn't do it in that generation."

"Back then, you stuck things out," Bill said.

The fact that his parents drifted apart left a void.

"I would not want to see a kid go through what I went though," Bill said. "I always felt different from the other kids, from my buddies, because nobody got divorced or separated in those days. Now, they say 50 percent of marriages fail, which is probably true. But you're talking about the 1930s. It was unheard of, and I always felt like an outsider, like I was really missing something. All the guys I hung around with and played sports with and went to the movies with, they all had regular homes with two parents. And I didn't. And I always felt cheated. It was difficult. That's why I developed lousy study habits early because I was on my own all the time. We ate in restaurants all the time and we moved in and out of places."

Growing up, Bill Campbell felt disjointed. Maybe that's why he enjoyed working on the radio in later years. It gave him power of sorts, gave him control. It was the opposite feeling of his youth, the opposite feeling of being an outsider.

In the mid 1930s, Bill Campbell drapes his arms around his sisters, Julie, and Polly (right). Polly became a nun. At left is Bill Campbell Sr., the trio's dad.

On the radio, he was an insider who was looking out.

———•———

The separation wasn't amicable, but the children tried to make the best of it. Every weekend, Bill would visit his mother and sisters, or his sisters would take the subway to visit Bill and their dad.

The sisters visited a lot of undesirable "homes." Broken-down hotels. Raggedy apartment buildings. If the hot water worked, it was a bonus.

"I lived all over the place with my father," Bill said. "All kinds of abnormal conditions."

First, they rented a North Philly apartment that was about five miles from the home where his mom and sisters lived. Then they rented a few rooms in a house, then back to a hotel. At one point, they lived at the Monterey Hotel on Ridge Avenue, a one-room place with two beds and a bath. The bugs were free.

While Bill Sr. gradually got back into the work force, Margaret became a social worker and later was hired by the Atlantic Refining Company to chart their fleet as it traveled up and down the coast. "She was a college graduate," Julie said, "so she could get jobs that other women couldn't."

When Bill entered seventh grade, his father had enough money to send him to boarding school at St. Aloysius in West Chester, where he stayed for two years. He then lived at Archmere Academy in Claymont, Delaware, during his first two years in high school. "I loved it and wish I could have finished there," he said. "But my father ran out of money."

With funds low, Bill moved back in with his father — who was renting a couple of rooms in a private house — and attended Philadelphia's Roman Catholic High School as a junior. Julie remembers visiting her brother and father, and feeling hollow because of a matter-of-fact statement made by her dad. The statement wasn't said with malice, but the words pierced her heart.

"Do you know what I was doing when you were born?" she recalled her father saying to Bill during one of his birthday celebrations, "I was picking out a cemetery plot and a casket for your mother."

Bill doesn't remember his father making the statement. Maybe the hurt of those words was so crippling that he buried them deep in the recesses of his mind.

Julie, though, says she can still see the anguish on Bill's face after his dad's comment.

———

Bill and his dad liked talking about sports and enjoyed each other's company. Just after Bill turned 13 in 1936, his father told him if he did well on one of his tests, he would take him to see heavyweight Joe Louis, who is generally recognized as the first African-American sports hero, fight Philadelphia's Al Ettore. Bill aced the test. Louis aced Ettore, knocking him out in the fifth round before more than 40,000 fans at Philadelphia's Municipal Stadium.

In the summers of his early teen years, Bill would travel with his dad as he drove up and down the East Coast and help unload sample cases of his paintbrushes into the various hotels.

The conversation was always light. Sports and school were the main topics. When there was a lull in the conversation, Bill would dial-hop and listen to the different radio stations.

Even at 14, he had a plan. One day, it would be *his* voice coming out of the speakers that a dad and his son would be hearing, he thought. That's why, while his dad peddled paintbrushes at conventions, Bill would hop a bus and visit radio stations in Maine or North Carolina or Florida — wherever the trip had taken them — to get a firsthand look at how things worked.

"Like most kids, I always wanted to be a ballplayer, and I realized at an early age that that wasn't going to happen," Campbell said. "So I figured that being a broadcaster was the next-best thing."

———

At Roman Catholic, which he attended for a year before transferring to another school in Center City Philadelphia, Brown Prep, Bill seemed different than the other high school students. More mature. More self-motivated. He had gone from school to school and home to home, but somehow it didn't set him back. If anything, it made him feel as if he could handle any challenge.

Campbell wasn't an exemplary student — "just average," he said — but he seemed to have an inner peace, seemed to know what he wanted out of life. He was too small to play sports in high school, but he continued to compete on the playground and on intramural teams, and he continued to dream about a radio career.

During his junior year at Roman, the future "Voice of Philadelphia" got his start in the radio business. Every Saturday morning, he did a 15-minute high-school sports show on WTEL, an AM station on Roosevelt Boulevard. Bill reported on Catholic League and Public League athletes, writing copy with crisp, short sentences — a style that would become his trademark.

His salary: zilch. His experience: priceless.

"It was a foreign-language station that broadcast in German and Italian," Campbell said, laughing. "I might have been the only English-speaking guy on the station."

"I remember thinking how impressive it was that a high-school student — someone from *our school* — was on the radio," said one of Campbell's Roman classmates.

It wasn't a big station, and most Philadelphians couldn't understand the programs that were being broadcast. But for William Thomas Campbell Jr., it helped build the foundation of the most remarkable radio career in Philadelphia history.

That foundation became stronger during the summer between Bill's junior and senior high school years. It would be a summer when he worked alongside Frank Sinatra and Glenn Miller and Tommy Dorsey and entertainers who would become a part of Americana.

🎙

CHAPTER THREE

Greetings From Atlantic City

Before jet travel made Florida, the Caribbean islands, and Europe such popular tourist sites, before Las Vegas became the nation's entertainment capital, Atlantic City ruled. Bill Campbell had a love affair with *that* Atlantic City.

Long before casinos tried to revive the run-down resort, Atlantic City was arguably the world's No. 1 summer spot. It was retreat for Philadelphia's upper crust — women in furs would be pushed on Boardwalk rolling cars as they enjoyed the saltwater night air — and its skyline was an international symbol of opulence, glamour, and architectural brilliance. Atlantic City, a playground for the rich and famous, was the home of the Miss America pageant and eight miles of pristine beaches. It was also the home of amusement rides like the Flying Chairs and the Mexican Hat Bowl, and the place that hosted some of the best entertainment acts of its time.

Al Jolson, Fanny Brice, and Duke Ellington played Atlantic City. So did Frank Sinatra, Benny Goodman, and Jimmy Durante. And Sammy Davis Jr., Pearl Bailey, and Harry Houdini. And on and on.

Atlantic City was also the home of the world's first Boardwalk. The wacky, wonderful, rickety Boardwalk. Built in 1870 to keep people from tracking beach sand into the legendary luxury hotels and railroad parlor cars, the Boardwalk was a place where you could buy saltwater taffy and hot roasted peanuts — or hundreds of other goodies — and enjoy the carnival of outrageous attractions that would have rivaled McNabb-Owens. Hucksters competed for paying customers by offering entertainment that had two themes: weird and weirder. There were midget boxers and fighting kangaroos and dancing tigers.

The Boardwalk also featured many colorful sections that offered a respite from the freak shows: Heinz Pier, Ocean Pier, Million Dollar

Pier, Garden Pier, and Steeplechase Pier. Some offered the latest amusement rides; one offered a sun parlor with reclining chairs, writing desks, and a demonstration kitchen with free hot and cold food samples; another boasted the world's largest electric sign, 27,000 light bulbs advertising Chesterfield cigarettes. The most famous attraction was the Steel Pier, which showcased 16 hours of continuous entertainment for one admission. Vaudeville stars and some of the most renowned Big Bands performed at the Steel Pier, but they frequently found themselves being upstaged by a diving horse that, several times a day, would jump from a 60-foot tower into the ocean. A scantily clad female rider would be aboard for the dive, which was performed at an ocean stadium filled with cheering spectators.

This is the Atlantic City that Campbell remembers. This is the city, immortalized when the board game Monopoly was created in the 1930s, where he stayed with his aunts each summer and, through good timing, found himself auditioning for a radio job.

Strange but true: Bill Campbell's voice may not be famous if it wasn't for a tryout at an Atlantic City radio station in which he was asked to give a lively description of a couch.

Yes, a couch.

The year was 1940, and Bill was an ambitious 16-year-old who was spending the summers with his Aunt Mae and Aunt Marge. They were the sisters of his deceased mom, Nan, and they felt protective of Bill ever since he was born. "They were two little angels. Maybe they're the ones who inspired him and instilled goodness in him," said Jo, Bill's wife. His aunts' hearts still ached because of the loss of their sister, but having their nephew around their Virginia Avenue apartment made things more bearable. Bill had his mother's looks, his mother's charming personality.

Bill had just completed his junior year at Roman Catholic — he would transfer to since-closed Brown Prep, located at 15th and Race in Philadelphia, for 12th grade — when he headed to Atlantic City to spend the summer with his aunts and an uncle and grandfather.

Little did he know that the summer of 1940 was about to become a high-water in his life. He had doting aunts, the beach, and, as it turned out, his first paid radio job. He also had a seemingly endless amount of dates that included a romance with a Miss Atlantic City.

Campbell landed the radio job by accident. It was the classic case of being at the right place at the right time.

While listening to the radio in his aunts' apartment, Campbell stumbled over a show on a brand-new station, WFPG. George Thomas, an acquaintance of Campbell's who also had done work on Philadelphia's WCAU radio, was the station's chief announcer. "George had a great voice, but he didn't know sports," Campbell said. "He had no interest in it."

Campbell had met Thomas when he worked at WCAU radio.

"I used to go around and visit the radio stations to see how they operated and what they did," he said. "And 'CAU was the best station in town. There was an axiom in those days that 'CAU was the best station in America. Their announcing staff was the best and George was a terrific announcer. They had announcers like John Franklin and Hugh Ferguson. I used to go visit those guys all the time and when I went there to see how they operated, they were very nice to me. I'd go there and I'd go to WIP and saw John Facenda and those guys. I was really interested in what they were doing because this is what I wanted to be — a radio announcer."

On this day in Atlantic City, Campbell cringed as he listened to Thomas try to announce a lifeguard boat race.

"He was stumbling all over the place. He didn't know one crew from the other," he said.

Campbell headed to the beach, but by the time he arrived, the race had just ended. He told Thomas he was living with his aunts for the summer.

Thomas, knowing that Campbell was a sports enthusiast, had an idea. "You want a job? I can try to get you one," he said.

Thomas introduced Campbell to Harry Zoog, the station's general manager.

"I'll never forget him," Campbell said with a laugh. "I've never seen him since."

Zoog took Campbell into the tiny studio and gave him an on-the-spot audition.

"Describe everything in this room," he said.

"I described the blinds and the chairs and the couch and whatever else was in there," Campbell said. Apparently, Zoog liked

Campbell's in-depth description of the slipcover patterns that draped the couch. Midway through the description, he interrupted Campbell and told him he was hired.

For $15 a week.

"Great!" Campbell said.

George Thomas got $20 a week as the main announcer. Campbell was thrilled just to be getting paid to talk. He spun records for a radio show that originated on the Steel Pier, covered the Miss America pageant, and did dance band remotes from two Boardwalk piers.

Ironically, he did a little of everything in his 72-hour work week — except sports.

"That was," he said, "the GREATEST, GREATEST summer of my life! I did the beauty pageant. I dated a lot of girls. We did all the dance bands on the Steel Pier, and Tommy Dorsey and Glenn Miller and Frank Sinatra and Ray Eberle [did shows there] and I would introduce them. I met a lot of girls in Atlantic City, and George was single, too, so it was just a wonderful summer. We'd go from the Steel Pier to the Million Dollar Pier. I did a disc jockey show called 'The Midnight Jamboree.' We did it right on the beach, from midnight to two in the morning."

After the show, Campbell and his friends would stay out until the sun started to rise. Ah, life was awfully good for the young radio star — that is, until word of his lifestyle drifted back to Philadelphia.

One night, as Campbell did a radio show from a balcony that overlooked the beach on the Steel Pier, a middle-aged man walked into the scene and watched the dancing and late-night commotion that was being created by the young announcer. The man was Bill's dad.

"He came right in there and said to me, 'Get the hell home.' " Campbell said, smiling at the memory. "It was one of the most embarrassing moments of my life, and some of the kids down there never let me forget it.

"I finished the show and then I went home."

The next summer, after graduating from Brown Prep, the 17-year-old Campbell announced Class B minor-league baseball games for the Lancaster Red Roses in the Interstate League. It wasn't as much fun as Atlantic City, and he didn't get to hang out with Sinatra and his pals. But it *was* a job that set the foundation for his later success.

Campbell's love for baseball started at a young age. After his father remarried, the Campbell family settled in the Logan section of North Philadelphia and lived next door to John Nolan, who happened to be the Philadelphia Athletics' baseball writer for *The Evening Bulletin.*

Campbell's father was a big baseball fan and he became friendly with Nolan. The Athletics, who were a baseball dynasty in those days, and Phillies always gave them something to talk about, and, even at a young age, Bill felt comfortable joining their conversations and talking about the strengths and weaknesses of each team.

Nolan took a liking to Bill. "Most of the kids in our neighborhood were girls," Campbell said. "I was one of the few boys, and John Nolan would take me to games."

The first major-league baseball game Campbell ever attended turned out to be an epic. A little over a month after his sixth birthday, Bill and his father went to Shibe Park, which later became known as Connie Mack Stadium, to watch the fourth game of the 1929 World Series between the Athletics and Chicago Cubs. The A's faced an 8-0 deficit before scoring 10 seventh-inning runs en route to a 10-8 victory that paved the way for their championship.

It was the most runs ever scored in a World Series inning — and that record still stands today. Jimmy Dykes, a 32-year-old third baseman who hit a club-high .421 in the Series, snapped an 8-8 tie with a two-run double in the inning, one that featured an infamous Cubs moment: Centerfielder Hack Wilson lost Mule Haas' fly in the sun, resulting in a three-run, inside-the-park homer.

"That's how I got my interest in baseball," Campbell said. "My father took me to games, and John Nolan took us both to games. I was around the press box a lot in those days."

Nolan couldn't get Campbell into the press box, "but he took me as close as he could. He introduced me to all the writers and all that. I don't remember any broadcasters much in those days; they didn't broadcast many games except for the World Series."

Campbell went primarily to A's games during that era. The Phillies were an afterthought. "I saw a lot of the A's," he said. "I could give you the whole history of the A's."

Dykes, Jimmie Foxx and Max Bishop were A's who were Bill's heroes. So were Lefty Grove and Al Simmons. And Mickey Cochrane and Bing Miller, among others.

Years later, after he became established in broadcasting, Campbell was a member of the Bala Golf Club, where he played countless rounds with Dykes. "He told me some unbelievable stories — that the best curveball hitter who ever lived was Bing Miller. Stuff like that," Campbell said.

It was Dykes who erupted with emotion during the historic 10-run inning in the 1929 World Series, a game that helped Campbell get hooked on the sport.

During the rally, Dykes excitedly slapped a person on the back so hard that he tumbled off the bench and landed on the dugout floor with the bats.

Connie Mack, the A's dignified 66-year-old manager, dusted himself off, laughed, and told a remorseful Dykes there was no need to apologize. The A's were on their way to a championship and their manager was feeling a little giddy.

So was six-year-old Billy Campbell.

———————

Fast-forward to 1937 and another sporting event that steered Campbell toward a career as a sports broadcaster.

Campbell was not a big tennis fan, but he found himself listening to the Davis Cup matches on the radio of his father's navy-blue 1936 Dodge. "Don Budge was playing Baron Gottfried von Cramm of Germany. I've never forgotten it," Campbell said.

Tennis historians call the fifth and deciding match — won by Budge, 8-6 — the most scintillating in Davis Cup history. Budge came back from a 4-1 deficit and had match point five times before he sprawled to the ground while making an epic winning shot. He thus defeated von Cramm, 6-8, 5-7, 6-4, 6-2, 8-6 in the deciding match of the Davis Cup semifinal between the United States and Nazi Germany. Minutes before the match, von Cramm received a good-luck phone call from Adolf Hitler, the Chancellor of Germany.

The German star "came out pale and serious and played as if his life depended on every point," Budge was quoted as saying. The next year, when Hitler was preparing for Germany to launch World War II, von Cramm declined to speak for Nazism in his tennis travels and was imprisoned by the Gestapo.

Campbell wasn't thinking about any of the political ramifications when he listened to von Cramm battle Budge in that 1937 broadcast. All he knew was that two of the all-time tennis greats were playing a match for the ages. Campbell, then 13, became so enthralled by the announcer's description that, when he arrived home in his father's car, he ran inside and turned on the radio to listen to the rest of the match.

"Somewhere in the third set, the announcer came on and said that Ted Husing, who was broadcasting at courtside, was interrupting the players' concentration and they asked that Mr. Husing move back three or four feet and lower his voice to almost a whisper," Campbell recalled. "So Ted, whom I got to know a little later, obliged and moved back and whispered for the last two sets."

Even now, nearly 70 years later, Campbell gets excited as he remembers the broadcast.

"I'm telling you, it made the hair stand on the back of my neck," he said. "It was the most dramatic thing I have ever heard in my life. Ted had a magnificent voice. He whispered the last two sets and I can still hear it. He whispered it and it left a lasting impression."

And even though Bill wasn't a tennis buff, Husing's dramatic style planted a seed: Bill Campbell wanted to have the same impact on listeners.

Years later, Bill would pinch-hit for an ill Husing as the CBS radio announcer at the Penn Relays at Franklin Field. As he broadcast the event, memories of Husing's tennis broadcast echoed in his head.

In 1941, at the tender age of 17, Campbell found himself broadcasting minor-league baseball games on WGAL for the Lancaster Red Roses, a Class B team that included third baseman George Kell, who later played for the Philadelphia A's and became a Hall of Fame player; catcher Frank Reagan, an all-American back at the University of Pennsylvania who would play seven years in the NFL; and short-stop Don "Red" Kellett, who later became the head basketball and baseball coach at his alma mater, Penn, and also wound up as a general manager of the NFL's Baltimore Colts. Kellett was instrumental in signing legendary quarterback Johnny Unitas.

The summer of '41 was right around the time that Major League Baseball and America were starting a radio romance. The sport was perfect for the medium — a slow, relaxing pace that made it possible for the listeners to feel a connection to the announcers. At first, Major League Baseball frowned upon having the games

Bill Campbell, shown here in an early WCAU promotional photo, began broadcasting professionally for WFPG in Atlantic City in 1940, when he was 16. He received $15 a week.

broadcast. Why would fans pay to see the games if they could listen to them on the radio for free?

By the time Campbell was broadcasting in the Interstate League, he had been listening to local role models like By Saam, who did games for the A's and Phillies. Around the league, Red Barber (one of Bill's idols) was becoming a legend as the Brooklyn Dodgers' voice, as was Mel "How about that!" Allen with the Yankees. Russ Hodges — who would later become famous for describing Bobby Thomson's "Shot Heard 'Round the World" in 1951 — was just establishing himself, and former pitching star Waite Hoyt was starting a distinguished broadcasting career.

While Campbell was working Lancaster's minor-league games and getting paid $70 per month, several future broadcasting icons had yet to work in the majors. That group included Harry Caray, Jack Brickhouse, Ernie Harwell, Bob Prince, Vin Scully, Jimmy Dudley, Jack Buck, Lindsey Nelson, and Milo Hamilton. They would become Campbell's contemporaries.

This was decades before cable television brought numerous baseball games into your living room each night. TV was still emerging. Radio ruled. So did its colorful baseball announcers.

The baseball announcer became part actor, part storyteller. He had to entertain and inform between the pitcher's deliveries — although that wasn't the case with Harold Arlin, who did baseball's first radio broadcast in 1921 on KDKA in Pittsburgh.

"No one told me you had to talk between pitches," he once said. (Coincidentally, Arlin's grandson, Steve, pitched in the Phillies' farm system in the 1960s, when Campbell was doing the big-league team's games.)

When Campbell announced minor-league baseball games in 1941, he was just out of high school and had no experience doing play-by-play. The Lancaster Red Roses only broadcast one or two games a week, but Campbell went to all the home games to gather background information on the players and be prepared to make prescient comments. "We only did 20 games the whole year and we didn't do any road games," Campbell said. "I didn't do a lot of games, but it was a good experience."

Campbell said he doesn't remember anything extraordinary about his inaugural broadcast with the Red Roses. There was nothing that stood out, like in Saam's debut. "Hello, Byrum Saam," his first game began, "this is everybody speaking."

Saam displayed many other malaprops, but he had a magical voice and he was so charming, so innocent, so prepared that he became a well-loved announcer — and a man who helped pave the way for Bill Campbell's success.

Campbell would always have a soft spot for Saam….and for that Atlantic City couch.

CHAPTER FOUR

Finding love at the radio station...
and being mesmerized by Mr. Mack

In the 1940s, Jo DeCesaris' job title at WIP radio was the boss'
"secretary," but the strikingly pretty young woman nearly ran the station, which was operated by Ben "B.G." Gimbel and located in the
thriving Gimbel Brothers department store on 9th and Chestnut in
Philadelphia. B.G. was a nephew of one of Gimbel Brothers' founders.

Jo did a little of everything at the radio station, including lining
up famous guests — such as actress Ella Logan — and escorting them
through Gimbel's department store and making sure they received dis-
counts on their purchases. In addition to her myriad of administrative
duties, Jo was the editor of the *WIPeroo*, a company newspaper that
kept people abreast of the comings and goings at the station.

Bill Campbell had worked as a WIP summer relief announcer
for a year and had been a casual acquaintance of Jo's. Nothing more.
When he left his part-time gig at WIP and went into the Coast Guard
in October of 1942, he followed the station's fortunes in Jo's snappily
written newsletter. It was a good diversion from the atrocities that
World War II was producing.

In the Coast Guard, Campbell spent 18 months in Florida and
six months in Atlantic City, where he went to radio-communications
school. That was followed by convoy duty in the Atlantic and several
ports in Europe and North Africa. Campbell was en route to the
Pacific Theatre, "and as we were going through the Panama Canal, the
war ended," he recalled. He was shipped to Delaware and was a radio
communications director aboard a navigational tender.

When he came home on leave, Bill would stop by the WIP
studios.

"He looked so cute in his sailor suit," recalled Jo, who was
known as "Miss Dee" around the radio station.

During one of his leaves, Bill went to visit his sister, Polly, who was nearly three years younger than him. Bill had a letter informing him that Polly was becoming a nun.

He read the letter twice to make sure he hadn't misunderstood. He could have envisioned his baby sister, Julie, joining the convent. But Polly? Loud and opinionated Polly? Bill thought the letter was a joke.

"I went to visit her and I said, 'What kind of order would have *you*?'" Campbell said with a laugh. "Polly and I were always going at it. We were average students and we were always getting into trouble. Brother-and-sister stuff. Julie, on the other hand, never did anything wrong. She was an angel. She was always above the fray — never gave me, or anybody, anything to argue about. She was always low-key. Still is. Never gets too excited. Never gets ruffled."

Bill had a pleasant visit with Polly, wished her well, and returned to the Coast Guard.

The time in the service, Campbell said, "taught me responsibility and taught me to be respectful of other people. I really grew up in the service. I was a smart-aleck kind of kid who really didn't have any roots at home and didn't have any discipline at home like most kids had. The service was a good thing for me. I had a commanding officer who taught me that I was responsible not only for myself, but I was responsible for the lives of the guys around me."

When his Coast Guard stint ended in May of 1946, Bill figured he would see if WIP would take him back.

"WIP did not owe me a job because I had only been a temporary employee when I left," Campbell said. "Under terms of the GI Bill, they did not have to take me back."

To Campbell's surprise, the station had a spot for him. He would get a few lines in Jo's *WIPeroo*.

The job offer altered Campbell's plans to return to St. Joseph's College, which he had briefly attended before entering the service.

"I had applied for the GI Bill and had every expectation to go back to school," he said, "but when they had a job for me, I had a decision to make. We didn't have any money at home; my father was having all kinds of financial problems. I was afraid that if I turned down this job, there wouldn't be any other jobs."

He took the position as a general staff announcer at WIP. He would serve as a DJ, read commercials, and give the newscasts. Whatever was needed, he did it. He would also fill in when Stoney McLinn — the sports director and the man who would shape Campbell's career — wasn't available to broadcast his sports reports. Campbell also was given a chance to do recreations of Philadelphia Athletics baseball games.

It was a hectic schedule, so college was put on hold.

Getting a college degree to work in radio "probably wasn't the necessary thing that it is now, but I've always wanted to go back," Campbell said. "I've always felt that I've lacked something in education. I've worked hard to make up for it. I've listened to a lot of people and I think I've learned a lot. But I've always regretted that I didn't go back to school. It's something I didn't accomplish and I don't even like to talk about it."

Irony of ironies: Without a degree, he became the most lasting radio voice in Philadelphia history — a man who deserves a doctorate in communications.

"Even if I had attained a college degree, I still would have been a sports broadcaster," Campbell said. "It was the only thing I ever wanted to do."

———•———

Jo DeCesaris grew up in South Camden and attended Woodrow Wilson High in East Camden. She worked for a while at a Camden radio station, WCAM, but the hours were scattered so she went to WIP in January of 1941.

By 1946, she was firmly entrenched at the station, which featured Big Band music and call-in contests designed to gain more listeners. The station even had its own orchestra that performed on the radio. Joe Frasetto was the band leader.

"Swing and sweat with Joe Frasett," was the WIP slogan.

Back then, the airwaves were filled with more entertainment and fewer sales pitches.

"In those days, the law only allowed one commercial before the station break and one after the break," Jo said. "It was much more pleasant than it is now, where they give you five or six commercials at a time. And they're long. At that time, they were only 30-second commercials."

In the 1940's, WIP was vastly different than the all-sports station created on December 7, 1987. By the same token, the WIP of the 1940s bore little resemblance to the one that became the first Philadelphia radio station in 1922. One of the station's most popular early programs was called "Uncle WIP" (rhymes with ship), a show in which radio personality Christopher Graham — and later Wayne Cody — would read bedtime stories to children. The Gimbel Brothers department store owned the station. At the time, other department stores, such as Strawbridge & Clothier (WFI) and John Wanamaker (WOO), owned other radio stations; they promoted their stations in their department-store ads.

WIP is credited with broadcasting several "firsts" to Philadelphia audiences, including a college football game (Penn-Cornell in 1922), an opera, and a church service. In its early years, the station featured the basics: time updates, weather reports, and musical recitals. Before long, boxing matches, baseball scores, budding crooners, news reports, and theatre pickups were added to the repertoire.

This is the radio industry that Bill Campbell remembers as a youngster. If he didn't make it as a pro baseball player, he figured, this is where he belonged.

When Campbell got out of the service and returned to WIP in 1946, he was greeted by an announcers' strike. Dutifully, he walked with a strike placard outside the station's Center City studio. But he hated the strike, hated not being behind a microphone. The strike ended quickly and Campbell and the rest of the WIP announcers — including the legendary John Facenda — were back in business.

In September of that year, just a little less than four months after Bill's return to the station, Jo found herself working late when Ben Gimbel told her he wasn't able to use tickets to *What Every Woman Knows*, a comedy that was playing at a Center City hotel that night.

"If you want them, they're yours," he told her.

She wanted them, but it was already 7 o'clock — an hour before the curtain would rise.

"Why didn't he tell me earlier?" she muttered in a low tone as she walked down a long WIP hallway and headed home. "How can I find someone so quickly? What a shame to have these tickets go to waste."

As she approached the elevator, the door opened. Out walked Bill. Jo was still mumbling to herself.

"What's wrong?" Bill asked.

"Oh, I just have these two tickets and I have to get someone to go with me," she said. "At this late hour, I'll probably just throw them away."

"I'll go with you," Bill said, cheerfully.

"Oh, come on."

"I'd be happy to go," he insisted.

"Really? Swell."

They went out that night and a few days later, Bill asked her to go to an Eagles game at Shibe Park. Jo bought a new coat for the occasion and sat with Bill in the stands. From that day, they sat at a lot of ball games together.

It was a whirlwind romance. Bill felt secure with Jo's nurturing and motherly personality. Jo was attracted to Bill's honesty and kindness. The way he cared for Stoney McLinn, the handicapped sports director who had hip and leg problems and used a cane to get around, made her heart melt.

"Just the way he treated Stoney was enough to make you love him," she said. "He was so kind to him. Stoney leaned on him to walk. I mean, *literally* leaned on him."

About three months after their first date, Jo and Bill attended *Finian's Rainbow*, a musical starring Ella Logan. Again, B.G. got the tickets, though this time he gave them to Jo far in advance of the show, which was held a few days before Christmas.

There was another difference. While the show was being performed, Bill wrapped his arms around Jo and handed her a box. As she opened it, she squinted hard and used the reflection of the stage's spotlight to get a glimpse of what was inside.

It was an engagement ring, which Bill had purchased at a Philadelphia jewelry store. His father had gone with him to help pick the ring.

Less than six months later, on June 7, 1947, Bill and Jo were married at Our Lady of Mount Carmel Church in Camden. The night before the wedding, Bill slept at the home of his best man, Jim McQuaide, the brother of the altar boy who had died when he was crushed by the religious statue. Bill became panic-stricken that night when he realized he didn't have black shoes to go with his tux. Campbell and his best friend hurried to find a shoe store that was open on Germantown Avenue. They found one. Bill wouldn't have to wear brown shoes.

At the wedding, a beaming Jo wore an elegant gown that she had made. The *WIPeroo* reported that the priest who married Bill and Jo was "such a dead ringer for John Facenda that one wag remarked, 'What John won't do for a commercial fee…' "

The newsletter also gave an account of the reception, which was held at Deighan's in Camden: "All had a gala time because every-thing was just right. Nice orchestra, pretty hall, charming people and lotsa kickapoo juice."

Nearly 60 years after their wedding, Bill says the highlight of his radio career was that it allowed him to meet his wife.

"Best thing that ever happened to me," he said.

By the time Bill and Jo were married, neither was working at WIP.

Bill had left WIP to become the sports director at WCAU radio in October of 1946. "I was given $75 a week and I thought it was more than God," Bill said.

With such a comfortable salary and their marriage around the corner, he asked Jo to stop working. They could make it without her $50-a-week paycheck.

This was an era when a man's pride was hurt if he couldn't support his wife on his own salary.

Jo and Bill Campbell in their 1947 wedding photo.

Ben Gimbel, Jo's boss at WIP, was furious at Bill's decision. Jo was his point person; she made the station run smoothly and he didn't want to lose her.

He phoned Bill at WCAU and asked if he would meet him for lunch.

Bill was stunned to get the call. "When I worked at WIP, he never talked to me," he said with a smile.

They met for lunch at the Ben Franklin Hotel. Gimbel made an impassioned plea.

"He *begged* me to let her work, and I said no," Campbell said. "Ben Gimbel didn't want to be bothered by all the details of management and he really depended on her a great deal. If you wanted to get anything done at WIP, you went through Jo. Jo didn't care whether she stayed or not. He said to her, 'Why don't you want to work? You run the station?' And she said, 'I want to have a baby.'"

"Anyway, it was a dumb thing. We should have let her work. We didn't have a baby for five years or so, and in the meantime, every time Ben Gimbel would see Jo, he would say, 'Where's the goddamn baby?!'"

Campbell let out a robust laugh.

"If I had to do it all over again," he said, "I would have let her work."

———•———

Bill blossomed into one of the area's most respected sports authorities during his time at WCAU from 1946 to 1963, a period that included stints doing the sports on Channel 10's nightly newscasts. Facenda did the news, Phil Sheridan, Hugh Ferguson, and Herb Clark were among the weathermen, and Jack Whitaker and Campbell did most of the sports reports. TV was a new medium on those days — in 1948, Facenda, whose baritone voice commanded your attention, did the nation's first local 11 p.m. news broadcast.

Though he became a part of the TV crew, Campbell still did radio work at WCAU.

"I felt more loyalty to radio because that's where I started," he said. "I didn't want to just jump out of radio and go to TV. Maybe it was a mistake, but that's the way I felt. I liked radio because you had to be more descriptive and I enjoyed that aspect. You were both the ears and eyes of the listeners."

Before landing at WCAU radio and TV, it was Stoney McLinn, the WIP sports director, who put Campbell's career in motion.

Campbell became a proverbial walking encyclopedia of sports. He asked a gazillion questions, digested the information, and saved it for just the right time. He had an insatiable hunger for knowledge. McLinn was his unofficial teacher. Even when Campbell wasn't working, he would be in McLinn's office, watching how he prepared for his nightly sports show, learning how to write tight scripts, and how to punctuate broadcasts with perfectly timed inflection in his voice.

McLinn, a colorful character, had been a sportswriter at the *Philadelphia Record* before being hired at WIP radio. He had been around the sports scene for decades and he took a liking to Campbell and nurtured him. "He helped me get to know a lot of people," Campbell said. "He knew everybody. He had been Ty Cobb's ghost-writer through all kinds of things, so that's how far back he went."

There would be stories in newspapers, magazines and books that had Ty Cobb as the author, but it was Stoney McLinn who wrote the words, Campbell said.

"Someone who could write was the person who wrote the stories for the players. That's how it was in those days," Campbell said. "Those guys never wrote things themselves. Therefore, Stoney knew everybody. Chief Bender, the great A's pitcher, was a great friend of his. The guys whom I met — Lefty Grove, Rube Walberg, George Earnshaw and all those guys from the A's — I met through Stoney. I got to know Mr. [Connie] Mack and the A's and the Phillies through Stoney. Stoney went to a lot of games but he couldn't operate physically on his own. His only support in his life was his wife, Bess, and she was just a terrific lady. Some days she couldn't make it and I would go. She would call me up and say, 'Can you drive Stoney to the game?' "

Bill and McLinn combined to do a WIP sports show that was called, quite simply, "The Kid and the Oldtimer." It was a half-hour show that centered around the sports world and had a Philadelphia flavor. They later did the show on Channel 3.

McLinn, a former president of the Philadelphia Sportswriters' Association, had been one of the A's and Phillies radio announcers; he had contacts all over the city and he informed Bill when WCAU was looking for a sports director.

"Stoney and someone in the 'CAU newsroom recommended me for the job," Campbell said.

Campbell went for the tryout but didn't get a vote of confidence from his mentor, McLinn.

"I want you to audition; it'll be good for you," McLinn told Campbell.

"I'll do it."

"You're not going to get it. You're too young and inexperienced and I'm sure they're going to hire someone who's worked somewhere else," McLinn replied, "but it'll be a good experience for you. See how you do. But I don't want you to get down if you don't get it."

"OK."

Campbell wowed them at the audition. And he didn't even have to describe a couch or office drapes, like he did at his Atlantic City tryout. At the tender age of 23, he was hired as WCAU radio's sports director. He did a sports show every night at 6:15, interviewed visiting major-league baseball players who came into the city, hosted a sports quiz show, made personal appearances, and soon did Penn football broadcasts, among other things.

WCAU sent Campbell on a two-week trip to Florida to cover the Phillies' and Athletics' spring-training camps in 1947. The Phillies were in Clearwater, the A's in West Palm Beach. Campbell spent the last two days of the trip covering the Mackmen (as the A's were affectionately known) face the Phillies in a pair of city-series exhibition games.

Before Campbell left for Florida, the *Philadelphia Dispatch*, in its March 9th edition, trumpeted his coverage plans:

Bill's sunny, southern observations will be transcribed and airmailed back to WCAU for incorporation in the live portion of his sports broadcast heard daily at 6:15 p.m. His Sunday "Weekly Sports Roundup" also will be transcribed by Bill while he's away, the newspaper reported.

The 24/7 information highway was still decades away, but Bill Campbell was becoming a media star. At around the same time, he was doing a Saturday morning "Time Out" radio show on WCAU with Joe Thomas and some local sports guests. The sports quiz show was for teenage boys, and sports equipment was awarded as prizes.

"And to this day, I bump into somebody at least once a month who tells me they were on that show," Campbell said.

Campbell was praised by *Variety* for "keeping the show fast-paced with his rapid-fire chatter."

A few months later, *Variety* mentioned that Campbell was part of a national sports radio show that was under the direction of Red Barber. The show featured reports from various sportscasters who worked for CBS affiliates. *Variety* gave Campbell high marks for his "punchy, economical style."

Bill was becoming so well-known — he was also making appearances and presentations and numerous local functions, and he was vice president of the Philadelphia Basketball Writers' Association — that newspapers carried an ad that read: "Bill Campbell Has Switched to Calvert Because Calvert Whiskey Tastes Better."

At around the same time, Campbell was doing numerous reports from Philadelphia A's games. For the first time in his life, he was nearly awestruck as he interviewed "Mr. Baseball," the legendary Connie Mack, who was the A's owner and manager.

The Philadelphia Athletics' Connie Mack (left) is a guest on "Time Out," the Saturday morning youth-participation show that Bill Campbell (right) hosted on WCAU radio in the 1940s.

"One of the biggest thrills I ever had was meeting Mr. Mack after I became a broadcaster. And having Mr. Mack call me Mr. Campbell," he said. "Here I was, a 20-some-year-old kid, and I'm walking around like I knew what was going on, and Mr. Mack called me Mr. Campbell. He called all his players Mister, too. He called everybody Mister."

Campbell remembers sitting in the dugout when the phone rang before one particular game, and Mack nodding to him, as if to say, 'Answer the phone.' Campbell complied.

"It's the press box; they want to talk to you," Campbell told Mack.

Mack talked for a half minute, hung up the phone and had a proposition for Bill.

"Well, you're a broadcaster, and you can do me a big favor today."

"What would you like me to do?" Campbell asked.

"The public-address announcer is sick and we need someone to fill in. Would you like to do it?"

You didn't turn down Cornelius Alexander McGillicuddy, who had shortened his name to Connie Mack during his playing days so it would fit on the scorecard. Campbell said he would happy to do it.

In those days, the P.A. announcer sat in a submerged area that was next to the A's dugout. You sat on a bench with a microphone and you went about your business. "It wasn't very taxing. You announced the starting lineups and you informed the crowd when there was a change of pitchers or a pinch hitter. But that was the extent of it," Campbell said. "You really didn't have much to do; it's not like nowadays and all the duties that Dan Baker has with the Phillies."

The best part, he said, was that you could hear the byplay of all the players. "It was a great place to watch the game; it was like being in the dugout. And you got to hear all the comments that everybody was making: 'Lay off this pitch' or whatever."

During this particular game, A's first baseman Ferris Fain made a rare error and it started a chain of events that Campbell has never forgotten.

"Fain made the 3-5 play better than anyone," Campbell said. "He was utterly fearless in bunt situations. If anybody ever pulled back and took a swing and hit it at him, they would have killed him because he was in so close every time, and he'd field the bunt and throw the guy out at third. Hank Majeski was the third baseman."

With Bill in the P.A. area next to the dugout and an opposing runner on second, Fain fielded a bunt and threw the ball 10 feet over Majeski's head at third.

"And the whole inning fell apart," Campbell said. "Mr. Mack was very disturbed and they came in at the end of the inning and Fain was prancing up and down the dugout, mad as hell; he had a hair-trigger temper. And he's pacing up and down in the front of the dugout, and every time he would come to a stop, he would stop right in front of the old man [Mack]. And the old man couldn't see the game and he knew the old man was a little upset. So he turned around and said to the old man, 'What would you rather have me do with the ball, stick it up my ass?' And Mr. Mack said, 'It would have been a lot safer there.' "

———————

When Mack died in 1956 at age 93, Campbell did a heartfelt WCAU radio show that was titled "Connie Mack: His Life and Death."

Here are some snippets of the 10-minute tribute:

"The news that baseball and the world of sports has dreaded to face for a decade or more came to pass today. At 3:20 this afternoon in suburban Mount Airy, Connie Mack died....

"The patriarch of baseball had concluded a 71-year career in the game just 15 months ago; 71 years as a player, manager and team president, a career unparalleled in anything in America. And a career that was sadly climaxed by the sale of his beloved Athletics to Kansas City. After the sale, Mr. Mack started downhill. He suffered a definite mental and physical setback...."

Campbell mentioned that, as a teenager, Mack — who was born during the Civil War — worked at one of the shoe factories in his Massachusetts town.

"At the age of 19, he became a foreman and before he was 21 he was an assistant manager. But then he discovered baseball. From that day, the

only interest shoes held for him were to keep his feet warm. Baseball was not long in discovering Cornelius McGillicuddy, either, and the partnership was something fabulous. Those of us who were blessed with his personal friendship were the recipients of a gift that can never be equaled. We are much poorer tonight for having lost him.

"The biggest thrill I used to get every year was spring training with the A's at West Palm Beach and those hours we used to spend in the hotel lobby just sitting there and listening to him. Mr. Mack made an impression on me that no one will ever equal. I never completely got used to being on informal speaking terms with him; and if several weeks or months would pass between visits, it always struck me as completely remarkable that he would remember my name. Just about two years ago — before he stopped granting interviews because of his failing memory — I went up to see him in The Tower at Shibe Park. I knocked on his door and he told me to enter. As I approached his desk, and in an effort to be helpful, I put out my hand and told him my name. He frowned at me rather severely, I thought, and he said, 'William, you must really think I'm getting old. Don't you think I know your name?' Such was the greatness of this man. His greatness, I always thought, was in his simplicity."

Campbell talked about Mack taking over the A's in 1900 and how Mack loved reminiscing about his first pennant in 1902 and his second in 1905. And many times, Campbell told listeners, he heard Mack describe the famous court battle when Larry "Nap" Lajoie, one of the greatest second baseman in baseball history, jumped from the Phillies and joined the A's — and the National League team subsequently obtained an injunction to prevent him from playing in Pennsylvania. Campbell talked about the A's players who became stars under Mack, and how Mack used to say that A's outfielder Bing Miller "could hit the curve better than any batsman he ever saw. These days, a fellow swinging a bat at the plate is called a hitter. Mr. Mack always used the term batsman. I never heard anyone else use it. It was one of his words."

Over the airways, you could *feel* the sincerity and admiration in Campbell's voice.

"This is at best a horrible, feeble, and rather inept effort to tell you something about Mr. Baseball. It has not yet been three hours since he died.

It is physically impossible to cram 71 years of devoted service to baseball into three hours of thinking. And it is completely preposterous to believe that it can be inserted properly into any 10-minute program. A Mack memory builds on a Mack memory. You can just go on and on....

"He left us today. It's an irreparable loss for baseball; it's like some-body stealing home plate. And yet the game will go on. It will continue and it will survive. This reporter voices the hope that it will continue in the tra-dition of Cornelius McGillicuddy, whose book of life was opened in East Brookfield, Massachusetts, in 1862 and closed this afternoon in Philadelphia in 1956. Many other things of note happened in sports today, but in a phrase — who cares? This program, too, is completely devoid of any com-mercial message. Which is as it should be. Everything around town seems to be standing still. It was a bright, sunny day, but since 3:20 this afternoon it's clouded up a bit. But then it had to. For at 3:20 this afternoon, Connie Mack died. May he rest in peace."

While Campbell did nightly sports broadcasts and filed reports on the A's and Phillies in the late 1940s, he also provided the color for play-by-play announcer By Saam at Penn football games. Penn was *the* football team in Philadelphia in those days. Yes, bigger than the Eagles. Much bigger.

"I tell my grandson that and he looks at me like I belong on the funny farm," Campbell said. "We would get 70,000 every Saturday for Penn football at Franklin Field. The Eagles were playing at Shibe Park and would get maybe 20,000 fans. The emphasis was on the college game back then.

"Penn was playing a national schedule. Harold Stassen was the president of the university and he was lusting for the Republican nomination for president. He had been the boy-wonder governor of Minnesota. He had a great, great future in national politics and there wasn't any doubt about the fact that he was headed to the White House — at least that was his ambition," Campbell said.

Stassen, who died in 2001 at 93, ended up seeking the Republican presidential nomination nine times. Nine times, he lost. Stassen managed to keep his good humor, despite being lampooned

— one political cartoon showed his supporters gathering in a phone booth — and sometimes being called "the Grand Old Party's grand old loser."

When he was Penn's president, Stassen was indirectly trying to get the football team to win him some votes, Campbell assumed.

"I guess Stassen figured it would bolster his chances of getting the nomination for president if he played a national schedule. We would play Notre Dame, Southern Cal, Ohio State, Wisconsin, Minnesota, Northwestern. It was terrific. And every Saturday was a big game. They were packing the place at Franklin Field."

Campbell was content to be Saam's sidekick for several years.

"I read the commercials and made a few comments at halftime and during timeouts. That kind of thing," Campbell said.

Saam and Campbell would later work together for eight years in the Phillies' broadcast booth, but it was during their days at Penn that Campbell realized the secret to Saam's success.

"Nobody prepared for a game — baseball or football — like Byrum Saam," Campbell said, fondly. "He was unbelievable and I really learned about preparation from By and tried to prepare like he did. He was always ready."

In addition to Penn games, Saam had also been working the Eagles' broadcasts during football season. But in 1955, he left his job at Penn to concentrate on the Eagles. Campbell waited patiently to find the identity of Penn's new play-by-play man. About a month before the season, he was called into the WCAU radio offices and told that the exhaustive search had finally ended.

He was the new play-by-play man.

"I want to tell you, I was scared to death," he said. "The opening game was around the corner and I'm shaking in my boots. I didn't know what to do. I wasn't going to turn it down, but I didn't know what the hell to do."

Campbell says he made perhaps $100 for doing the play-by-play, which was $50 more than the color man. He didn't care about the increase.

He just didn't want to embarrass himself.

"The only time I did play-by-play was when I did Catholic League and Public League high school games," he said.

Concerned that he was overmatched, Campbell phoned Steve Sebo and explained his predicament to the Penn football coach.

"I knew him because I had been the Penn color man, and I told him what my problem was," Campbell said. "I said, 'I'm afraid I'm your guy.' "

"What are you afraid of?" Sebo asked.

"To tell you the truth, Steve, I don't know if I can handle it."

Campbell had received excellent guidance over the years from former Penn head coach George Munger, but he still had doubts about doing the play-by-play. Sebo asked Campbell to come to Penn's practice at 4 o'clock that afternoon.

"If we can make you sound good, it'll be good for the football team and good for the university," he told Campbell.

Sebo invited Campbell to attend as many practices as he wanted, adding that he and assistant coach Paul Riblett would take turns helping him.

"We're going to make a football coach out of you," Sebo said.

Campbell went to practice every day for the next three weeks. "At the end of three weeks, I not only knew the whole Penn system, I knew Notre Dame's," Campbell said of the Quakers' opening-game opponent. "Still, I was scared to death of the opener."

Penn's Frank Riepl took Paul Hornung's opening kickoff and, on the first call of Campbell's career as a college football play-by-play announcer, raced on a 108-yard touchdown return — an unofficial NCAA record.

"That's the first play I described, and I was fine after that," Campbell said with a laugh. "I described everything. Every detail, every move Riepl made, every missed tackle."

Like a football player who gets rid of the jitters after the initial hit, Campbell's nervousness disappeared when the opening kickoff was over. As a kid, he had walked around his Logan home using a rolled-up towel as a pretend microphone while he created the play-by-play. Now he was doing the real thing. He was officially Penn's football announcer. He was a star was in the making.

A few weeks later, Riepl was a guest on the popular network TV show, "I've Got a Secret", hosted by Garry Moore.

The panelists would ask questions to figure out what the person had accomplished. Riepl stumped the first three panelists before Bill Cullen correctly guessed his secret.

"I won $60 but I donated the money to a club on campus so I wouldn't lose my amateur status," Riepl said from his home in Vero Beach, Florida. Riepl became an executive with a New Jersey utility company before retiring in 1998 and moving from central New Jersey to south Florida. In 2005, Riepl, along with his family, returned to Franklin Field to be honored at a Penn-Cornell game; the university was celebrating the 50-year anniversary of his miracle kickoff return.

And, yes, there on KYW radio was the same voice that had described his famous touchdown. Fifty years after making the call, Bill Campbell was still going strong.

———•———

At WCAU in the '50s and '60s, Campbell would also do play-by-play work for the Philadelphia Warriors, the Philadelphia Eagles, and Big 5 basketball.

But it would take a while before anything came close to matching the excitement of Riepl's return. This was an era when Campbell seemed to be at every Philadelphia sporting event. If you turned on your radio or TV, there was a good chance Campbell was there. In addition to doing play-by-play for Penn football and Warriors and Big 5 basketball in 1955, Campbell did 11 radio shows and three TV shows each week.

The demands on his time didn't cause him to take any shortcuts. He was always at the teams' practices, always picking the coaches' brains, always reading as many newspapers, magazines, and books as time would allow. Anything to make himself a better announcer.

He carried that same work ethic into any broadcast that he worked, including college and pro basketball, Eagles football, and Phillies baseball.

"I've really been fortunate in my career that I've been around people who really knew what they were doing," Campbell said. "I learned more about football, particularly on the offensive side, from Norm Van Brocklin than I ever thought there was to learn. The same thing with baseball and Gene Mauch."

And basketball with Jack Ramsay.

Campbell was doing a lot of Big 5 basketball games in those days. In fact, he did college games of the Big 5 teams before the "Philly league" was officially established in 1955-56.

In the Big 5's first season, Ramsay was beginning a highly successful 11-year tenure at St. Joseph's, where his Hawks rarely died. They went 232-72, won or shared seven Big 5 titles, and reached the post-season 10 times. That led to a Hall of Fame coaching career that took him to the NBA's 76ers, Buffalo Braves, Portland Trailblazers, and Indiana Pacers.

'When I was doing basketball, the biggest problem I had was trying to tell the difference when a team switched from a zone press to a man-to-man press, and vice versa," Campbell said. "I couldn't get it into my head when I was doing play-by-play whether it was a zone or 'man' press. Jack Ramsay had written a book called *Pressure Defense* and it was a pretty widely accepted book. And I bought the book and read the damn thing cover to cover and got absolutely nothing out of it. It just went right over my head and I couldn't absorb it. I was doing a lot of St. Joe's games and I finally went to Jack at a practice one day and asked how you tell the difference between a zone and 'man' press. Jack walked me though it at a gym and I finally got it through my head."

Bill Campbell was never afraid to show his vulnerability, never afraid to ask questions. Unknowingly, his listeners were the ones who benefited.

CHAPTER FIVE

Soupy's ticket to fame

When Bill Campbell was told he was receiving the Curt Gowdy Media Award from the Naismith Memorial Basketball Hall of Fame in 2005, his mind revisited snapshots of many magical (and a few forgettable) moments of his basketball broadcasting career.

Joe Fulks taking what was then a revolutionary shot — a jumper — for the old Philadelphia Warriors.....Julius Erving skying toward the rafters, holding the ball high above the rim as he prepared to throw down one of his highlight-film jams for the 76ers...The legendary 1966 Big 5 game where little-used Steve Donches hit a 29-footer at the buzzer, lifting St. Joseph's past Villanova, 71-69, at the frenzied Palestra....The futility of the 9-73 76ers....Jack Ramsay taking time from St. Joseph's practices to explain his intricate defensive scheme to a young broadcaster....The night in Hershey, Pennsylvania, where 4,124 fans attended a meaningless regular-season game between the Philadelphia Warriors and lowly New York Knicks.

"And over the years, I've talked to at least 40,000 people who claim they were there that night," Campbell said.

That night — March 2, 1962 — 7-foot-1 Philadelphia center Wilt Chamberlain scored an NBA-record 100 points in the Warriors' 169-147 victory. Campbell's broadcast has become a part of sports lore:

"In to Chamberlain. He made it! He made it! He made it! A dipper dunk! He made it! The fans are all over the floor! They've stopped the game! People are running out on the court! One hundred points for Wilt Chamberlain!"

It has become a famed sports broadcast, sort of like Russ Hodges announcing Bobby Thomson's dramatic three-run homer in 1951. ("There's a long drive! It's going to be, I believe! The Giants win the pennant! The Giants win the pennant! The Giants win the pennant!)

That broadcast is one of Campbell's calling cards and undoubtedly played a role in helping him land in the Hall of Fame in Springfield, Massachusetts.

Oddly, it was a game Campbell said "seemed more like an exhibition."

The game was played in Hershey — Chocolatetown, USA —- because the Warriors were having problems attracting fans to Philadelphia. The Warriors, who called Convention Hall their home, weren't drawing well, so they decided to play three "home" games that season in Hershey, along with one in Syracuse, New York, and another in Utica, New York.

This particular game was the Warriors' third and final trip that season to Hershey, the town where they had held their training camp.

And, yes, at times, Campbell thought he was watching an exhibition game that night.

"There was no doubt, certainly in the second half, that they were going for a record for Wilt," Campbell said. "It was more of that than a competitive game. Wilt was in pursuit of a record and he had a lot of cooperation from his teammates. Paul Arizin, who was a hell of a shooter, passed up open shots and gave the ball to Wilt." The same goes for Tom Meschery and Al Attles. And Guy Rodgers was at his playmaking best, dealing 20 assists.

Darrall Imhoff, one of the many players who unsuccessfully guarded the 25-year-old Chamberlain that night, called the game a joke because of the way the Warriors bypassed open shots and fed the ball to the Dipper almost every time down court.

Maybe that's one of the reasons the Basketball Hall of Fame, on its website, says that Campbell "called Wilt Chamberlain's infamous 100-point game."

Looking back on it now, Campbell says the game was more amusing than anything else. But infamous? It depends on your point of view. To some, the game was a farce because the Knicks, despite facing a huge fourth-quarter deficit, weren't trying to score as quickly as possible to slice the lead.

Instead, they tried to waste time and keep the ball out of Chamberlain's hands.

Regardless, the game made Chamberlain's legend grow and it helped put Campbell on a national stage. To this day, it remains the most quoted broadcast of Campbell's career.

Still, the game does not rank high on Campbell's list of favorite broadcasts.

"It doesn't because it wasn't a real competitive game," he said. "I have a lot of baseball and football games that I'd put ahead of that. To me, the team is more important than any individual. But this was strictly in pursuit of a record.

"I don't get all fired up about that game; he made it look so easy. He was unmatchable."

In *Wilt: Just Like Any Other 7-Foot Black Millionaire Who Lives Next Door*, Chamberlain said he dated a woman in New York the night before his historic game and that "by the time we were done enjoying ourselves, it was 6 o'clock in the morning."

Chamberlain boarded a train from New York, where he lived, to Philadelphia at around 8 a.m. He said he ate and talked during the entire trip and never slept. When he arrived in Philly, he said, he had lunch with friends and, when he finished, it was almost time to board the team bus to Hershey for that night's game.

When he arrived in Hershey at 5 p.m., he played some pinball — winning several bets in the process — and then headed to the Hershey Sports Arena locker room, where Warriors coach Frank McGuire showed Chamberlain two New York newspaper stories that quoted some Knicks saying Chamberlain was slow and didn't have any stamina.

"Let's run 'em tonight, Wilt," McGuire said in Chamberlain's autobiography.

Chamberlain, the most physically imposing player in the NBA, could not be contained by Imhoff, Cleveland Buckner, or Dave Budd. Nor by Willie Naulls or Jumpin' Johnny Green.

By the half, he had 41 points; he lifted his total to 69 with a 28-point third quarter.

From the WCAU radio studios, By Saam introduced Campbell, who set the scene for his listeners: "This is the big fourth quarter and everybody's thinking, 'How many is Wilt gonna get?' "

The fans in the drafty old arena realized they might be in the middle of a historic development. As the fourth quarter started, they could not contain their enthusiasm. "Give it to Wilt!" (CLAP) "Give it to Wilt!" (CLAP) they chanted.

The Warriors complied. The Knicks tried milking the 24-second clock and began fouling other Warriors to keep the ball away from Chamberlain. The Warriors then started committing their own fouls to get the ball back.

After a few minutes of the final quarter, Chamberlain had increased his total to 75, breaking his own NBA record for points in a regulation game. "The players on the Warriors' bench are jumping for joy for him," Campbell gushed.

The game no longer was feeling like an exhibition to Campbell, whose voice became giddier than usual.

"We're just conjecturing here how many he can make. He's got nine minutes and 24 seconds left, and the guesses are running as high as 100. Wouldn't THAT be something?"

Old announcers' axiom: When a pitcher is throwing a no-hitter, do not mention it to the listeners because of fear you will jinx his accomplishment.

Did Campbell fear he would jinx Chamberlain by daring to mention the words that everyone was thinking — *one hundred?*

Campbell didn't subscribe to the jinx theory— not when a pitcher was throwing a no-hitter and not when an NBA player was on the verge of reaching triple digits for the first time in history.

"That jinx stuff," said Campbell, his voice getting fiery, "is a bunch of crap. Red Barber put that to rest a long time ago."

Barber is regarded as one of the best baseball announcers to ever grace a microphone. Barber also hosted national radio shows and Campbell used to file reports for him.

"When I worked for Red Barber he said, 'Don't do that superstitious crap.' " Campbell said. So when a pitcher was throwing a no-hitter, "he would tell people that so-and-so has not given up a hit, fans. We had no control over what was happening on the field. Red's point, and I agree with it, was that there's a guy who just jumped into his car after a real tough day at the office and he puts on his radio, and that guy is entitled to know what's going on just as much as somebody who has been there since the first pitch. And to deprive that guy that a no-hitter is in the works, well, you're not doing your job as a reporter."

Campbell used that same theory with Chamberlain's 100-point game. He continually gave running updates on his point total, and, even in the opening minutes of the fourth quarter, he wasn't shy to mention that 100 was on everyone's mind.

Chamberlain made an inside bucket and was fouled with about eight minutes left. His point total was at 77.

"Field goal, Chaaaaaam-ber-lain, is gooooooooooooooooood!" public-address announcer Dave "The Zink" Zinkoff told the crowd.

Campbell supplied Chamberlain anecdotes during the final quarter.

"This guy is just a magnificent athlete, there's no question about it. He's quite a runner; he's a good high-jumper. He handles the weights and takes excellent care of himself and it pays off here. Jimmy Brown of the Cleveland Browns was telling me just yesterday — he's a great friend of Wilt's — and he was saying how Wilt really works at physical conditioning. He said it's no surprise that he's so great; he works so hard to attain it.

"Jimmy Brown says he has one distinction: He's the only guy who's ever beaten Wilt Chamberlain in hand wrestling, and Jimmy Brown says it took him 23 minutes to get his arm down.

"Chamberlain with a jumper from the circle. GOOD! He's broken all kinds of records now. 141 to 124 is the score; he had 78 in triple-overtime [against Los Angeles nearly three months earlier]; he's past that now in regulation. He has 79."

A short time later, as Chamberlain went to the foul line to shoot two free throws, Zinkoff announced to the crowd that he had just set an NBA record for points in a game. The fans stood and screamed, but Wilt didn't pay much attention, Campbell told his listeners.

"And during the announcement, Chamberlain goes right ahead through the announcement and makes a foul. They're still making the announcement, he makes ANOTHER foul. Chamberlain didn't even listen to it! He just made two straight fouls and he now has 81 points. Eighty-one."

After Chamberlain scored his 84th point, Campbell became even more enthusiastic.

"If you know anybody not listening, call them up. A little history you're sitting in on tonight."

For most of the fourth quarter, the Knicks played keepaway to kill some clock. The game may have been 90 miles northwest of Philadelphia, but the fans knew the sound that made that city famous:

Booooooooooooooooooo!!!

Campbell leaned into his microphone at courtside.

"They are not taking the shot," he said. "They are eating up time."

Less than seven minutes remained, and Campbell told listeners that Wilt had scored 23 in the first quarter, 18 in the second quarter and 28 in the third quarter. He had already accounted for 15 fourth-quarter points and had lifted his total to 84.

"You know what's in the fans' mind, they're thinking of the magic number — 100…Six and half minutes to go, it's possible. Nothing is impossible with this big man."

A short time later:

"New York is really trying to screen Chamberlain off and trying to prevent them from getting the ball into the big man."

With 3:22 to play, Chamberlain had 89 points but had been scoreless for nearly the last two minutes. The Knicks worked the clock before Rodgers was charged with a foul.

"The Warriors figure the only way to combat the New York stall is the come out and foul."

Chamberlain finally reached 90 as he hit a free throw following a foul by Imhoff.

Before Chamberlain hit the foul shot, Zinkoff — who had been building up the crowd's anticipation by frequently announcing Chamberlain's point total — hammed it up. Like always.

"And that is the lim-IT…." Zinkoff said into the P.A. microphone, telling fans that Imhoff had just drawn his sixth foul. Imhoff was booed loudly as he walked off the court and was replaced by Johnny Green.

On New York's next possession, Willie Naulls was fouled by the Warriors' Joe Ruklick.

"And they almost came to blows. You can understand the Knickerbockers' feelings; they're a little upset having it rubbed in a little bit like this with a guy on a scoring rampage."

With 2:28 to go, Chamberlain made one of two foul shots, but still had another one coming.

"This," Zinkoff proclaimed, "is the pen-al-ty shotttttttttt."

Chamberlain canned it. He was eight points shy of 100.

The next time down the floor, Chamberlain put the crowd on its feet.

"Wilt's got the ball. Heeeeee's going up. He shoots. It's GOOOOOOOD!! A deep bank shot from 12 feet out on the left, he hit it."

Campbell chuckled into his microphone, telling listeners that Chamberlain's smiling expression was priceless.

"As if to say, 'What am I doing out here?!'"

Campbell's chuckle turned into a hearty laugh.

"He KNOWS what he's doing out here. He's gone for One Zero Zero."

Wilt had 96 points when the Warriors sped downcourt with about 1:30 left. Philadelphia guard York Larese looked for the Big Fella.

"Larese with the ball down the right side, passes to Chamberlain; he's open, he shoots, he scores! Dipper dunk. [It's] 167 to 145. He has 98. Chamberlain STEALS THE INBOUNDS PASS! SHOOTS!!!! No good! Johnny Green has it. Down to Guerin. Chamberlain stole the inbounds pass and took a shot that went in and out. New York with the ball. Into the backcourt now."

After Guerin hit a foul shot with 1:01 remaining, the Warriors had possession and had one thought: Feed Wilt, and never mind that he was breathing heavily and laboring mightily.

"Let's see if they foul somebody quick. Rodgers throws long to Chamberlain. He's got it. He's trying to go up. He SHOOTS. No good. The rebound [Ted] Luckenbill. Back to Chamberlain. He shoots, up. NO GOOD! In and out. The rebound Luckenbill. Back to Ruklick. Into Chamberlain. He made it! He made it! He made it!"

The guy who, just seven years earlier, had scored 90 points for Philly's Overbrook High — including 60 in a 10-minute span that led to a 123-21 rout of Roxborough — had just reached tripled digits.

"....They've stopped the game! People are crowding him, hounding him, banging him. The Warrior players are all over him! Fans are coming

out of the stands! Forty-six seconds left. The most amazing scoring perform-
ance of all time! One hundred points for the Big Dipper! People are all over
the floor, they're taking pictures, flashbulbs are going off! They're hollering
on the P.A. to clear the floor, but it's going to take a few minutes. He has
100 points, ladies and gentleman, with 46 seconds left!"

In all the on-court commotion that followed the game, a 14-year-old boy named Kerry Ryman stole the ball that Wilt supposedly had used to score his 100th point, then raced out of the arena with police in pursuit. Harvey Pollack, the Warriors' public-relations director at the time, says that ball was not the one Wilt used to score any of his 100 points.

When Chamberlain scored his 100th point, Pollack said, referee Willie Smith brought the ball over to the scorer's table. "He said to me, 'Harv, you better take this ball out of the game. It's a collector item for the Hall of Fame,' " Pollack said. Pollack said he gave the ball to equipment manager Larry Jacobs, who passed it along to the head ballboy, Jeff Millman. Millman put the ball in Wilt's duffel bag in the locker room. After the game ended, Millman passed around the ball and players and team officials signed it.

The ball that the 14-year-old stole, Pollack said, apparently was one that was used for the game's final 46 seconds. That ball, he said, came from a bag that was beneath his press-row seat. "And that ball was never touched by Wilt," he said. "Technically, Wilt was still in the game, but he stayed off the court for the final 46 seconds and just leaned on the bench. He didn't want to score anymore. He was smart enough to know that 100 had a better ring to it than 102." (Ryman's ball sold for $551,844 at a 2000 auction, but the sale was voided when its authenticity came into question; it was resold for $67,791 - or nearly a half million dollars less.)

When the final buzzer sounded that night, Chamberlain didn't even do a post-game show with Campbell. "I guess we couldn't get to him and had to get off the air," Campbell said.

Campbell was surprised that Chamberlain didn't take the bus back to Philadelphia with his teammates. "After the game was over and the celebration had ended, I couldn't believe that he walked out of the building

Wilt Chamberlain celebrates his 100 point performance.

and got into a car with three New York Knick players," Campbell said. "They went back to New York, like their day at the office was over."

Naulls sat in the front seat of a shiny Cadillac, next to the man he had guarded for portions of that night. "I figured Wilt would go back on the bus and they were going to celebrate, but he just walked out, got into the car and drove to New York," Campbell said. "He lived in New York, so he didn't even come back to Philadelphia."

Chamberlain, the adrenaline overriding his sleepiness, headed to the Harlem nightclub in which he was one of the owners, Big Wilt's Smalls Paradise. It was only about 11:30. The night was still young.

———•———

Chamberlain shot 36 for 63 from the floor that night in Hershey, but the astounding part was his 28 for 32 marksmanship from the foul line. That's 87.5 percent — far above the 51.1 percent that he would shoot in his career.

"The thing that really made you think that something unusual was going on here was the fact that Wilt was one of the all-time worst foul shooters and he made almost every foul shot in the first half," said Campbell, mindful that Chamberlain was 13 for 14 from the line in the first half, and 21 for 22 after three quarters. "I remember thinking, 'What's going on here?' Normally, he was like Shaquille O'Neal at the line, not even coming close."

The poor free-throw shooting aside, when Chamberlain retired in 1973, he had rewritten the NBA record book. During his near-mythic 14-year career, he led the league in rebounding 11 times and in scoring seven times. Aided by the 100-point outburst in Hershey, Chamberlain averaged an incomprehensible 50.4 points per game in 1961-62.

And just to show he was more than a scorer and rebounder, he led the NBA in assists in 1967-68.

"Wilt could do anything he made up his mind to do," Campbell said. "And this may sound like a ridiculous thing to say — with all the records he established — but I honestly think he could have been even better. He loped down the court. The other four guys waited for him to get there and then set up what they were going to do. But to his credit, he played 48 minutes every game and he never fouled out of a game. I guess if he ran full speed, he wouldn't have made it. But to me, what Wilt did was a scratch in the surface, and for a guy who averaged all those numbers, that sounds like a ridiculous thing to say."

As for Chamberlain's 100-point game toward the end of the 1961-62 season, it didn't save the Warriors. After the season, they left Philadelphia and went to San Francisco.

Campbell was only mildly disappointed to see the Warriors leave; it wasn't like when the Athletics left Philadelphia for Kansas City after the '54 season.

"The A's had been here forever. The Warriors had only been here for 16 years. It wasn't a big deal when they left, especially since there was talk of bringing the Syracuse team here," Campbell said. "We were without a team for one year and then they brought Syracuse here."

The departure of the A's, however, left him feeling jilted. "I felt really badly when they left. I grew up with the A's. I was a little kid and started following baseball as an A's fan. I was an American League fan, and the Phillies were really pathetic at that time."

Sort of like the New York Knicks on March 2, 1962.

———————

Chamberlain's 100-point game highlighted a season in which the Warriors went 49-31 and finished in second place. They lost to the Boston Celtics, four games to three, in the Eastern Division finals and then were San Francisco-bound. Owner Eddie Gottlieb sold the team for $850,000 and went along as a consultant. Campbell often wonders if the Warriors would have remained in Philly if they had beaten the Celtics — who won the championship that year — in the seventh game of their dramatic playoff series.

In any event, Philadelphia was without an NBA franchise for the next year. In 1963-64, the Syracuse Nationals moved to Philadelphia and the 76ers were born.

When the Warriors went to the West Coast, they ended a 16-year stay in Philadelphia that included league championships in 1947 and 1956. Campbell worked both of those championship series.

In 1946-47, the inaugural year of the Basketball Association of America (the forerunner to the NBA), the Warriors finished second in the regular season but won the league's first title, beating the Chicago Stags in five games and earning a bonus of around $2,300 per player.

Campbell, naturally, was filing reports on the games.

The Warriors averaged just 68.6 points per game in the league's initial season, and Joe Fulks totaled more than a third of them as he led the BAA with a 23.2 points-per-game average. Philly received balanced scoring from guys like Angelo Musi and Howie Dallmar. Musi, a 5-foot-9, 145-pound guard out of Temple who specialized in the two-handed set shot, became one of Campbell's closest friends. They were golf buddies and their families would vacation together in Florida and Ocean City. In 2006, nearly 60 years after the Warriors' historic championship, Musi, 87, and Campbell, 82, were still in constant contact.

Musi became the godfather of the Campbells' daughter, Chris; Musi's wife, Lydia, and Bill's wife, Jo, also became close. To this day, Bill Campbell is grateful that the Musi's don't hold grudges for an oversight that has haunted him for years — since 1947, to be exact.

Gottlieb, the Warriors' owner and founding father of Philadelphia basketball, was holding a victory party for the champions in Fairmont Park. Bill, who was engaged at the time, was dancing with Lydia Musi, and the two made small talk.

"So you're going to get married?" Lydia asked.

"Yes, in a few months," Bill replied. "And, we've got to have you and Ang come to the wedding."

"Sure, we'd love to come."

Campbell is embarrassed by what happened next. Or what didn't happen.

"I told her I would send her an invitation and then I promptly forgot all about it. Forgot *completely* about it! Never even mentioned it to Jo."

Campbell smiled.

"But we've been great friends all these years, and they've never let me forget that invitation; they have teased me unmercifully over the years."

The mail must really be slow with that invitation, Bill. Yadda. Yadda. Yadda.

In 1997, at a party celebrating Bill and Jo's 50th wedding anniversary at the swank Tavistock County Club near the Campbells' Haddonfield, New Jersey, rancher, Bill and Lydia Musi again danced together.

"Lydia," he told her, "you finally made it."

It apparently took a half century for the invitation to arrive.

———•———

Angelo Musi was a rookie who earned $5,000 on the 1946-47 Warriors' team that won the championship. He was Philadelphia's second-leading scorer with a modest 9.4 points-per game average, behind only the incomparable Fulks.

"Joe Fulks," Musi said, "was the Babe Ruth of basketball."

Campbell agreed. He listed Fulks on his all-time NBA team, along with Chamberlain, Michael Jordan, Larry Bird, and Magic Johnson.

"Joe was an unbelievable player," Campbell said. "They discovered him in the service during World War II. Petey Rosenberg, who had played high school ball in Philadelphia and at St. Joe's, had met him during the war." Rosenberg had played for Gottlieb's Philadelphia

SPHAs in the old American Basketball League and had heard the Gottlieb was starting the Philadelphia Warriors in the newly formed Basketball Association of America.

Rosenberg told Gottlieb that Fulks was a special player.

"And he was right," Campbell said.

Fulks' numbers paled in comparison to the latter-day stars. But his 23.2 average in 1946-47 — remember, this was a time when teams rarely reached 70 points — might have been closer to 35 or 40 points a game in today's era.

For one thing, there was no three-point shot when Fulks played. "And there was no restriction on how long teams could hold the ball," Musi said. "There was no 24-second clock. You could hold it for a week if you wanted — and teams would hold it against us; as a result, passes were very important. Dribbling was almost unconstitutional."

Players are bigger and stronger and more athletic now, but they don't play as much defense as they did in the Fulks era, Musi said. "In those days, defense was the most important part of the game," he said. "If a guy faked past you, it was almost sacrilegious. You could not let that happen. Now it looks like a cop on Broad Street waving people by. Everything has changed. I still enjoy the game, but it sometimes gets a little monotonous because it's all about strength and the ability to jump and run. There were different types of shooters in my days."

In the 1940s, the set shot was popular. Fulks helped revolutionize the game. "He was the first person I ever saw take a jump shot," Campbell said.

Campbell was filing reports for WCAU radio the night Fulks scored 63 points in a 1949 game against the Indianapolis Jets. The 63 points established a league record that lasted until Elgin Baylor scored 64 in a 1959 game.

"After the game, everybody was in the locker room interviewing Joe, and we had a guy named Elmore Morgenthaler" — a center who stood just a shade under a then-unheard-of 7 feet — "and while everybody was making a fuss over Joe, I'll never forget Elmo saying, 'My God. Joe got 61 more points that I did!' " Campbell said.

The respect that players had for Fulks was immense. Campbell remembers Paul Arizin, who would become an NBA legend himself, attending the Warriors' games and sitting in the front row while he was still a player at Villanova. Arizin would rest his chin in his hand and stay transfixed on Fulks the entire game.

"He would watch every move that Joe made. Every move," Campbell said. "He studied Joe like you couldn't believe."

Arizin emulated what he observed. He became a superb jump-shooter. In 10 years with the Warriors, he made 10 NBA all-star teams, won two scoring titles and was eventually selected to the Hall of Fame.

With Arizin, Neil Johnston, and rookie sensation Tom Gola leading the way, the Warriors won the NBA crown in '56. It was the first season Campbell had done the Warriors' play-by-play, and it gave him the "triple crown" of sorts.

In the *Evening Bulletin*, Frank Brookhouser wrote that Campbell had been doing radio reports when the '49 Eagles won the NFL title and when the '50 Phillies took the National League pennant. "This WCAU sportscaster, Bill Campbell, must be a good luck omen," he wrote. "....If they ever put this guy on horse races, we're going along."

———

One of the best things about Campbell is his perspective. Having been around the Philadelphia sports scene longer than any-one, he can give a unique stance on virtually any topic. He's like a lovable grandfather with an endless supply of stories.

If you're looking to compare players (Chamberlain and Kobe Bryant, for instance) or teams from different eras (the '50, '64, '80 and '93 Phillies), no one is better qualified than The Dean.

The Wilt-Kobe comparison became a natural topic after the stunning developments of January 22, 2006. That night, the Los Angeles Lakers' Bryant erupted for 81 points, including 55 in the sec-ond half, in a 122-104 win against the Toronto Raptors. Afterward, it was only fitting to turn to Campbell. After all, he was the announcer in the only game when a player scored more points in NBA history.

On KYW radio, Campbell's commentary touched on the Chamberlain and Bryant performances:

"I didn't see Kobe Bryant's 81-point sizzler the other night, but I saw and broadcast Wilt Chamberlain's 100-point performance in 1962.

>   "The comparisons I've seen and heard are interesting. Wilt's perform-
> ance was more in pursuit of a record rather than in a competitive game. The
> NBA was still young in 1962, needing a headline. Why do you think they played
> in Hershey? Because the Warriors weren't drawing that well in Philadelphia.
>
>   "Last Sunday, Bryant's team was down 18. The game was in doubt
> in the fourth quarter. The Lakers apparently needed most of Kobe's points.
>
>   "The Lakers have become a one-man show, despite coach Phil
> Jackson's team concepts. The Shaq is gone. It's all Kobe now.
>
>   "A lot of people feel that way about the 76ers. Let's hope Bryant's
> performance doesn't fire up Allen Iverson's trigger finger.
>
>   "This is Bill Campbell, KYW Newsradio."

Bryant scoring outburst was needed, so his performance was
more impressive than Chamberlain's, Campbell said. And, yes, he
thinks another 100-point NBA performance — whether it's by Kobe,
some player still in college, or a hotshot who is now in grammar
school — is going to occur.

Wilt Chamberlain (left) signs his first Philadelphia Warriors contract while owner Eddie Gottlieb enjoys the moment at the club's office in the Sheraton Hotel in 1959. Chamberlain signed for a reported $30,000 a year, plus incentives that brought the deal to between $40,000 and $50,000.

"After Wilt's 100-point game, I thought we'd see quite a few of them, but I was dead wrong," he said. "The three-point shot was coming, the lane was widened and the players were getting bigger and stronger. I always thought we'd see more of them and I still do."

If it happens, chronicling the performance will be quite different than that magical night in 1962 when Wilt Chamberlain became legendary. If it happens, the news will spread, instantly and probably with a theme song, around the world on the Internet; the video replay will be shown *ad nauseum*, with studio hosts analyzing and re-analyzing; and TV specials will be built around The Event.

When Chamberlain scored 100, the performance became larger than life — and, to this day, it still percolates with intrigue and mystery — because most of the country never saw it. And never will. There were no television cameras that filmed the game, and the New York newspapers didn't send a single reporter. *The Daily News* sent Jack Kiser, the *Evening Bulletin* sent Jim Heffernan, *The Inquirer* sent no one.

Pollack, the Warriors' publicity director, wrote the story for *The Inquirer*, United Press International and the Associated Press. He also scribbled "100" on a piece of paper and asked Wilt to hold it up for a photographer, an AP guy who happened to be attending the game as a spectator with his son.

The newspaper stories have yellowed and faded. Campbell's broadcast, however, is still crisp, still electric, still one of the most memorable moments of his broadcasting career.

Even if it did seem like an exhibition game.

CHAPTER SIX

Van Brocklin and the '60 Eagles (Oh, Baby!)

Quarterback Norm Van Brocklin had a reputation for not getting along with others. He was abrasive, tough on his teammates, and had verbal battles with management.

Sort of like a modern-day version of Terrell Owens — without the touchdown-celebrating theatrics.

In the late 1950s, Van Brocklin was fed up with the amount of playing time he was getting and asked to be traded. The 32-year-old Van Brocklin was near the end of his career and didn't want to play for a non-contender. That's the main reason he told the Los Angeles Rams' management that he didn't want to go to Philadelphia.

And, so, naturally, he was traded to the Eagles.

In the middle of this 1958 drama was Bill Campbell.

Campbell had been the Eagles' broadcaster for the dismal 1956 and 1957 seasons. The Eagles were a combined 7-16-1 in those years and were looking to change their fortunes.

They wanted a new (albeit old) face to lead the team as they moved from their old home, Connie Mack Stadium, to historic Franklin Field in 1958.

Van Brocklin was the face.

The Rams were having a problem finding playing time for both Van Brocklin and Billy Wade, so they sent the Dutchman to the Eagles for defensive back Jimmy Harris, offensive tackle Buck Lansford, and their first round pick in 1959.

Van Brocklin arrived in Philadelphia a night before he was going to be introduced at a press conference. Eagles' general manager Vince McNally asked Campbell — who, at the time, was covering Phillies games as part of his duties as WCAU radio's sports director — if he could do him a favor. McNally figured that since Van Brocklin was a big baseball fan, he would enjoy watching a game at Connie Mack Stadium.

"Would you be good enough to meet Van Brocklin at the front gate and sit with him in the press box?" McNally asked Campbell. The Phillies were playing the Milwaukee Braves, and Van Brocklin was friends with one of the Braves' stars, third baseman Eddie Mathews.

McNally knew Campbell was an engaging sort, someone who would make Van Brocklin feel welcome and feel good about being in Philadelphia.

Campbell sat with the Dutchman in the Connie Mack Stadium press box, and after the game they went into the Milwaukee clubhouse. "He introduced me to Mathews and Johnny Logan and some of the other Braves," Campbell recalled. "And that's how Dutch and I started together."

Campbell and Van Brocklin seemed like an odd couple. One was tall and loud, the other was short and dignified. Yet, they became inseparable. They became golfing buddies and their families became intertwined.

"My dad has a tremendous amount of natural curiosity. He always wants to learn," said Campbell's daughter, Chris, who became close with Van Brocklin's three children — all girls. "And if it was football that he was broadcasting, he would find the best football minds around and talk and ask questions and really listen and learn and learn and learn. I think that's how he first struck up a friendship with Uncle Dutch. But they really just liked each other. They enjoyed each other's company and they could tease each other, rib each other. They were men's men and they just hit it off."

In Van Brocklin's first year with the Eagles, he and Campbell did a weekly pregame show on Channel 10. As they prepared for each show, they listened to Campbell's play-by-play radio broadcast of the previous week's game.

Van Brocklin turned into a teacher. A nasty, critical teacher.

Campbell would describe a play and Van Brocklin would stop the tape.

"Draw play, my ass! God damnit, can't you tell a draw play from a delay," Van Brocklin fumed.

Years later, as he recalled Van Brocklin's biting criticism, Campbell smiled. "Every week, I used to hear, 'You have to be *the worst* football announcer of *all time*," Campbell said. "Every week!"

The criticism, Campbell said, was justified. He said Van Brocklin made him a better announcer. "I learned more football from Dutch than anybody," Campbell said. "And when I was doing a game, I almost got to the point where I knew what he was going to call because of the way the defenses presented themselves. I spent so much time with him and some of it rubbed off."

Football, he said, was his most challenging sport to broadcast. "It demands more of your concentration because you have to worry about a lot more players than the other sports," he said. "Plus they were always tinkering with the rules and that kept you on your toes."

So did Van Brocklin.

In 1958, Van Brocklin's first season in Philly, the Eagles went 2-9-1. "Let's get the hell out of here," The Dutchman screamed to the team's bus driver after one lopsided loss, "before they score another touchdown."

Still, there was hope. Van Brocklin had an all-pro season and young receivers Tommy McDonald and Pete Retzlaff showed promise. The next year, the Eagles improved to 7-5. Expectations were high when the 1960 season rolled around.

And then Van Brocklin had three of his first six passes intercepted in a season-opening 41-24 loss to the Cleveland Browns. Boos echoed around Franklin Field.

Undaunted, Van Brocklin led the Eagles to ten wins in their final 11 regular-season games to capture the Eastern Conference crown and earn the right to face the Green Bay Packers, champions of the Western Conference, in the NFL title game at Franklin Field on December 26, 1960.

On Christmas Day, Van Brocklin told Campbell the Eagles were going to be NFL champions.

"He said to me, 'Relax. Don't worry. We're going to beat these guys.' He always had this expression, 'Never give up on the old

Dutchman,' " Campbell said. "He was a tremendous leader. And without a doubt, the best of any sport I've ever been involved with. If you wanted someone to demonstrate the essence of leadership, he was it. He really led. He'd chew out guys for not protecting him and all that. But, boy, they looked up to him. They really did. He was a great, great leader. Even to the extent that if a teammate was injured and he had a good drive going, he would raise hell if the officials called a timeout. The players used to tell me he would go up to the referee and say, 'Can't you see I have a drive going? Get this guy off the field. Take care of him, but pull him over there on the sideline and do it.' That's the kind of competitor he was."

———•———

As you listen to a recording of the 1960 championship game, you notice a glaring difference when compared to today's broadcasts: The touchdowns, sacks, defensive stops, and timeouts aren't sponsored by airlines or potato-chip makers or insurance companies. Oh, there are a few commercials that Ed Harvey, who was Campbell's sidekick for that game, delivered for the Yellow Pages. But they were during breaks in the action, not *part* of the action. Hence, Campbell's play-by-play description was more lively, more dramatic, more flowing than today's broadcasts.

The game was not televised locally, though some fans drove to outlying areas, such as Trenton, to beat the blackout. The game was shown in Philadelphia on a tape-delay broadcast later that night. Campbell did the game live on WCAU radio and his audience was huge. After announcing the starting lineups and giving the players' heights, weights, and colleges, Cempbell told listeners:

"We have over 67,000 people jammed into Franklin Field today. We've gotten a tremendous break in the weather. You know what freezing temperatures we've been putting up with in this neck of the woods for the last 10 days or so. The temperature is in the high 40s. The sun beating down in all its majesty and brilliance. But the field — the tarp was removed only today — is extremely hard and in some spots, quite muddy. In front of the Eagles' bench, on the south side across the way, from the 35 to the 50,

very heavy going. And I assume that the hardness of this field will disappear into a little goo, probably by the second half as these big thundering players move around on it."

Campbell then introduced Harvey, who told listeners that the Eagles and Packers had met 14 times in NFL history — with Philadelphia winning just once, a 28-14 victory in 1947. Harvey congratulated Van Brocklin and Buck Shaw for being named the NFL's player and coach of the year, respectively, by United Press International.

Van Brocklin and Shaw, each of whom joined the Eagles in 1958, had already announced that they would retire after the 1960 season, thus adding drama to the championship game.

Seconds before the Eagles' Timmy Brown took Paul Hornung's opening kickoff, Campbell's voice filled with the excitement of a six-year-old on Christmas Eve.

"Ladies and gentlemen, the Green Bay Packers and the Philadelphia Eagles are about to play the biggest game of their lives. And there will be bedlam coming out of your loudspeakers for the next several hours. We hope you'll enjoy the play. We hope we can make it enjoyable for you. Here is Hornung booting off, a deep one....and the championship of the world is underway...."

The muddy field made yards difficult to gain that afternoon. The Eagles, in fact, had just two first downs as they started a drive from their 43-yard line with eight minutes left in the second quarter. Though they had been badly outplayed, they faced only a 6-0 deficit when Van Brocklin, who was named the league's MVP that season, jump-started the drive with a 22-yard pass to future Hall of Famer McDonald.

"And the Eagles show signs of coming out of it. This is their best penetration and the best spot they've had the ball to date. First-and-10 at the Packer 35. McDonald goes wide right....First-and-10 at the Green Bay 35. Here's Van Brocklin back to throw; he's LOOKING. He tries to go LONG. He throws it and HE'S GOT A MAN OPEN. It is McDonald. TOUCHDOWN!!"

For the next 24 seconds, Campbell went silent and let the crowd's euphoria tell listeners the story.

"Well, as they predicted before the game started, the big bomb can often overcome a lot of ball control. And Van Brocklin threw the home run. Thirty-five yards. McDonald, running a deep sideline pattern, ran by Hank Gremminger and makes a catch at the five and slides into the end zone. It's 6-6. Walston has a chance now to untie it. Midway through the second quarter — Jurgensen to hold, Walston to attempt the conversion. Bednarik snapping. Here's the point, it's up, it is GOOD! It is GOOD! Score: Eagles 7, Packers 6."

It was a tense, fierce-hitting game in which both teams jockeyed for field position. Green Bay, which dominated the statistics and finished with a 401-296 edge in total yards, took a 13-10 lead on a seven-yard touchdown pass from Bart Starr to Max McGee early in the fourth quarter. But Ted Dean, who played his high school ball at Radnor, returned the ensuing kickoff 58 yards to put the Eagles on the Green Bay 39. That set up Dean's five-yard TD run — he followed the blocking of guard Gerry Huth for the first touchdown of his pro career — to help give the Eagles a 17-13 lead.

The Eagles were five minutes and 21 seconds away from an improbable championship. Improbable because the team had a lackluster running attack that season and ranked 10th out of 12 NFL teams in defense.

But they had the leadership of Van Brocklin, the master of late-game comebacks. Six times the Eagles overcame fourth-quarter deficits to win games that season.

McDonald said he felt a guardian angel was watching over the team. Van Brocklin was the guardian angel.

"He willed that team to wins," Campbell said.

With eight seconds left in the title game, Starr, the Green Bay quarterback, lined up the Packers at the Eagles' 22-yard line. The Packers had no timeouts left, so this had a chance to be the game's final play. Campbell's account painted the picture for his radio audience.

*"I wish you could be here to see 67,000 people standing. STAND-
ING! What an ELECTRIFYING finish to a great game and a great season.
Starr is over the ball. This will be it! Starr's back to throw. He takes time.
He throws over the middle. It's caught at the 15. Running hard to the seven-
yard line and DOWN ON THE SEVEN is Jim Taylor. DOWN on the seven.
The game's OVER! The Eagles are champions of the world! LISTEN!!!!!"*

An announcer with a big ego might have pontificated for a
minute or two. Not the classy Campbell. He respected the fans too
much for that. And, so, for several seconds, he let his listeners feel
the excitement by hearing the crowd's unyielding roar.

This was more than a championship for the Eagles. It was also
for their fans, the ones who hugged and screamed at joy-struck
Franklin Field and the ones who were jumping up and down in their
living rooms. Nobody understood that better than Bill Campbell.

The Eagles' 17-13 win over the slightly favored Packers — their
first NFL title since 1949, when they traveled three days on train and
then beat the Rams in the pouring rain in Los Angeles — ended with
Chuck Bednarik refusing to let Taylor get up until the final seconds disappeared. Bednarik and defensive back Bobby Jackson made the tackle.

"You can get up now; this f—ing game is over!" Bednarik told
Taylor when the game ended.

"I never got the feeling that Taylor was going to score on the
play," Campbell said, remembering Taylor's run after he made the
catch. "I didn't think he had a chance. I guess with a missed tackle
he scores, but they didn't miss."

Bednarik, a Hall of Famer who was the last of the 60-minute
men, played the championship game as a linebacker and center. He
was 35, the oldest player on the field, and he played an amazing 59
minutes. At the time, he was one of the most popular Eagles. Over the
years, however, he and the Eagles had a very public parting. During
the Eagles' training camp in 2003, Bednarik said he asked club owner
Jeffrey Lurie if he would buy copies of his book, *Bednarik: The Last of
the 60-Minute Men* to give to his players. According to Bednarik's

account in a *Philadelphia Inquirer* story, Lurie declined, saying the NFL contract states "we can't give our players gifts."

Bednarik became incensed. He publicly criticized the Eagles at every opportunity. He said he purposely went to bed early and didn't watch the Eagles' 2004 NFC title game against Carolina; the next year, he repeatedly said he was rooting for the New England Patriots to beat the Eagles in the Super Bowl.

"I covered Chuck when he was a player at Penn, and I knew Chuck pretty well," Campbell said. "He was a great, great player — one of the best I've ever seen. He was always a little bit distant [with the media]. I can't ever remember having an incident with him; there was nothing remarkable about our relationship. I'm really saddened and shocked that he has adopted the attitude that he has; it's all about money. He's not the only one of the players from that era" who didn't make a lot of money.

Campbell thinks Bednarik is bitter about the salaries of today's players. The Eagles' 1960 team payroll was about $500,000; the club's average payroll each year from 2003 to 2005 was $85 million.

In his heyday, Bednarik made about $15,000. By comparison, 6-foot-4, 345-pound guard Shawn Andrews received a reported $6.1 million signing bonus when the Eagles made him their top pick in 2004.

"And the first thing he did when he got his bonus money is buy seven cars," Campbell said, laughing. Andrews broke his right leg in the Eagles' 2004 opener and missed the rest of his rookie season. Reportedly, he ballooned to near 400 pounds.

"You wonder what you're dealing with now," Campbell said before the 2005 season. "I would not like to be around these guys that much. In most sports."

He had an exception.

"If they asked me to go back and do baseball, I'd go in a minute," said the 82-year-old Campbell.

Baseball was his passion, but the Phillies never won a world championship with Campbell behind the microphone. Campbell announced games for four Philadelphia pro teams — the Eagles, Phillies, 76ers, and Warriors — for a combined total of 33 years.

The '60 Eagles and '56 Warriors were the only teams to win overall titles during Campbell's play-by-play years. The Eagles won the championship in the only season that Campbell was paired with Ed Harvey.

"I had one great year with you and the Eagles, the championship year, and you carried me all the way through because I didn't know a damn thing about football," Harvey once told Campbell.

"I guess I should have kept Ed around a little longer," Campbell said. "I come from a long line of losers. I have one year with Ed and we won the championship. He might have been a good-luck charm and I didn't have enough sense to realize it."

Campbell says chemistry, not talent, carried the Eagles to the 1960 championship.

"They got the most out of their ability and played way over their heads, no doubt about it," he said. "I've never seen a team that had so much camaraderie. Those guys really loved each other. They fought like hell among themselves sometimes, but at the same time, they loved each other….They weren't the best team in the league and weren't the best in their own division. But they were the best every Sunday."

The players even bonded with their play-by-play announcer.

"When he traveled with us, he wasn't considered a member of the media," said Tom Brookshier, a standout defensive back on the '60 team. "He was one of the guys."

On most Mondays, Van Brocklin and some of the Eagles would stop at Donoghue's, a tiny tavern on Walnut Street, and rehash the previous day's game. "Monday was our day off, so we'd go over there and have a few beers," Brookshier said.

On this particular Monday, one day after the Eagles had defeated St. Louis, 20-6, to clinch the 1960 Eastern Conference title, Van Brocklin had invited at least a dozen teammates to the bar, including Brookshier, Billy Ray Barnes, and Bobby Walston; he also invited Campbell.

"The Dutchman had set him up," Brookshier said.

And with good reason.

On the plane ride home from St. Louis the previous day, several players were razzing Van Brocklin about a TV commercial had had done for Vitalis hair tonic. The players were drinking and having a grand old time "and someone wanted somebody to pour beer on

Dutch's head and say, 'Work like Vitalis?' " Campbell said.

Nobody volunteered.

"Brookshier or Billy Ray Barnes or somebody said to me, 'Why don't you do it? He won't get mad at you,' " Campbell said.

Campbell had put down a few cocktails and was feeling pretty good. With the players howling with laughter, he emptied a beer atop the head of a startled Van Brocklin.

"Work like Vitalis, Dutch?" Campbell said.

Van Brocklin was furious.

"You wait. I'll fix you," he said. "You be at Donoghue's tomorrow at noon, and, remember, if you're not there, I know where you live."

Campbell figured he didn't want his house being ruined, so the next day he decided to meet Van Brocklin at the bar. Van Brocklin had placed a bucket of beer on the transom, so when the door was opened, the bucket would empty.

As Campbell headed for the door, Van Brocklin took a drag on his Camel cigarette and smiled. Van Brocklin's teammates were peering out the window, and they told him Campbell was approaching.

"He walks in and the beer comes down all over him. All over his sportscoat, all over his hair," Brookshier said. "Dutch walked over and gave Bill a big hug and we all hugged him. After that, he knew he was part of the team."

Van Brocklin could be acerbic, tough on his teammates, and a practical joker. But there was also a soft side to the man.

After Tom Dowd, the Eagles' beloved team physician, died of a heart attack in 1959, it was Van Brocklin who gathered a half-dozen Eagles players and painted the house for Dowd's widow, Peggy. He also kept close tabs on Dowd's children, becoming a guardian of sorts.

It seemed that some of Campbell's kindness rubbed off on The Dutchman.

On his WCAU radio show — presented by "Schmidts: beer as beer should be," the announcer said — Campbell eulogized Dowd:

"I realize that not many of you knew Dr. Tom Dowd. I wish you had, for the privilege of his friendship is something you would have treasured all the days of your life. Tom Dowd's life, which came to an untimely end last night at the age of 52, revolved around three things: his family, the practice

of medicine, and football. Specifically, Eagles football. Dr. Dowd was the team physician for the Eagles. At least that was his title. But it was a flagrant misnomer. He was so much more; he was doctor, lawyer, teacher, consultant, adviser, big brother, and friend.

"To those of us who have lived and traveled with the Eagles over the years — the players, the coaches, the owners, the executives, the reporters, the broadcasters, and anyone who has ever set foot in an Eagle dressing room from coast to coast — Tom Dowd was the human crutch who got us over the rough spots. The problem could revolve around anything, not necessarily around medicine. But Dr. Dowd wanted to hear about it. I spent some time with him this past Saturday afternoon and we got around to discussing a problem. As usual, it was a problem of mine. It didn't occur to me until last night, when I had heard that he had died, that none of us had ever gotten around to listening to problems that were his. But even if we had, Tom Dowd would never have discussed them. There was always someone else.

"His weekly day off from his practice was devoted to the Eagles. On Sunday, game day, he was the first person in the locker room. His annual vacation was spent flying around the country and taking care of the team on exhibition trips. As Vince McNally so often said, 'He is the only Eagle I'd never trade.'

"Tom Dowd died last night of a heart attack while treating a patient in his office. To me as a layman, it is inconceivable that Tom Dowd's heart could ever have failed him, because it was the biggest heart in town."

When the Eagles won the 1960 championship in the mud, the conditions were much better than the last time they had captured a title on their home turf, back in 1948.

Campbell was at that 1948 game, too. (Has there been a major sports event in the last 60-plus years that he has not attended?) He was doing sports reports for WCAU radio when he worked that championship game against the Chicago Cardinals. The Eagles won that game, 7-0, before 28,864 frozen fans at snow-swept Shibe Park.

During the game, the snow became so heavy that players couldn't see each other. The sidelines were obliterated with snow, making it nearly impossible for officials to figure out when a player was out of bounds. And icy spots made it treacherous just to *walk* on the field. "You couldn't even stand up," Eagles legendary running back Steve Van Buren, who took three trolleys and walked six blocks to get to Shibe Park before scoring the game's lone touchdown, once said. "I fell twice going from the huddle to the line of scrimmage."

Before the game, players from both sides shoveled the snow off the tarp so the championship could be played. And, no, Campbell couldn't picture Terrell Owens and his teammates doing the same thing.

This was a different era, an era when the players didn't think they were bigger than the game. An era when players (read: mini corporations) didn't create bombastic touchdown celebrations with the hope that they would be replayed on ESPN and would lead to an endorsement.

Campbell says a lot of players in the T.O. era don't have the same connection to fans that their predecessors did, like the Eagles teams that won NFL titles in 1948, 1949, and 1960. Back then, players felt they were winning for their city — many of the players, after all, lived in the same neighborhoods as the fans — and not for themselves.

———————

The 1960 team, Campbell said, was extremely close-knit. They hung out together and enjoyed each other's company. As corny as it sounds, they considered themselves a family.

Maybe that's why they were able to win six games in which they trailed in the fourth quarter that season. They believed in each other.

They especially believed in the Dutchman, Van Brocklin, whose death in 1983 left a void at the team's 25th anniversary party in 1985.

"Without ol' No. 11," McDonald said, tearfully, at that reunion, "I don't know what Tommy McDonald ever could have been."

In three years, Van Brocklin took the Eagles from last place to champions.

Yes, he was demanding. Yes, he had an acerbic tongue. And, yes, there were times when his own offensive linemen "wanted to punch his lights out," Brookshier said. "But at the end of a game, they would be thanking him."

"Guys just believed in him," Campbell said. "I've never seen a team where everybody on the team believed so much in one guy. He used to call McDonald 'Squeaky' because he could squeak through defenders — he had a name for everybody. And Tommy would come back to the huddle and tell Dutch that he had so-and-so on a revolving door and was wide open. So what else is the quarterback going to do but get him the ball? And that's what he would do."

As they prepared for their TV show before a regular-season game in 1960, Van Brocklin was listening to Campbell's description of a contest against the New York Giants. The Eagles fell into a 10-0 halftime hole at Yankee Stadium.

"I guess I was moaning about how things were going," Campbell said. "And he said to me, 'You really didn't believe in us. Let me tell you something, never give up on the Dutchman.'"

The Eagles had rallied and won, 17-10. The game became famous for a clean, blindside tackle that Bednarik made on the Giants' Frank Gifford, knocking the running back unconscious and causing a game-clinching, fourth-quarter fumble that was recovered by Philadelphia linebacker Chuck Weber. In the celebrated photo that was taken, Bednarik is standing over a fallen Gifford, pumping his right arm and doing a dance.

Campbell remembers the play — Bednarik says he wasn't celebrating that Gifford was injured, but rather that the hit had clinched the win — but he gets more excited about another aspect of that game. Specifically, the way Van Brocklin moved the Birds down field after the intermission, a development that coincided with Bednarik replacing Bill Lapham at center and picking up the Giants' blitz.

"Dutch was just murdered in the first half; he couldn't do anything. In the second half, he took [end] Bobby Walston and just dropped in pop passes a couple yards beyond the line of scrimmage. *Pop, pop, pop.* And the Giants had Jim Katcavage and Andy Robustelli and all those great guys," Campbell said. "He'd let them come through the line and, boom, a quick pop pass to Walston. He kept doing it. He knew how to pick apart defenses."

And he knew how to be a charmer when he was away from the football field.

"Uncle Dutch was a handsome man with this booming kind of presence, a physical presence. With those icy blue eyes. Beautiful blue eyes," said Bill's daughter, Chris. "He was a room-filler. He walked in the door and you knew he was there. And he'd roughhouse and tease and he'd play and enjoy his daughters, and he treated me like one of them after a while. He was often over the house to pick up dad to go hit some golf balls or look at game films, so he was in and out a lot."

Van Brocklin and his wife, Gloria, were also at the dinner parties that Jo and Bill hosted quite frequently during the days that Campbell announced Eagles games. During one November party, with a handful of Eagles coaches and players present, Dutch picked up Campbell's daughter and plopped her atop the refrigerator.

"Chrissie," he said, "how come you don't have a dog?"

"My daddy won't let me."

Van Brocklin seized the opportunity.

"When's your birthday?" he asked.

"July 24th."

"Well, on July 24th, your Uncle Dutch will get you a dog."

Campbell was in earshot and heard the whole conversation. He took his daughter up to bed, tucked her in, and didn't mention the dog.

"Dutch is down in my rec room, drinking my beer, and making all these promises," Campbell said. "When I got downstairs, I said, 'Norm, you should never ever make a promise to a child that you don't have any intention of keeping. And he says, 'What do you know about this?' I said, 'Dutch, in July, you're going to be shooting quail or something out in Oregon.' "

"Why don't you just mind your own business?" Van Brocklin countered.

As the seasons changed, Campbell forgot about the conversation. Five months later, on July 24, the doorbell rang in the Campbell's Broomall, Pennsylvania, home at 7 a.m.

It was Van Brocklin. The man whom some of his teammates compared to General Patton was holding a tiny puppy under his massive arms.

Chrissie, who was celebrating her eighth birthday, heard Uncle Dutch's voice and ran to the door.

"Do you want to hold her? She's yours," Van Brocklin said.

About a week earlier, Van Brocklin had cuddled with the dog in front of his TV set as John F. Kennedy won the Democratic presidential nomination in Los Angeles.

"This is my little delegate from Pennsylvania," Van Brocklin told Chrissie. "She watched the whole Democratic Convention with me, waiting for you to come back from the Shore."

Van Brocklin would throw a career-high 24 touchdown passes and lead the Eagles to the NFL championship later that year, but for Chrissie Campbell, the Dutchman had reached the pinnacle when he handed her the three-pound cocker spaniel/beagle.

"I just looked at her and I loved this puppy instantly," she said. "And I looked at Uncle Dutch and he rose from like a saint to God. And I looked at Dad and said, 'Am I allowed to keep her?' And he said, 'Yes, honey. Happy birthday. This is from Mom, Dad, and Uncle Dutch.' "

Van Brocklin retired after the '60 season, but he didn't want to leave Philadelphia. He had told Campbell the Eagles had promised him the head-coaching job. Instead, the job was offered to assistant Nick Skorich. Van Brocklin went to Minnesota and became the first head coach in the Vikings' history, and he later coached the Atlanta Falcons. While living in Georgia, he and his wife adopted three youngsters whose parents had died in a car accident.

The Dutchman suffered a heart attack and died in 1983 at age 57.

Campbell thinks about him frequently.

"He was an incredible character and we really got along," Campbell said. "If he liked you, there was no limit as to what he would do for you. But if he didn't like you, you'd know about it in five minutes."

———————

Nearly midway through the 2005 NFL season, Campbell sat in the Lincoln Financial Field press box and watched the first quarter of the Eagles' improbable 20-17 win over the visiting San Diego Chargers.

The game would be remembered for its frantic finish — the Eagles' Quintin Mikell blocked a field-goal attempt and teammate Matt Ware scooped up the ball and scored on a stunning 65-yard return with 2 minutes, 25 seconds left.

Media members (left to right) Tom Cardella, Bill Campbell, Dan Baker, Merrill Reese, and Bill Bransome pose for a photo during a Big 5 basketball luncheon in the 1980s.

Campbell would remember the October 23 game for another reason: His eyes started to fail and he became so upset — he couldn't decipher the players' uniform numbers — that he left before halftime.

This was supposed to be an enjoyable afternoon for The Dean. He wasn't at the Linc because of a KYW radio assignment. He was there because his long-time friend, Eagles broadcaster Merrill Reese, had asked him to be his guest. Campbell, whom Reese called his hero, liked to show his face in the press box, liked to be with his media pals and exchange stories, liked to get a first-hand look at the Eagles.

The Eagles had given Campbell some of his most rewarding professional memories. Had it really been 45 years since he described Ted Dean's game-winning five-yard touchdown run in the NFL title game against Vince Lombardi's Green Bay Packers? Had it really been that long since The Dutchman and Concrete Charlie and Squeaky had made Franklin Field come alive?

Not that every Eagles season was memorable. Campbell announced his share of losing seasons. The Eagles had just a 47-64-5 record in his nine-year career — 1956 to 1964 — as the Birds' play-by-play man.

The defeats were so common that this became a typical scene in the early part of Campbell's broadcasting days with the team: A tired Campbell would come home after a game, take off his hat and tie, sigh loudly, and give what seemed liked his weekly proclamation: "Another loss," he would moan to his wife and young daughter.

The disgust in his voice was sincere. No matter. Chrissie Campbell, though only six years old, decided her dad didn't need to be consoled. He needed a good laugh, needed to forget about the Eagles' latest drubbing.

So, on this particular Sunday, she waited until her parents were in the kitchen before she put on her dad's hat and tie — and his deep voice. The hat draped over her forehead and seemed to cover half her face. In a sweet moment that Bill would remember a half-century later, Chrissie mimicked her dad's all-too-familiar routine.

With a playful, exaggerated gait, she walked into the kitchen and displayed her best "man" voice.

"Another loss," she said, shaking her head in mock disbelief. Her tone had just the right amount of disgust to make her dad burst into laughter.

Fast-forward to the October afternoon in 2005, the day Bill Campbell's career flashed before his failing eyes. He had undergone cataract surgery earlier in the year and, for the most part, his eyesight had been adequate.

Until this autumn day at Lincoln Financial Field.

Bill's vision became so bad that he decided to walk to a different part of the press box so he would have a better view of the stadium's oversized screens that televised the game. It didn't help. If something was close to him, his vision was fine. From a distance, however, Bill was lost — at least on this frightful afternoon.

For more than seven decades, most of them from press boxes all across America, Campbell was not only Philadelphia's voice, but also its eyes.

Now, at age 82, those eyes were abandoning him.

For Campbell, his seven decades of work flashed in front of him. Would he ever be able to enjoy another game from his long time second home, the press box? Was his eyesight going to get worse? Was age catching up with him?

All those games, all those vivid descriptions, all those famous play-by-play calls over the years.... A lot of them sped through Bill's mind as he tried to make out the action during the second quarter of the Eagles-Chargers game.

Frustrated at his inability to see what was happening, he decided to go home, where he could clearly see the game on his den TV.

Bill Campbell was too distraught to tell Merrill Reese he was leaving. He left the press box, walked slowly to the parking lot and got into his powder-blue Buick. On the ride home to South Jersey, as he listened to Reese's lively account, Campbell's mind kept drifting away from the football game. Forget the game. Campbell was pondering more serious matters. Tears trickled down his cheeks and he headed to Haddonfield. He needed comfort, needed to share his fears with his devoted wife, needed to find out why his long-distance sight was disappearing.

A few days later, an eye doctor changed the prescription in his glasses. It didn't help much; his long-distance sight was poor and he still had problems seeing at night. Bill went for a retina test and eventually had laser surgery. The surgery didn't improve things, but Bill was learning to accept the fact that couldn't do much nighttime driving anymore. His eyesight in the day was now fine and his vision still enabled him to read. For Campbell, at age 82, the eye problems were a roadblock that he could negotiate. He wasn't even *thinking* about retiring from KYW radio.

Eagles quarterback Norm Van Brocklin (right), who became one of Bill Campbell's closest friends, helps give coach Buck Shaw a playful hoist during the 1960 preseason. Bobby Walston (left) and Chuck Bednarik join in the fun. By the end of the season, the Eagles were still smiling: they were NFL champions.

CHAPTER SEVEN

Double-duty: The Eagles and Phillies
(and red-eyes and ulcers)

Announcing Phillies games got tricky when Bill Campbell was also expected to be doing the play-by-play for the Eagles. That was Campbell's plight in 1963 and 1964.

In August, Bill was juggling Eagles exhibition games and Phillies regular-season contests. September was difficult since both teams were playing in the regular season. The preparation and grind wore on Campbell.

There was the time he rushed out of the press box following a Phillies Saturday afternoon game at Connie Mack Stadium and took a short flight — the plane was flown by Jack Clements, the WCAU program director and a man who had his pilot's license — to Hershey, where the Eagles were playing an exhibition game that night.

"He'd land the plane right next to the stadium," said Campbell, adding that WCAU general manager Jack Downey, who later opened Downey's restaurant in Society Hill, was also on the plane. "And after the game, I'd get back in the puddle-jumper and fly back to Philly."

Ah, that was easy compared to when the Phillies were playing on the road and Campbell was broadcasting their Saturday game and the Eagles' home game the next day.

In late September of 1963, Campbell was in such a predicament. He was working the Phillies' game in Houston on September 21; the next day, he was expected at Franklin Field in Philadelphia to broadcast the NFL team's matchup against the St. Louis Cardinals.

Because he had to leave after the Saturday game, Campbell missed the drama that occurred in the Phillies' 2-1 loss to the Houston Colt .45s on Sunday — a game that became noteworthy because tiny Joe Morgan, in his second major-league game, delivered the winning hit in the bottom of the ninth and caused Phils manager

Gene Mauch to go ballistic in the losers' clubhouse.

After the game, Mauch became enraged as he watched his players casually line up at the buffet table and fill their plates with spare ribs, barbecued chicken, and all the trimmings. Mauch startled his players, yanking the tablecloth from under the spread and sending food across the otherwise silent room. Barbecue sauce splattered all over the place and covered several of the players' clothes.

"Have you no shame?" Mauch screamed. "You just got beat by a guy who looks like a bleeping Little Leaguer!"

The "Little Leaguer," all 5-foot-7 of him, turned into a Hall of Famer.

Campbell didn't witness any of Mauch's theatrics — or Morgan's game-winning hit off reliever Johnny Klippstein.

The previous day, Campbell left the press box at mosquito-infested Colt Stadium and weaved through the stands late in the Phillies' 4-3 win; he then walked onto the field in foul territory and made a quick stop in the Phils' bullpen, where he was storing his suitcase. He picked up his luggage, flagged down a cab, and headed to the airport.

He had a football game to broadcast.

Groggily, Campbell took a flight home and went to Franklin Field to broadcast the Eagles' game. This became a routine. Broadcast the Phillies on a Saturday, take a late flight or a red-eye home and arrive in Philadelphia, sometimes at 6 a.m. or 7 a.m. on a Sunday. Drive to his home in Broomall; shower, shave, and then head over to Franklin Field to broadcast the Eagles.

On one such coast-to-coast "doubleheader," Campbell had dark circles under his eyes as he arrived at Franklin Field after an all-night flight from Los Angles. When he walked into the locker room before the game, he was greeted by Mike Mandarino, the Eagles' physician.

As he finished taping a player's ankle, Mandarino looked up and saw the weary-looking Campbell.

"Hey, didn't I just hear you doing the baseball game in L.A. last night?"

"You did," Campbell said.

"You don't look too good, Bill."

Campbell threw some water on his faced and toweled off.

Mandarino walked over and sort of gave him a pep talk. Literally.

"He pulled out a little blue pill, and he said, 'Around halftime, you may need this. Wash it down and it'll pick you up,' " Campbell recalled. "I said OK."

Sure enough, Campbell started to drag as the first half concluded. He took the doctor's advice. The blue pill seemed to have a wonderful effect, he said.

"I did the second half, and you always know whether you did a bad job or a good job," Campbell said. "That was the best second half I ever did! I should have taken that pill every week. It was great."

He swears it was the only time he took such a pill. What kind was it?

"I don't know," he said. "I was afraid to ask."

In the second half of that game, he said, "I was right on top of every play. You know when you're doing it and everything is running smoothly. After the game, I drove down to the airport to fly back to California and re-join the Phillies on their trip."

"Would you like a drink?" the stewardess asked Campbell as he boarded the plane.

"Sure, I'd love a Manhattan."

The stewardess left two little airplane bottles on Campbell's tray. It had been a long weekend. He quickly polished off the drinks.

"And the next thing I remember, this gal is shaking me and waking me up, and she says, 'Please buckle up! We're going on arrival in San Francisco.' It seemed like a 20-minute flight! Greatest flight I ever had. I recommend it."

Doing the Eagles and Phillies was a grind, and it took its toll on Campbell's health.

"It got to be really tough doing both jobs," he said. "And [Phils owner] Bob Carpenter was a real good guy, but I don't think he was too happy about me leaving a baseball game to do a football game. He never confronted me about it, but I heard through the grapevine that he wasn't happy about it. And, physically, it was draining. It was tough, and I did wind up in the hospital with ulcers. It really took a lot out of me and I gave up on the Eagles a few years later."

"He was overlapping things and it was wearing him out," said Jo, Bill's wife. "I remember my older sister, Lillie, seeing him on TV. She called me and said he just looked terrible. She said, 'I want you to get him out of there and go on a vacation. He needs some time away from that schedule.' "

Added Jo with a laugh: "So I told Bill what my big sister said and that I had to listen to my big sister. And he said, 'Not a bad idea.' " Bill, Jo, and their young daughter, Chris, eventually went on a cruise to the Bahamas.

"It did a lot for him; he got a lot of reading done and really rested," Jo said. "But at the same time, I remember Mike Grant, who was his boss and program director at WCAU, was on the phone with him a lot. He wouldn't leave him alone. He must have called the ship five times and they would page him."

Despite the interruptions, Bill seemed re-energized.

———

Campbell did play-by-play of Eagles games from 1956 to 1964, a nine-season span in which the Birds went 47-64-5, went through four head coaches (Hugh Devore, Buck Shaw, Nick Skorich, and Joe Kuharich) and had just three winning records. Over the years, his colormen included Bill Bransome, Ed Romance, Ed Harvey, Tommy Roberts, Bobby Thomason, By Saam, and Tom Brookshier.

Brookshier said Campbell didn't appear stressed during the hectic years in which he did Eagles and Phillies games.

"In those days, you didn't think much about it. You just thought that's the way it was and you did it," said Brookshier, the former Eagles star who played on the 1960 championship team.

If you needed to do double-duty, you just did it. No questions asked. Take John Facenda, for instance. Facenda, who would achieve immortality as the voice of NFL Films, was doing radio news on WIP in the 1940s and 1950s while he also anchored the Channel 10 news.

But Campbell's double-duty became a bit extreme when it involved coast-to-coast travel and it played havoc with his eating and sleeping schedule. "If you look back on it now, it's almost impossible to do baseball and football," Brookshier said. "You couldn't do it. Baseball is such a grind. I used to work with Lindsey Nelson and Jack Buck [on football telecasts] and they used to say that baseball was so much more demanding because you did it every day, and when you weren't doing it, you were traveling and you were away from your family."

In other words, it was difficult enough doing baseball games without having to fit football — and all the preparation time that went with it — into your schedule.

It was even more difficult to do a football game when the conditions made it tough to see the field. A blizzard of snow wasn't the culprit.

Instead, it was a blizzard of insects.

Brookshier said it was one of the first games he ever did with Campbell, an exhibition against the Chicago Bears in 1962. The Bears were the team that had broken Brookshier's leg and caused him to retire from football the previous season.

Time did not ease Brookshier's hatred of the Bears. When Chicago made a big play against the Eagles in this exhibition game in Cedar Rapids, Iowa, Brookshier — still a player at heart — was so upset that he began pounding the desk-like table in the rickety wooden press box.

Brookshier had no way of the knowing that several hornets' nests were underneath the table. The broadcaster had just given them a wake-up call.

"Hundreds and hundreds of hornets start flying all over the press box," Brookshier said. "I mean, they were all over the place."

Campbell and Brookshier used newspapers and their press notes as ammunition; their arms resembled windmills as they tried swatting away the hornets so they could view the action.

"And Bill took it like a pro; he actually announced it on the air," Brookshier said. In a calm voice that was interrupted by a few hearty chuckles, Campbell told listeners: "You won't believe what we're going through up here in the press box, ladies and gentlemen."

In 1983, Brookshier sent Campbell a letter to congratulate him on his 60th birthday. The letter, naturally, included mention of the night they were almost swallowed by hornets:

"The main thing I remember, William, is you starting me out in this 'life of crime' and that we did a game right after I had suffered my self-inflicted wound. The game happened to be between the Eagles and the Chicago Bears, the team that jumped up and down on my right leg.

"....Since it was August and there had been no game obviously played in this ball park, nobody had thought to spray for insects. Early in the second quarter, your rookie analyst began to regress and become the player again, and when he jumped up and down and beat on the desk and other areas around the press box, giant hornets began to come out in formation. The closer and tighter the game got, the more the former Eagle beat [the desk] and ranted and raved, and the hornets continued to come.

"Your coverage of this action sequence should go into a space capsule. Your coverage of what was happening on the field, but more importantly, what was happening to us in the booth, was some of the most colorful and animated commentary of all time. The highlight being [that] a local Iowa farmer attempted to save the two city slickers by coming in with a DDT bomb and throwing it under the desk.

"What a game! What a night! And what a great broadcaster you always have been...."

From the fellow you started on the 'road to ruin.'

Tom

———

The Eagles weren't the first NFL team that Campbell broadcast. That distinction went to the Pittsburgh Steelers. Bill filled in for a few games during the 1952 season, and worked alongside the colorful Bob Prince, who also did Pirates baseball games.

During a game in late November that season, Prince, following orders from the NFL commissioner, Bert Bell, reminded the referee that he was supposed to delay the start of the 1:30 p.m. game to 1:35 p.m.

"Bert Bell used to tell us that it was incumbent of the announcers to remind the officials to hold the kickoff for five minutes," Campbell said. "That way, they could get five minutes of commercials in. So Bob goes down and tells the referee and the ref says OK."

At 1:30 p.m., radio commercials filled five minutes. The broadcast went on the air at 1:35 p.m., as planned.

One problem: The referee forgot about the instructions. He started the game at 1:30 and Pittsburgh's Lynn Chandnois took the opening kickoff and scored on a 91-yard return, sparking a 63-7 upset of the New York Giants. Chandnois got a running start by racing down the Forbes Field pitcher's mound, located outside the end zone, before catching the ball in full stride.

"So we get on the air, and Prince says, 'Good afternoon. Most football games start with the score 0-0. This game will start with the score 7-0 because you have just missed the *greatest* play in the history of the Pittsburgh Steelers. And you can thank the knucklehead referee for not listening to our orders to start the game at 1:35,' " Campbell said.

Bell heard what happened and called a meeting in Philadelphia the next day; he met with Campbell in Philly and talked with Prince on the phone.

"It wasn't our fault," Campbell said, "but he chewed us out."

———

When the Phillies offered Bill the broadcasting position in 1963, he knew this was the job he had wanted his whole life. He had a history with baseball; it had been his favorite sport since he went to the 1929 World Series game with his dad and his next-door neighbor, John Nolan, the baseball writer for the *Bulletin*.

Still, he wondered if he was taking on too much responsibility if he accepted the Phillies' job. On one hand, he was already doing Eagles games and nightly sportscasts. On the other hand, his schedule had eased a bit because the Warriors had left Philadelphia for Syracuse and he would no longer be broadcasting their NBA games.

Complicating matters was the fact that, if he took the Phillies job, he would have to stop his nightly sportscasts on WCAU. He was making $25,000 at 'CAU; the Phillies had offered him $15,000.

Bill went to his wife, Jo, for advice.

"I told him, 'Baseball is what you've always wanted to do your whole life, and now that you have the opportunity, don't pass it up,' " Jo said.

Bill's sister, Julie, remembers her brother picking up objects — whether it be a wooden spoon or a rolled-up towel or newspaper — and pretending it was a microphone as he did play-by-play of an imaginary game during his childhood. Jo has heard all the stories about little Billy, the wannabe announcer.

"He was always sports-conscious, but he was always too small to play anything seriously, and he realized it," she said. "They tell me he used to fool around with a tin can with a string on it and hold it up to his face and pretend he was broadcasting a ball game. And it was always baseball. That was his love."

Bill felt comfortable doing baseball games. As a 17-year-old in 1941, he had done the Lancaster Red Roses' minor-league games and he had been filing radio reports on the Phillies (and, at one time, the A's) since the 1940s. He had covered the Phils' improbable run to the National League pennant in 1950 and had been a fixture at the ball park ever since.

Campbell had also done radio recreations of Philadelphia Athletics away games, filling in for By Saam in the late '40s. A Western Union operator sat next to Bill at the radio station and handed him a ticker-tape that would provide the play-by-play of each pitch. Bill would take the information and add his own color.

Foul ball, said the ticker-tape. Bill would make it sound exciting.

"Chapman fouls the pitch off on the left side — oh, he almost got a fan in the third row behind third base! That guy just got out of the way!"

Lucky the guy had such great reflexes, you thought as you listened at home — unaware that the announcer was bending the truth.

"There were no sound effects when I did it. Just talk," Campbell said. "You got the basic information from the operator and then you made stuff up that you didn't even see. You'd say, 'There's a curveball in the dirt for a ball.' Stuff like that. You didn't know it was a curveball and you didn't know it was in the dirt, but you had to do something to make it sound somewhat entertaining. You really got to use your imagination, which was very helpful for a broadcaster. It helped you be able to ad-lib in almost any situation."

The operator's tape would read: "Groundout to shortstop. Two outs." Campbell would supply the details.

"There's a smash into the hole at short; Eddie Joost backhands, sets, throws. Got Rizzuto by a step! TWO outs!!"

Listening to your radio at home, you felt as if you were sitting in those old seats with the peeling paint at Shibe Park.

One of the best parts about doing Phillies games was spending six weeks in sunny Florida for spring training. Campbell and one of his broadcast partners, By Saam, would drive down together each year. That way, they'd have two cars in Clearwater — the one they were driving and the one the team's sponsor had assigned to them.

One year, Bill would take his car; the next year, it was Saam's car that went down.

Early in Bill's tenure with the Phillies, the two men were driving south and had reached Maryland when Saam came up with an idea. They had some time to waste before they had to be in Clearwater, so why not make a pit stop at one of the most famous golf courses in the world.

"Ever seen the Augusta National Golf Course?" asked Saam, who, like Campbell, was an avid golfer.

"No."

"Well, why don't we take a ride there then?"

"OK."

They took turns driving and headed to Georgia.

"Now this was before I-95 was built," Campbell said. "We had to go three hours out of our way to get there."

When they arrived at Augusta National and pulled Campbell's dark green Chrysler into the main driveway, they were greeted by two guards."

"Can I help you," one of them asked.

"Well, hello. Yeah, we just wanted to stop by and look at the golf course," Saam said in that rich baritone voice.

"Sorry," the guard replied. "You cannot come in here unless you're accompanied by a member."

Saam, who was known for his easygoing nature, was dumbfounded.

"Now wait a minute. You don't understand. We're baseball broadcasters from Philadelphia."

The guard was not impressed.

"We're on our way to spring training and we just thought we'd stop by and look at the golf course."

"I don't mean to be impolite, sir, but I can't do it. I have a job to do here. You *must* be accompanied by a member."

Saam didn't understand. He got out of the car and pulled out his wallet. He showed the guard his Phillies credentials and his press cards.

He pulled out every card that he had for the last 30 years, Campbell said.

The guard still wasn't impressed.

"I don't care who you are! You *cannot* come in here without a member."

Saam was persistent.

"I'll tell you what," he said in his Texas drawl. "I'll bet I can walk over to the clubhouse over there and when I show a member these credentials, *any* member will be glad to take me out on the veranda and let me look at the fairway."

Still, no taker.

"I'm sorry, I cannot let you do that. It's cocktail hour and dinner hour and I cannot let you do that."

To this day, Campbell bursts into laughter when he recalls Saam's disbelief that they wouldn't allow deeply respected baseball announcers on their sacred golf course.

"Byrum was wild. The guy would not let us in and we had gone three hours out of our way to get there. We never got in."

Well, not that day. But a few weeks into spring training, Campbell remembered that the guy who directed the Masters' telecast was Frank Chirkinian, with whom Bill had worked for numerous years at Channel 10.

Campbell called Chirkinian from the spring-training press box and told him what had happened to him and Saam as they tried to visit Augusta.

"On the way home, Frank, can you get us on the golf course?" Campbell asked.

Back then, when the Florida spring-training days ended, major-league teams played exhibition games as their buses traveled north and headed for home. The Phillies, for instance, would frequently stop in Spartanburg, South Carolina, and play either one of their minor-league affiliates or another major-league team.

Hitting the links has been one of Bill Campbell's favorite hobbies. From left to right, Campbell, Jack Whitaker, Walter Tillman, Ed McMahon, and John Facenda. Tillman was a TV Guide executive, while the others worked for WCAU TV. McMahon became famous as Johnny Carson's Tonight Show sidekick.

Campbell told Chirkinian they had a few extra days as they headed to Philadelphia, and he wondered if they could see one day of the Masters.

"No problem," Chirkinian said.

It paid to have connections. Take that, Mr. Security Guard!

Chirkinian told Campbell that CBS had rented 10 or 12 golf-course houses for their technicians. "I can give you a house with one condition," he said. "Get here on Thursday night and you can stay all day Friday, but you have to get out when my crew comes to televise on Saturday and Sunday."

"Great," Campbell said.

The house and the setting, Campbell said, "was like something right out of *Gone with the Wind*. We had a butler, we had a servant, we had cocktails made for us."

The course was spectacular, too. Campbell and Saam arrived at Augusta National at 8 o'clock Friday morning and as they got to the first tee, the public-address announcer's voice could be heard for miles:

"Now teeing off at Augusta National Golf Course — Ben Hogan."

Like Saam, the legendary Hogan was from Texas. Saam idolized the man. He ran over to the first tee to watch Hogan. Campbell followed.

"Would you believe that we followed Hogan for every single shot?" Campbell recalled. "I mean, every single shot. And it was like watching golf balls come out of a machine. It was incredible. He was on the green in regulation on every single hole — and never made a [birdie] putt! He was at the end of his career then. He shot a par 72. And he stayed over his putt *forever*! You thought he was never going to take the club back. He hit every fairway, every green, but he *never* made a putt."

No matter. Saam and Campbell had a memory that would last a lifetime.

Saam, Campbell, and Richie Ashburn seemed to be the perfect broadcasting trio. Saam was the straight man to his sidekicks' Martin and Lewis routine. But the chuckles that Campbell and Ashburn provided couldn't mask their unmatched insight and knowledge of the game.

The biggest problem that the trio had wasn't broadcasting the action, it was seeing it — and that had nothing to do with Saam's eye problems that occurred later in his career.

It had everything to do with the cloud of smoke that settled over the press box each night. Saam smoked cigars, Ashburn puffed a pipe, Campbell smoked Chesterfields.

"We're lucky we could even see," Campbell said. "We had a very cloudy booth each night. It's a miracle I have any voice left."

A typical at-bat with Campbell, his right hand cupped over his right ear — a habit he developed while trying to do play-by-play over the sounds made by 60,000-plus Franklin Field fans — sitting behind the microphone:

"The pitch to Tony Taylor is high, ball one." Puff.

"Cloninger's fastball is a little outside; Joe Torre didn't like the call." Puff.

"Taylor ahead, 2 and 0. Tony takes a late swing and fouls it off on the right side; Aaron has no play." Puff.

"Phils lead, 3-1, we're in the fifth. Cloninger is ready, here's the pitch.

A ground ball and it's THROUGH, past Menke at short, and into center field for a base hit." Puff, puff, puff.

"That'll bring up Dalrymple with no outs and the Phillies trying to get some more runs."

Restart puffing sequence.

"I smoked a pack and a half or two packs a day for a lot of years," Campbell said. He quit smoking in 1978 after a two-week hospital stay caused by Crohn's disease, a gastrointestinal disorder. "If I had not stopped smoking when I did, I'm sure I would not be here right now," he said.

Campbell had other habits when he announced games. As the action intensified, his right leg would wobble like a bowl of Jell-O™ and his right foot would tap the floor rhythmically. When the game got extra tense, he began picking the skin off his thumb as a stress reducer. "It was just this nervous habit he had," said his daughter, Chris, who sometimes sat next to her dad in the Connie Mack Stadium press box. "His thumbs would be bleeding by the end of the night; that was just his intensity."

She smiled.

"After a while," she said, breaking into laughter, "you didn't want to sit next to him."

Brookshier doesn't remember Campbell destroying his thumb when he was his broadcast partner with the Eagles in the '60s, but he does recall his ever-active right foot.

"He would jiggle it like crazy," Brookshier said. "He would be so calm on the air, but you look down and his foot was going like mad. I used to think, 'Is this foot attached to the same guy who is so calm when he talks?'"

Campbell's voice was calm but, at the same time, filled with gravelly enthusiasm. He would start out a sentence in simple descriptive terms — *"Van Brocklin has McDonald over the middle near midfield...."* — and then his voice alternated from conversational tone to euphoria in a split second. Up and down, up and down it went as he intensified the drama with each stride taken by the Eagles' receiver. *"....McDonald shakes off a tackler, AND ANOTHER and he's IN THE CLEAR!!!!! McDonald is IN THE CLEAR! And they're NOT GOING TO CATCH HIM. TOUCHDOWN!"*

There was a melodic rhythm to Campbell's football descriptions — much like the broadcasts done by Merrill Reese, who in 2006 was scheduled to begin his 30th year as the Eagles' play-by-play announcer. Like the 5-foot-7, 150-pound Campbell, Reese is a small man — 5-8, 140 pounds — with a booming voice. Growing up in West Philadelphia, Reese used to listen to the Eagles broadcasts done by Campbell, a man who is now his close friend.

Reese calls Campbell his hero.

"He is, by far, the greatest announcer this city has ever had," said Reese, a broadcasting legend in his own right. "No one comes close to him."

CHAPTER EIGHT

The Phillies' collapse of '64

Phillies fans know the 1964 numbers. They're ingrained, like your date of birth, your social security number, your wedding anniversary.

With 12 games to play, the over-achieving Phils were in first place with a 6 1/2-game lead and were helping to keep peoples' minds off of the racial unrest that plagued the city.

Philly was abuzz. World Series tickets were printed. Hotels were being booked. The Chestnut Street Association unfurled 100 large red flags proclaiming "Go Phillies Go," and Center City stores proudly displayed photos of Phils players in their windows.

Less than three seasons after they had lost 23 straight games and finished with the worst record in the majors at 47-107, the Phillies were the talk of the baseball world.

What followed was the greatest late-season collapse in major-league history. A 10-game losing streak that broke their fans' collective hearts. In less the two weeks, the '64 Phils went from being maybe the most beloved team in the club's history….to the most infamous.

Bill Campbell has a unique perspective on that season. It was his second year as one of the Phils' play-by-play announcers and he spent a lot of time with the club's fiery manager, Gene Mauch. They lived near each other — Campbell in Broomall, Mauch in Newtown Square — so they drove together to the airport at the start of a road trip.

Campbell cherished those rides, cherished those conversations.

"We would talk about a lot of things; he would let his hair down and talk about his players," Campbell said. "It was really off the record, most of it. But I picked up things he said. I had been at 'CAU for 16 years when I went to the Phillies and I had been to a lot of ball games. I went down there every night and I thought I really under-stood the game. But I learned more about the game, particularly studying the body language of players, from Gene Mauch than I thought there was to know.

"The only thing that mattered to Gene was baseball and his family. When he wasn't with his family, he was at the ballpark. He'd be there at 1 o'clock for a game that started at 8 that night and I started getting there at that time because I really liked being around him and listening to him. And he made me a better broadcaster. He made me look for things that I never paid attention to before."

Mauch was one of the first managers to use double-switches (strategically inserting substitutes into different spots in the batting order) and he loved to employ the suicide squeeze. He always seemed to be ahead of the opposing manager, always seemed to know the rules better than the umpires. And he did everything in his power — *everything!* — to give his team an advantage. For instance, he moved the Phillies' bullpen from left field to right field so his relievers could wave a towel if a fly ball was going to hit off the gigantic wall. If the third-base coach saw that a reliever was waving a towel, he was usually waving his runners around the bases.

"I learned so much from Gene, and I learned a lot from Richie's throwaway lines," Campbell said.

Campbell had always been identified by his unique, gravelly voice and his ability to make each listener feel as if he was having a conversation *with them*. His knowledge, his preparation, and his ad-libbing skills were also part of his success formula. He became an even better broadcaster, however, after he was in the daily company of Mauch and Richie Ashburn. They broadened his insight, broadened his appreciation for a sport that he loved to its core.

The 1964 season started in stunning fashion. By May 1, the Phils were 10-2 and sitting atop the 10-team National League standings. By the all-star break, this odd mix of players had a 1 1/2-game lead as they remained in first place with a 47-28 record.

As the season progressed, Mauch, who turned platooning players into an art form, pushed all the right buttons. If he inserted versatile Cookie Rojas into the lineup, he seemed to make a big defensive play or get a clutch hit. If he needed a ground-ball double play from Jack Baldschun or Ed Roebuck or any of his relievers, he got it. If he needed a timely late-inning hit from Richie Allen or Johnny Callison or Wes Covington, they usually delivered.

If his offense had an off night, his starter (particularly if it was Jim Bunning or Chris Short) pitched brilliantly and overcame the lack of run support.

"Mauch always had the defense positioned perfectly. They always moved runners. Fundamentally, they did every-thing right," Campbell said.

Sport World's Magazine *named Bill its sportscaster of the month in its April, 1964 edition. Bill (center) is flanked by Phillies manager Gene Mauch and broadcast partner By Saam.*

Everything was clicking, and it made Campbell think back to the time in 1963 when he, Mauch, Phils coach Peanuts Lowrey, and Jimmy Dykes, the former A's infielder who managed six major-league teams from 1934 to 1960, were on the golf course. "We're playing at Bala, and Gene and I are riding in one cart, and Dykes and Peanuts are in the other cart," Campbell said. "And Gene turns to me and says, 'You know how much I love Jimmy, Bill. I think Jimmy Dykes is one of the best guys in the history of baseball. But you know what? He never won a banner [as a manager]. He never won a damn banner. I'm gonna win a lot of banners. I'm here to win *banners*.' "

Campbell kept thinking of Mauch's words as he watched the Phils take control of the National League race in 1964. Heck, the year even included a memorable gem by Bunning — the league's first nine-inning perfect game since 1880. Twenty-seven batters up, 27 down — 10 on strikeouts — as the Phils defeated the woeful New York Mets, 6-0, in the first game of a June 21 doubleheader at sweltering Shea Stadium. Fittingly, the game was played on Father's Day; Bunning was the father of seven children. (He and his wife would have two more children, bringing the count to nine.)

Campbell missed that perfect game because he had returned to Philadelphia two days earlier to be with his ailing mother, Margaret Campbell.

Margaret had settled in with a good job at the Atlantic Refining Company, but she was plagued with breathing problems. Years of smoking had taken its toll. Plagued with emphysema, she had been in and out of hospitals for five years. Bill would be on the road with the Phillies and would get the inevitable phone call from his wife, Jo: "Your mom is back in the hospital."

These oxygen treatments became a part of Margaret's life.

Campbell remembers one of his mom's emphysema attacks in the late '50s and how it led to her meeting Norm Van Brocklin for the first time. Back then, Bill would go to the Eagles' office, located at 15th and Locust, on Mondays and do a voice-over or some promotional work for the team. Van Brocklin, being the club's most visible player, frequently joined Campbell. On this particular blustery November day, Campbell and Van Brocklin had just finished eating lunch at a downtown restaurant and were heading back to the Eagles' offices. Bill planned to work for another hour and then visit his mother, who lived in the nearby Touraine Apartments.

As Bill, the little Irishman, and the Dutchman walked down Spruce Street, Van Brocklin noticed a drunk woman staggering across the sidewalk on the other side of the road. Every few steps, the woman would grab onto a fence or a storefront or whatever she could find in order to keep her balance.

"It's only a little after noon, and look at that lady. Damn, is she bombed," Van Brocklin said. "Pretty early in the day to be so snookered, isn't it?"

Campbell nodded in agreement. But after he took a few more steps, he recognized the woman.

"Dutch, you're not going to believe this, but, that's my mother!"

Campbell raced across the street to assist her. She wasn't drunk, but she was having an emphysema attack and she was huffing and puffing, struggling to catch her breath.

"Mom, where the hell are you going? Why would you leave your apartment when you're having problems breathing?"

Margaret looked up at her son sweetly. She struggled as she tried to get out the words between deep breaths.

"I...(heavy pant)....had (another heavy pant).... to.... get.... (more panting) to the hairdresser's."

Campbell was incredulous. The hairdresser's! The damn hairdresser's!

"My wife's the same way," he said. "Friday is like a holy day of obligation — the hairdresser's. It could be snow eight feet high and she'd get there. If we lived in New Orleans after Hurricane Katrina, I *guarantee* my wife would find a way to get to the hairdresser's."

On that windy afternoon nearly a half century ago, Campbell went back to his mom's apartment and got her wheelchair. While Bill was gone, Van Brocklin held her arm so she could balance herself. Bill and Dutch took Margaret home, administered some oxygen and calmed her down.

The hairdresser's appointment would have to be postponed because of breathing difficulties.

Bill Campbell's stepmother, Margaret (left), and his sister, Polly, circa 1950.

Van Brocklin stayed for a while and then headed back to the Eagles' offices. Campbell, after making sure his mom's breathing was normal, went grocery shopping for her; when he returned to her apartment, he told her Van Brocklin had originally assumed she was a drunk.

Margaret Campbell was amused. "She thought it was a riot," Campbell said.

Van Brocklin became her favorite player.

———•———

When Jo Campbell phoned her husband in his Chicago hotel room in 1964, Bill wasn't alarmed to learn his mother had been admitted into the hospital. This, after all, had been a recurring development.

Then Jo cut to the chase.

"I've seen her in the hospital a lot, but this time it looks to me like she's not going to make it," Jo said, tearfully. "She's really having a tough time."

It was late at night, but Bill called Charlie Meister, the Phillies' traveling secretary, and his broadcast partners and told them he was going home and would not join the team in New York. He arrived at Philadelphia's Jefferson Hospital early the next morning. As he walked into the room, his uncle — Father William Graham, a Jesuit priest nicknamed "Brick" because of his red hair — was giving last rites to Bill's mother. Brick was Margaret's younger brother.

Margaret died the next afternoon. Bunning pitched his perfect game the following day.

After rejoining the Phillies following services for his mom, Campbell watched in amazement as the club could not do much wrong.

Late rallies became part of the Phils' identity. "Richie Ashburn and I used to look at each other like, 'What is going on here?!' " Campbell said. "It was almost like it was fixed. It kept happening over and over and over. It was incredible."

Like the '60 Eagles, the '64 Phillies seemed like a team of destiny. First, there was Bunning's perfect game. Then Callison, the Phillies' handsome young rightfielder, won the All-Star game for the National League with a three-run homer in the ninth. You didn't have to be a hard-core fan to realize that a theme was building.

A Phillies theme.

What made the season even more remarkable was that it occurred during the heyday of the National League. Superstars — and, in many cases, future Hall of Famers — were everywhere. The Cardinals had Curt Flood, a blossoming Lou Brock, and Bob Gibson. The San Francisco Giants had Willie Mays, Willie McCovey, Orlando Cepeda, and Juan Marichal. The Cincinnati Reds had Frank Robinson, Vada Pinson and a brash kid named Pete Rose. The Milwaukee Braves countered with Henry Aaron, Eddie Mathews, and Joe Torre, while the Los Angeles Dodgers had Sandy Koufax and Don Drysdale, the league's most feared pitching duo. Even the Cubs — who finished eighth in the 10-team league — had stars like Billy Williams, Ernie Banks, and Ron Santo.

"It was just great, great baseball every night. Compared to what it is now, there's no comparison," Campbell said. "Baseball in the '50s and early '60s was the best I have ever seen."

Yet, it was the Phillies — a team composed mostly of castoffs, emerging youngsters, and veterans considered past their primes — that held first place for 134 days that season; the champion Cardinals held first place for six days.

On September 20, with their WFIL radio and TV ratings soaring, the Phils were perched in first place with a 6 1/2-game lead with 12 games remaining. And then Chico Ruiz stole home with two outs in the ninth inning — and future Hall-of-Famer Frank Robinson at the plate, for crying out loud — to give the Reds a 1-0 win.

"He steals home with Frank Robinson the hitter; it made no sense," Campbell said.

"That was just stupid baseball — running with a home-run hitter up there," said Frank Thomas, the Phillies' first baseman for part of the '64 season. "But that's the kind of thing that happened to us at the end of the year."

Ruiz' dash even stunned interim Reds manager Dick Sisler, a hero for the 1950 Phillies Whiz Kids — yes, Campbell covered him in those days — who was filling in for the ill Fred Hutchinson.

Ruiz ran on his own.

Said Campbell: "After the game, one of the writers in the clubhouse — Ray Kelly or somebody — piped up and said, 'Dick, what did you think when Chico started down the line with Frank Robinson the hitter?' Dick was a good guy. And he had a speech impediment and when he got excited, he stuttered. And Dick said, 'He b-b-b-b-b-b-b-b-b-e-t-t-e-r be safe.' "

That 1-0 loss started a chilling homestand at chilly Connie Mack Stadium. The Phils went 0-7, the worst homestand in the club's history. Three road losses followed, running the losing streak to 10.

The Phils would win their final two games, but it was too late. They finished in a second-place tie with Cincinnati, one game behind St. Louis. Ruiz, a utility player who stole just 34 bases in his eight-year career, became the face of The Collapse. As he broke for home on the steal, startled pitcher Art Mahaffey saw him out of the corner of his eye and delivered a fastball low and outside. The pitch sailed past lunging catcher Clay Dalrymple. Ruiz had dropped to one knee to slide, but then popped to his feet and stomped on the plate.

When Ruiz died in 1972, the headline in *The Philadelphia Inquirer's* obituary stretched over four columns: *Chico Ruiz Dies at 33 in Automobile Crash: Stole Home to Beat Phils in '64 Collapse.*

From 1963 to 1970, the Phillies' popular broadcast team was composed of By Saam (left), Richie Ashburn, and Bill Campbell.

"I think the team became vulnerable after they blew a couple of games at the start of the streak," Campbell said. "And Mauch was not a popular guy to opponents [or to some of his own players, for that matter] and they really geared themselves up every time they faced him; they wanted to deny him going to the World Series."

Opposing players despised Mauch because he did everything in his power to unravel them. From the dugout, he could be a foul-mouthed and caustic chatterbox as he tried to disrupt a rival's concentration. He was a man who did anything for a victory. (Two years later, he literally punched an opposing catcher, Jerry Grote, who had the audacity to chase a foul ball that went into the Phils' dugout.)

"I remember going into St. Louis during the losing streak and their third baseman, Ken Boyer — one of the nicest guys you'd ever meet and a hell of a player — was standing by the batting cage when I walked over and watched the Cardinals hit before the game," Campbell said.

Boyer had an impish grin.

"How's the Little General taking this, Bill?" Boyer said, referring to Mauch.

"Not very well, Kenny. Not very well at all."

Boyer seemed pleased.

"It couldn't happen to a nicer guy," Boyer said, sarcasm dripping.

Over the years, Mauch has been vilified for overworking aces Bunning and Short down the 1964 stretch. He used them a combined five times on two days' rest during the 10-game collapse.

Campbell prefers to look at Mauch's genius during the season's first 150 games, not at the infamous swoon. He does concede, however, that the one move he never understood happened in the sixth game of the losing streak.

The Phils took a 4-0 lead into the fifth inning and a 4-3 lead into the ninth of that game against the Milwaukee Braves. But right-handed-hitting Rico Carty hit a three-run, ninth-inning triple off left-hander Bobby Shantz to continue the Phils' misery, 6-4. On national TV, no less.

This happened to be Shantz' 39th birthday, and it wasn't the way he wanted to spend it.

The diminutive Shantz had been spectacular with the A's in the early part of his career, winning the American League's Most Valuable Player Award after going 24-7 in 1952.

Shantz, all 5-foot-6, 139 pounds of him, was an exception to the Whitey Ashburn Rule: Pitchers can't do a damn thing except throw the ball.

"Bobby could field his position; he was quick; he could run and you could use him as a pinch runner," Campbell said. "He could swing the bat and he had the best curve ball in the American League."

Shantz was at the end of his career when the Phillies acquired him from the Cubs in an August 15 cash deal in 1964. Mauch, who had a fondness for older players, thought Shantz could regain his old magic. And he did, but not in that fateful game against the Braves.

"We had some pitchers hurt and we needed a left-hander badly, so we picked up Bobby," Campbell recalled. "But Bobby will tell you, as he's told me on the golf course, he didn't have anything left. And Mauch put him in the game in the late innings and, all of a sudden, the bases are loaded and Rico Carty, a tough right-handed hitter, is coming up."

When Carty stepped into the box, Campbell said he was about to pause for a commercial.

Gene Mauch manages to force a smile, but the fiery Phillies manager was devastated by the late-season 1964 developments. Here, Mauch receives congratulations from some of the estimated 7,000 fans who greeted the Phils when they returned to the airport at the end of the 1964 season.

"We just figured there would be a pitching change, because I was sure Gene wasn't going to let Bobby Shantz pitch to Rico Carty. But it didn't happen. He never got out of the dugout," Campbell said. "Richie Ashburn and I just kind of gave each other a puzzled look. We couldn't figure it out."

Campbell can still visualize the missile that Carty launched.

"Carty hit it to the left of the scoreboard, up off the top of the fence," he said. "It was one of the hardest balls I've ever seen hit and it just destroyed us," he said. "I've always wondered why Gene didn't make a move. I guess he figured the guys he had in the bullpen had nothing left."

Roebuck, a right-hander who had been arguably the team's best reliever that season, relieved Shantz and got the final three outs. No matter. The losing streak had reached six and it wasn't close to ending.

Neither was the second-guessing.

"I have all the respect in the world for Gene Mauch," Campbell said, "but that was one of the worst moves he ever made."

In Mauch's defense, Shantz had a sensational 0.70 ERA in his previous 11 appearances. But he had pitched seven innings in one

relief outing, and seven and two-thirds innings in another relief appearance, so maybe that's why he told Campbell his 39-year-old arm was shot.

In any event, there would be no banner for Mauch. Not that year. Not ever.

———————

Campbell has a lot of memories from that 1964 season, including a September post-game interview with excitable rookie Braves reliever Clay Carroll, who went into a curse-filled explanation on how he retired Richie Allen. On live radio.

"One of the most unbelievable broadcasts of my life," Campbell said.

He also remembers a poignant moment from '64, when Cincinnati manager Fred Hutchinson was battling lung cancer and knew he was near death.

"Hutch was really ill and he was emaciated," Campbell said. "He and Gene Mauch were very good friends, and I'll never forget this: Hutch came up to the press box at old Crosley Field and he came up especially to see the visiting press and the visiting broadcasters — he apparently was doing this with each team — to say good-bye. He was dying and he looked like the wrath of God. He looked just horrible. And he came into the booth before the game and shook hands with Richie, By, and me and he thanked us for all the things we had ever said about him. He said, 'The next time you guys come back here, I won't be here, and I just don't want to pass up this opportunity to say good-bye to you.' I'll never forget that."

What Campbell remembers most about '64, though, is how the city had a love affair with the Phillies, like it did with the Flyers during the Broad Street Bullies days of the 1970s, or with the Eagles as they went to four straight NFC championship games in the early 2000s.

To Bill Campbell, that Popsicle summer of '64 — an innocent time when the Beatles' "I Want to Hold Your Hand" was the year's top-selling tune — brings joy, not sorrow.

That's typical of Campbell, said Callison, the rightfielder who finished second in the MVP voting in '64.

"If he didn't have anything nice to say, he didn't say it," Callison said.

Campbell is still amazed at the Phillies' efficiency for the first five-plus months of the '64 season.

"I've been around the game for a long time," he said, "and for 150 games, that team played the best baseball of any team I've ever seen. I don't know anything about the '27 Yankees because I was too young. The '29, '30, and '31 A's teams played great and had some great players, but I was just a little kid. I've seen a lot of really good teams over the years, but I'll tell you, for 150 games, the '64 Phillies were incredible. And you never saw that tailspin coming! Chico Ruiz stole home and everything went to hell after that; it wasn't the same team."

A few days after the '64 season ended, Campbell said, a friend of Mauch's drove the Phillies' manager to the airport, from where he would fly to California and be reunited with his family. Mauch's friend turned on the car radio and tuned into the Cardinals-Yankees World Series game. Mauch knew his friend was doing him a favor by driving, knew he should be grateful passenger. But he couldn't play the part. The Little General reached over and, without saying a word to his friend, turned off the radio.

It was too painful to listen.

————⋅———

Jo Campbell hears the stories about Gene Mauch's ranting and raving and she doesn't understand it. To her, Mauch was a sweetheart.

Jo and Bill would socialize with Gene and his wife, Nina. Off the field, Gene was pleasant, easygoing and nice to be around, Jo said.

The only time he was out of sorts, she said, was when one of the players "made eyes" at his pretty daughter, Leeanne.

"Gene adored her; he just worshipped her," Jo said. "God forbid if she ever took a shine to any of those ballplayers, I'm sure he'd kill her. The players would look at her and say, 'Um, not bad, not bad.' And he'd say, 'Better look the other way.' "

When Mauch died of lung cancer on August 8, 2005, the Associated Press story noted that he won 1,901 games while managing the Phillies, Expos, Twins, and Angels, "but became infamous for historic losses."

In addition to the '64 Phils collapse, Mauch managed the 1986 California Angels when they were within one strike of advancing to the World Series before losing a three-run lead to Boston in Game 5 of the American League Championship Series. The Red Sox won that game and two more to win the series.

Mauch also managed the 1982 Angels, who won the first two game of the then-best-of-five AL Championship Series against Milwaukee and then lost the final three.

"If it's true that you learn from adversity, then I must be the toughest SOB in the world," Mauch once said.

Campbell called the umpire-baiting Mauch "the smartest, brightest baseball man I've ever been around. I still can't believe that a man as qualified as him never got to the World Series."

Mauch set a dubious record — most seasons (26) managed without a pennant, breaking the mark held by his golfing pal, Dykes (21 seasons).

Two days after Mauch's death, Campbell eulogized The Little General in his KYW radio commentary:

"Last night's game was the first of 18 of 25 on the road for the Phillies, then home for a week, followed by two weeks out West.

"It's tempting to call it 'make or break' time, except that we've been saying things like that all season.

"Their inconsistency is baffling. My friend, the late Gene Mauch, would have called this team just a winning streak away.

"Much of my baseball knowledge — such as it is — came from Gene Mauch. I have often wondered how he would have described THIS team. I think he would have liked it, and would have loved to manage it.

"He wouldn't have blamed Ed Wade for all its shortcomings. He would have blamed some of the players who are the real culprits.

"Most people associate Mauch with the collapse of '64. That's our usual negative way of expressing ourselves. I choose to remember '64 — and I was there for every pitch — as the best baseball I ever saw played or managed....for 150 games. However you choose to think about it, it was Gene Mauch who woke up a sleeping franchise.

"Thanks, Skip, and rest in peace.

"This is Bill Campbell, KYW Newsradio."

CHAPTER NINE

A messy divorce from the Phils

Bill Campbell was running some errands as his wife, Jo, puttered around their Broomall kitchen and sang to the music that blared through the radio speakers on this December morning in 1970. While her thoughts drifted toward the Christmas shopping that needed to be done, she was staggered by two snappy sentences that were read by the WPEN announcer.

"There will be a new voice of the Phillies next year," he told listeners. "Harry Kalas will replace Bill Campbell."

Jo Campbell doesn't remember what the announcer said next. She was too busy feeling betrayed, too busy wondering how she would deliver the devastating news to her husband. Too busy crying.

"It was a shot in the heart," she said. "He didn't even know it. I had to tell him when he came home."

How do you tell a man he has lost one of the loves of his life, baseball? How do you tell someone he can no longer work with people whom he had considered his family?

"I don't even remember what I said to him," she said. "I was just hysterical. We had a little dog, and that poor dog" — Tootsie, the spaniel/terrier who had been a gift from Dutch Van Brocklin — "was running around in circles because I was screeching so much."

All day, people offered their condolences. Some called. Some showed up at the front door. All were incredulous.

No one was more incredulous than Bill and his wife. Just two months earlier, at the end of the season, the Phillies' advertising agency representative had complimented the three announcers — Campbell, By Saam and Richie Ashburn — for their work and had told them they would be back next year. The Campbells went out with friends and celebrated the news. "Here's to the Phillies!" said Jo, holding up a glass of wine and toasting the club. "Here's to the new stadium!" someone else replied.

Bill Campbell was excited to move into Veterans Stadium the next year. He loved the quaintness and the charm of Connie Mack Stadium, but the ballpark was old and in need of repair. So was the press box. It would be fun to help usher in a new era of Phillies baseball, fun to be part of the first broadcasting crew to work at what was then considered one of Major League Baseball's palaces, the Vet.

Reports that Campbell had been dismissed were all over the radio. Later that day, Phillies owner Bob Carpenter phoned Campbell and told him not to take the reports seriously.

"He told him, 'Don't take it so hard. It's not concluded yet. It's not finalized,' " Jo Campbell recalled.

Chris Campbell, then a freshman at Villanova, came home from college that night and she was aware of all the drama that had been unfolding. While she stayed home and studied, her parents went next door to spend time with neighbors. And, yes, Bill needed a drink or two.

Chris was alone when the phone rang in their split-level suburban home. Carpenter was the caller.

"Can I speak with your dad?"

"He's not here. He's next door."

"Do you think you can get him for me?"

Carpenter thanked Chris, gave her his number and asked if Campbell could call him at his home.

As she walked next door, Chris Campbell had a sick feeling in her stomach.

"I knew from the sound of Mr. Carpenter's voice," she said, "that what we heard was true."

Her beloved dad, she believed, was about to get fired and she felt helpless to do anything about it.

She walked next door and gave her father the message. Bill, Jo, and Chris returned home. Bill dialed Carpenter's number. Chris went upstairs and sat on the steps between the first and second floors. She was within earshot of the conversation. Part of her didn't want to hear it, but part of her wanted to be near her father to give support and comfort. Jo Campbell stood in the hallway, next to Chris.

"We just looked at each other," Chris said. "I think we both knew that life was about to change."

In a lot of ways.

"It's not just the job, but it's the people you work with," Chris said. "The players you see every day. The people you play golf with. My parents had fabulous dinner parties. There were always people in and out of the house. They happen to be ballplayers. They were their friends, and a lot of what you feel about yourself comes from the love and appreciation and acceptance of those in your life. People leave your life when jobs change; it's just the way things are. So many levels of his life were affected by it."

Carpenter told Campbell his back was against the wall and there was nothing he could do to save the announcer's job.

"That broke my father's heart," Chris said. "It broke my father's heart to lose that job."

She paused.

"And he was so damn good at it," she said with all-knowing conviction. "He was so good at it."

———•———

To this day, Jo Campbell and her daughter insist that Bill's long-time affliction with Crohn's disease — he had surgery in 1978 — was triggered by the Phillies' firing. That may be accurate, although such a chronic gastrointestinal disorder could not have been caused by stress. "But it certainly could have been exacerbated by stress," said Dr. Boris Libster, a South Jersey gastroenterologist.

To this day, Bill Campbell says he has never been told why he was dismissed.

There were plenty of theories, of course.

Theory No. 1: The Phillies were moving into a new balkpark, and one of their young executives, Bill Giles, wanted a new image to go with the club's new digs. Getting a new and younger broadcaster would add to that theme.

It was no coincidence that the man who was hired to replace Campbell, Harry Kalas, used to work with Giles with the Houston Astros. Late in 1969, Giles had joined the Phils from the Astros, where he worked in their publicity department.

All of the broadcasters were connected to Ballantine.

Theory No. 2: The Phillies were changing beer sponsors and that contributed mightily to the change in the broadcast booth. Ballantine was out. Schmidt's was in. Since Campbell was deeply identified with Ballantine, Schmidt's wanted a different announcer.

Close to four decades after the firing, Giles sat in his swank Citizens Bank Park office and tried to piece together why Campbell was dismissed from the $40,000-a-year job.

Giles, now the Phillies' chairman, was the club's vice president of business operations in 1970. He said Campbell was a "terrific" announcer. "I liked his enthusiasm. He was colorful. I thought he did a very good job."

Speaking in an authoritative tone, Giles recalled that Campbell's firing "was a very simple matter. He had done commercials for Ballantine Beer and he was connected to Ballantine because he did all those commercials….Schmidt's said they would give us millions of dollars — I can't remember the numbers — but we cannot have Bill Campbell on the air. We wanted a new face to do our commercials, so I was forced to fire Bill."

That puzzled Campbell, who said his broadcast partners, Saam and Ashburn, were just as connected to Ballantine.

"For some reason, Schmidt's didn't want Campbell," Giles said. He chuckled.

"To be honest about it, I thought Bill did a better job than By Saam. He understood baseball better. By had a great voice, but I enjoyed listening to Campbell a lot. But they insisted on having a new voice and insisted on not having Campbell."

Campbell said Giles never called to tell him he was fired.

"I didn't? Who told him?" Giles asked.

Told it was Carpenter, Giles suddenly backtracked on some of his earlier statements. "Now that you say Bob Carpenter called, the only thing I can vividly remember is that Schmidt's didn't want all three announcers back. And now whether Bob decided to fire Bill, for whatever reason, I don't know….The only thing I'm sure about is that Schmidt's had a problem… And I was in charge of selling the TV rights and I went out and sold Schmidt's a third of the television broadcasts to replace Ballantine."

Funny thing is, at around the same time, Schmidt's was also one of the leading sponsors of Big 5 basketball games that were telecast on Channel 17. The play-by-play man for those broadcast was Campbell. Why would Schmidt's think Campbell was acceptable to do college basketball games but not Phillies baseball games?

Campbell dismissed Giles' theory that he was fired because of pressure applied by Schmidt's.

"But what would be gained by making a big deal out of it now?" he asked.

Back in 1970, the newspapers had a field day with the Campbell controversy. The Phillies helped fuel things during a clumsy press conference that was designed to give details of the club's new $13.5 million television contract with Channel 17 and its parent, U.S. Communications Inc. As the club gave details of the TV deal, it made passing reference to the fact that Kalas would replace Campbell in the broadcast booth.

Giles seemed uncomfortable as he tried to answer why Campbell had been replaced. Leonard Stevens, representing Channel 17 and U.S. Communications, stood up and attempted to help. "I think you would have to concede that's an unfair question to be answered at this forum," he said.

"You are aware that the audience will want to know, aren't you?" a reporter asked Stevens.

"Not necessarily," Stevens replied.

A few dozen reporters groaned.

Wrote columnist Frank Dolson in *The Philadelphia Inquirer*: "It was a bad scene. An embarrassing scene. Surely the Phillies — or the station or the agency or somebody — had the right to make a change. But there had to be a better way to do so than this. There had to be some thought for the feelings of a man who had been a highly capable, highly professional announcer for eight seasons."

"*Firing of 'Voice' Strikes Bad Chord*," read the headline atop Dolson's column. Some other local headlines:

"*Static in Clumsy Ouster Widens Credibility Gap*"

"*Striking Out an Honest Voice*"

"*Phillies Put Campbell in Soup Line*"

Dolson, the *Daily News'* Stan Hochman and Bill Conlin, *The Trentonian's* Harvey Yavener, *The Trenton Times'* Bus Saidt, and the

Bucks County Courier Times' Paul Giordano were among the columnists who wrote stories that defended Campbell and vilified the Phillies.

The *Daily News* asked readers to write letters to express their feelings. Hundreds complied. For the next two weeks, the newspaper printed scads of the letters. Conlin reported that the letters ran 13 to 1 in Campbell's favor.

Some samples:

"The firing of Bill Campbell leaves us with a bad baseball team, worse announcers, and a rotten front office. Bring Campbell back and fire those who should go, Carpenter and [general manager John] Quinn."

"It is indeed a sad day when, in times when one hears cries for authenticity, believability, and sincerity in our plastic life, a man with the color and excellence of a Bill Campbell is removed from the air.....Bill Campbell gave Phillies, Eagles, and Warriors broadcasts an aura of excitement and entertainment that transcended the dreary performances of the teams he reported. He is a rarity among broadcasters in that he conveys a deep interest in the game. He was concerned and fascinated by the totality and complexity of the sports event he was describing. The beauty of a colorful man thoroughly enjoying his work will be sorely missed. I wish to register my deep protest."

Several fans wrote that they would no longer support the Phillies' sponsors because of the firing:

"I think Bill Campbell got a real bad deal. Don't know who to blame. However, no Atlantic/Arco in the car or Schmidt's in my refrigerator."

Wrote another reader: "I understand Campbell was fired on the advice of Bill Giles. Perhaps you should consider that a man who puts slats of wood into the hands of 10,000 people (as part of a giveaway promotion) and turns them loose in an emotional situation is subject to lapses of bad judgment. Perhaps it is Giles, not Campbell, who should go. Bring back Bill Campbell or you can write me off as a ticket-buyer, a Tastykake buyer, an Arco man, a Winston smoker, or a Ballantine drinker."

Boycotting Ballantine, of course, wouldn't affect the Phillies. Schmidt's was in, Ballantine was out.

Just like Bill Campbell.

Campbell still has a faded, oversized envelope that holds nearly 100 letters and cards of support that were sent to him after he was fired. Some of the letters were sent by recognizable names — Phillies coach George Myatt and Dallas Green, the assistant farm director who would climb the club's ladder; Penn basketball coach Dick Harter, who later advanced to the NBA; Ernie Casale and Al Shrier of Temple's athletic and sports information departments; and Jack Carty of the *Courier Post* — but most were written by everyday fans whose lives Bill had touched. Some folks attached copies of nasty letters they had sent to the Phillies.

Amid all the letters that supported Campbell and protested his firing was one written on Oct. 1, 1970. Back then, Campbell was expected to return to the Phillies.

Dear Bill:

I just finished listening to you, By, and Richie broadcast the last game played at Connie Mack. What a finish to a season that, hopefully, casts an exciting shadow of the future....But that's not why I'm writing. I want to take this opportunity to thank the three of you for bringing many, many hours of pleasure to me. I'm not a letter writer; in fact, this is the first time I've ever written a letter of this type and I'm no youngster. But I think the three of you have provided so many enjoyable moments — especially you, Bill — that I think it would be very selfish of me not to thank you.

I wonder if you've ever thought about the salesman on the road at night. Lonely, just starting toward Philly from some distant part of the state [and] hating the thought of the long, lonely drive. But then, great, great thought...the ballgame is on....and I have company and entertainment for the drive home. And how many times have the three of you been with me…while I got some chore done in my office or around my home. Radio on, or transistor plugged in my ear. And how many times with the earphones plugged in…laying in bed while a game was being broadcast from the coast.

By with his great voice and pleasant approach. Richie with his great sense of humor and his great knowledge of facts and the game. And you, able to bring emotion and a sense of excitement to the most commonplace of games.

Again, thank you and keep it up…for many, many years to come.
Sincerely,
Robert Siegel

The letter writer's kind words became oh-so-ironic when the Phillies pulled the plug on their popular voice a little over two months later.

Reflecting on it now, many people still remember their reaction to the firing.

"I was one of the fans who was really upset; I was one of Bill's most ardent fans," said Frank Catania, a retired purchasing manager from Marple Township, Pennsylvania. "I couldn't understand how the Phillies could do such a horrible thing. The banter that he had with Ashburn was so much fun, and he was one of the best play-by-play announcers I've ever heard. I came to love Harry Kalas, but at the time I couldn't figure out why they were getting rid of Bill. When it happened, some of my friends said they were done with the team, but I was too much of a baseball fan to give it up."

Catania, 67, remembered Campbell criticizing the team if it needed it.

"He called it like he saw it and didn't worry about repercussions," he said.

Like Catania, Steve McHugh recalled feeling confused by Campbell's dismissal.

"I was a 16-year-old kid at the time, and I was always a Bill Campbell fan and, all of a sudden, he wasn't on," McHugh said. "I remember saying to my dad, 'What happened? Why isn't he there?' And my dad said that he was too honest and too critical" of the Phillies. "That always stuck with me…and that concept, for a kid, was difficult to understand — that you could be *too* honest.

"Over the years," added McHugh, a gregarious 52-year-old actor and teacher who lives in South Jersey, "people have told me that I'm too honest, and I always attribute it to Bill Campbell."

It was more than his honesty that made Campbell such a favorite with listeners.

"His voice," said Tony Graham, a longtime Phillies fan from Central Jersey, "seemed to translate what my heart was feeling."

When Campbell was fired, a lot of hearts were feeling sad. This, of course, was long before 24/7 sports-talk radio, long before Internet chat rooms turned controversial issues (see Terrell Owens vs. Donovan McNabb and the Eagles in 2005) into a media circus.

If Campbell's dismissal had happened in today's 24-hour news world, said a smiling Larry Shenk, who in 2006 began his 43rd season in the Phillies' publicity department, "it would be worse than T.O. There would be news helicopters flying over Bill's house."

Campbell was popular with the media. He was a man's man. His storytelling made him fun to be around. He had an impeccable memory and his tales were priceless. He was classy and dignified, but he could mix in jokes and amusing stories with the best of them. And he had a voice that wasn't only known for his broadcasts, but for the

Bill Campbell (left) and fellow Phillies broadcaster By Saam sit in the brand-new Astrodome, home of the Houston Astros, and get ready to tour what became Major League Baseball's first indoor stadium in 1965. Ironically, the man who conducted the tour was Houston's Bill Giles, who later became a Phills executive and fired Campbell.

way it belted out tunes like "Fly Me to The Moon." When the Phils were in Clearwater, Florida, during spring training, it wasn't unusual to see Bill and *The Bulletin's* Ray Kelly or Saidt go up to the piano bar and entertain the patrons at the Beachcomber.

Bill was one of the guys. A Philadelphian, through and through. A guy who had paid his dues and worked up the ranks. A guy whose on-air candidness and honesty made him such a refreshing presence. He always looked for the good in people but, at the same time, didn't sugarcoat things. He oozed of integrity. Before he took the Phillies job, Campbell had not been shy to criticize the team, whose sad-sack play had made it a frequent target.

"It's easier to hire you than to fight you," Carpenter half-kidded Campbell when he got the announcer's job before the 1963 season.

Now, eight seasons and nearly 1,300 games later, the club was not going to fight to keep him; they pushed him out the door and never gave an explanation. Carpenter said he accepted the responsibility for the firing.

Shenk now says it was Giles' decision. Which is what everyone assumed all along.

Wrote Conlin after the firing: "...Bill Giles convinced Carpenter that a voice with a 'younger image' was needed, his Houston friend, Harry Kalas. That left one play-by-play man vulnerable."

The Phillies weren't going to dismiss Saam, Conlin said, calling him a company man and writing that, "Byrum Saam never made enough waves to capsize a peanut shell. No man has ever lasted so many years broadcasting baseball games in one city for one sponsor. He is a monument to the public's taste and the people who run the nation's media....There is no way you fire an institution. And Saam is a Philadelphia institution on the level of smog, the Expressway, and JFK Stadium."

Conlin wrote that "public opinion polls after the fact serve no purpose. But the Phillies claim listener polls influenced their decision. The feeling here is that a majority of you out there in Radioland enjoyed Bill Campbell's work as a baseball announcer. Then again, maybe the majority prefers to keep rolling along with a man who peaked when the A's were the big team in town. Anyway, let us know your feelings. You're footing a $50 million tab to put a 1920 baseball operation into a 1970 stadium. The least you can do is let Bob Carpenter know how you feel."

The readers responded. Hundreds of letters arrived at the *Daily News*. One guy said he had 250 signatures on an office petition that was threatening to boycott Phillies games. Conlin reported that letters were sent on fancy letterheads and on yellow-lined paper. He received letters from doctors and medical students, lawyers and law students, from housewives, school kids, senior citizens, and "fans so old they remember when the Baker Bowl had a fresh coat of paint." He even got a postcard from a monastery in New York City.

Campbell downplays the long-ago firing, but the hurt is deep. There is more than a twinge of sadness when he recalls the developments of 1970.

His daughter said that, because of the firing, she saw her dad cry for the second time.

His wife, to this day, holds a grudge against the man she sarcastically calls "dear Bill Giles."

Giles said he had been "very friendly" to Campbell in the years since the firing; they used to run into each other in the Phillies' press lounge at Veterans Stadium. "But I could tell from his facial expressions and his body language that he didn't like me." Giles said. "He thought I was the guy who fired him, and I don't believe that he believes it was Schmidt's that was pushing it. I felt very bad that he was mad at me. And I told him, 'Bill, it wasn't me, it was Schmidt's.' "

Things turned out favorably for Campbell. The day after he was fired by the Phillies, he was hired to do morning sports shows on WCAU radio, which, ironically enough, is the station that carried Phillies games that year. The station trumpeted the news by placing a half-page ad in newspapers:

"*Bill Campbell's Back!!!*" said the ad's huge headline.

He worked for WCAU until he was hired to do play-by-play of 76ers basketball games nine months later. In between, he broadcast some of the Pittsburgh Pirates' away games.

His career was back on track.

Campbell accepted the firing with dignity, but the hurt never left. The dismissal came at a time when he was in the prime of his career and recognized as one of the game's best announcers, along with the likes of Vin Scully, Jack Buck and Curt Gowdy.

Getting rid of Bill Campbell was like releasing Willie Mays after a 40-homer, .330 season.

Little did anyone know that Kalas, the man who replaced Campbell, would turn into the Barry Bonds of baseball broadcasters.

——•——

It was Giles' idea to bring in Kalas — who was named to the broadcasters' section of the Baseball Hall of Fame in 2002, 12 years after Saam received a similar honor — as Campbell's replacement.

"I definitely wanted Harry, and so when the Schmidt's thing cropped its ugly head, I was quick to make a move to get Harry up here, though I should say that Al Michaels at the time was making $25,000 a year as a broadcaster for the Cincinnati Reds and I did talk to the Reds about him," Giles said. "I heard he was unhappy and was going to leave, so I inquired about Michaels but he wasn't interested or something…and at the same time, I was in the process of hiring Harry."

When Kalas was hired, he was placed in an uncomfortable situation.

"It was awkward because I came here with the understanding that I was going to be an *addition* to the broadcast crew — that Bill would remain, By Saam would remain and, Richie, of course, would remain," said Kalas, who in 2006 was preparing to start his 36th season with the Phillies. "Well, when I got here, all of a sudden, I was replacing a legend in Bill Campbell."

Kalas let out his oh-so-familiar baritone cackle.

"I'm not saying I wouldn't have taken the job, because I probably would have," he said, "but still it was very awkward because Bill was a legend here. He's right up there with By Saam and Gene Hart and Merrill Reese and some of the all-time great Philadelphia announcers."

Kalas, who said his confidence sagged because of the swirling controversy, and Campbell worked around the awkwardness. After being hired by WCAU, Campbell frequently did interviews with players at Veterans Stadium.

"He always treated me so well. He didn't hold a vendetta against me at all; he was always so nice to me over the years and I'll never forget that," Kalas said. "When he would come to the ballpark, he would say hi and chat with me and he never ever showed any animosity toward me for what had happened."

Jo Campbell said the firing brought out the best in her husband.

"I'm very proud of the way he took it," she said. "He didn't blame anybody and he didn't take it to the press and take a stand. He didn't give any indication to the newspapers that he was heartbroken. And he didn't call Bob Carpenter to bawl him out or look for revenge. He just picked up the pieces and moved on."

Bill Campbell was told by his friend, Carpenter, that he was being dismissed late in 1970. For the next 20 years, their paths never crossed.

"The next time I talked to Bob was on his death bed," Campbell said.

That was in 1990, when Carpenter was battling lung cancer. Campbell had bumped into Carpenter's son, Ruly, who was the Phillies' president from 1972 to 1981, at a function and asked how his parents were doing. "He said my mother's fine, but my dad's not well at all and doesn't have long to go," Campbell said.

Campbell asked Ruly if he could phone his father.

"He'd love to hear from you, Bill. Give him a call and I would appreciate it and I know he would."

Bob Carpenter was in bed and incapacitated when Campbell called. "I talked to his wife, Mary, and then Bob got on the phone and he could hardly talk," Campbell said. "He knew who I was and all that; he thanked me for calling and he was gasping for breath; it was a brief conversation but we did talk."

Campbell said he always considered Bob Carpenter his friend. Carpenter was just caught in the middle of things during the tumultuous end of Campbell's association with the Phillies in 1970. The association resumed briefly in 1978, when Bill was the play-by-play man for PRISM — the cable TV operation that did 30 Phils home games that season — and had Jim Barniak as his sidekick. Campbell later returned to do Phillies pre- and post-game radio shows for WCAU radio in 1981.

It was nice to be back, but it was never the same.

CHAPTER TEN

Bouncing back with gusto

The season after he was fired by the Phillies, Bill Campbell was hired to announce some of the Pittsburgh Pirates' away games. Going from the sad-sack Phillies to a gifted Pirates team that included future Hall of Famers Roberto Clemente and Willie Stargell seemed like a pretty good gig. The Pirates would win the World Series that year, but Campbell never felt as if he belonged. His broadcast partners made him feel at home, but Bill longed to be in Philadelphia.

In the booth, Campbell worked alongside the legendary Bob Prince, who had been doing Pirates' games since 1948.

"He was the son of a military man and you'd expect him to be a by-the-book guy," Campbell said. "But he was wild man."

Campbell once went golfing with Prince and By Saam at the Bala Golf Club. Prince, on a par three, hit his tee shot into the lake, prompting him to heave his club into the same spot. "His caddy told him not to worry because he would dig out the club, and Bob said, 'Don't you dare,' " Campbell said. "And he went over and took his clubs out of the bag and, one by one, threw each of them into the lake."

Prince was more sedate when Campbell worked with him in 1971. Campbell did Pirates' broadcasts from New York, Montreal, and Philadelphia — yes, he got to work at Veterans Stadium, after all. He also remained at Philadelphia's WCAU, doing radio sportscasts from 6 a.m. to 9 a.m.

Ironically, the first game he ever did for the Pirates was at Veterans Stadium. Pittsburgh trounced the Phillies.

"For the first time I can ever remember, I'm nervous," Campbell told *The Evening Bulletin* before the game. "It's hard to believe. I guess I'm doubly on edge because of the conditions. I'm with another team and I wanted to work here."

Staying connected to baseball made Campbell happy, but it wasn't the same as working with Ashburn and Saam. "I didn't have the same feel for the team," he said in 2006. "It wasn't the same because it wasn't the Phillies. I determined after that season that I'm a Philadelphian."

Campbell grew up with the Phillies, knew their history, and felt comfortable doing their games. Ad-libbing came easy because he knew the subject and its audience. He was a Philly guy, simple as that. After one summer with the Pirates, he left the job because of a chance to return home and broadcast the 76ers' basketball games.

So what if it wasn't baseball. Bill Campbell was going back to Philadelphia, back to where he belonged.

Ironically, it was his replacement in the Phillies' broadcast booth, Kalas, who steered Campbell back on track. Campbell's confidence had been shattered by the firing, but Kalas gave him a pep talk one day at the Vet, told him how he was one of the best in the profession. It made Campbell feel rejuvenated and he soon landed the job as the 76ers' play-by-play man.

After he was hired by the 76ers, instigating Philadelphia reporters still kept asking Campbell if he felt any resentment toward the Phillies. Bill wouldn't take the bait.

"Nobody's ever really told me why I was replaced," Campbell told *The Evening Bulletin*. "But I've gotten over it. That's past history."

Even a man as religious as Bill Campbell — a daily churchgoer who serves as a lector at Mass — tells a little white lie every now and then.

The 76ers had a few superb teams during Campbell's nine years as the team's play-by-play announcer.

But Campbell doesn't get many questions about those winning seasons.

Instead, folks invariably ask him how he survived the infamous 1972-73 season, Bill's second year with the club.

In what was arguably the worst season of any professional team in history, the 76ers finished 9-73, a winning percentage of .110. Fred Carter, who averaged 20 points per game, was named the team's MVP.

Carter had mixed emotions about the award.

"Was it for leading the team to nine wins or for leading it to 73 losses?" he wondered.

Funny line. Funny team. Not ha-ha funny. But funny in the sense that they were so inept — and their coach, Roy Rubin, was so overmatched — that you had to laugh to keep from crying.

Years later, in 2004 to be precise, ESPN.com ranked the 10 worst teams of all time; it considered teams from the four major sports — baseball, football, basketball and hockey.

The 9-73 76ers were rated as the second-worst team in sports history. Only the 1976 Tampa Bay Buccaneers, an NFL expansion team, were considered worse. You could make a case, however, for ranking the 76ers as No. 1. The Bucs finished 0-14, but the 76ers managed to start their season with a worse record — they lost their first 15 games. (Three of the worst teams in sports history were from Philadelphia — the 1972-73 76ers; the 1916 Philadelphia Athletics, who finished 36-117, were ranked fifth; and the 1936 Eagles, who lost their last 11 games and finished 1-11, were ranked 10th. Campbell remembers cheering for the '36 Eagles as an optimistic 13-year-old.)

The 76ers ran off four double-digit losing streaks in 1972-73: 15, 20, 14, and a season-ending 13-gamer. They finished the season 59 games behind the Boston Celtics.

Repeat: 59 games behind.

Campbell called it "the longest year of my life."

"The team is standing still," Campbell would moan into his microphone. *"Nobody is moving to get open!"*

Throughout his career, Campbell's broadcasts were always per-colating with enthusiasm. The excitement came naturally. Campbell was someone who loved sports and didn't consider his work a job. All these years, he felt like a fan getting paid to describe the action, whether it was basketball, baseball or football.

The 1972-73 season was different.

"That was the only year in my career where I didn't want to go to the arena," he said. "It was a job. And when it becomes a job, you don't do it well. We had no talent. There was no way we could com-pete. And you knew that you had no chance. We even lost a game in which the other team was trying to throw the game."

Throw the game?

"We were told later that the Seattle SuperSonics were trying to get their coach fired," he said. "They hated their coach, Tom Nissalke. They threw the ball all over the place and we still lost. It was awful, just awful."

Nissalke was fired 35 games into that season. Campbell and his broadcast partner, Tom Lamaine, weren't as lucky. They were with the 76ers until the bitter end.

If Campbell had a difficult time going to the arena that season, he hid it from his listeners. And from Lamaine.

Lamaine recalled a close late-season game at lowly Cleveland and being uplifted by Campbell's professionalism.

"I remember looking over at Bill when we were playing the Cleveland Cavaliers — who that year, weren't a whole lot better than the 76ers — and he was broadcasting with the same fervor and pitch as if it was the seventh game of a playoff," Lamaine said. "And I'm looking over at him in amazement. When we went to a commercial, I said to him, 'I can't believe the energy and passion you have for this meaningless game.' I mean, he was really into it. And he looked at me quizzically, like, 'What do you mean?' He said, 'They all mean some-thing. If you lose the passion, you might as well not do the games.' And I tried to take that into everything I did.

"Bill was a taskmaster. He made sure you did things right. I remember Richie Ashburn stopped me after the basketball season and said, 'How you getting along with Soupy? Are you learning what he wants and feeding off him?' "

For Lamaine, working alongside Campbell was like going to class with a professor who had written the textbook.

"He's the guy I used to listen to with my transistor radio under my pillow when the West Coast baseball games were on late at night," he said. "I was the student and he was the teacher. He was a perfec-tionist and he would not let anything slip by that he thought should-n't be on the air."

You had to be prepared, like him. You had to add something to the broadcast that the listeners couldn't get from anywhere else. Bill Campbell drove Lamaine to do his homework, drove him to be a bet-ter color commentator.

"I had to do it right," he said. "And, looking back, I appreciate how he approached it. I'd give a stat and, during a break, Bill might say, 'Are you sure that stat is right? It just doesn't sound right.' And I showed him where it came from and he'd say, 'Oh, all right. I wouldn't have believed it if I didn't see it.' He was absolutely a perfectionist."

It wasn't easy trying to make the games sound exciting, though the Sixers, amazingly enough, had 10 players who averaged in double figures that season. But their defense was only a rumor.

"We'd go into a city and the people would feel sorry for us," Lamaine said.

Even the owner, Irv Kosloff, felt sorry for the 76ers — or at least for their No. 1 broadcaster.

"This is a highly competitive, dog-eat-dog business," Campbell said, "and I've always felt that maybe the nicest thing that's ever happened to me since I was broadcasting the various teams was something done by Irv Kosloff that year. We opened the season by losing our first 15 games. It was the worst year of my life; the team was really bad. We didn't have any talent, and it was the only year in my whole career where I really had to jack up some enthusiasm. I've always been enthusiastic about any game by nature. I think I'm a pretty enthusiastic guy and I think that's helped me more than any other quality I have. But that year, I really had to jack myself up every night and the enthusiasm sometime may have even been false."

Not only were the 76ers getting beat, but they weren't even competitive. "We were never in games; it was horrible," Campbell said.

By New Year's, the Sixers were 3-35. By mid-February, they were a mind-boggling 4-58, a winning percentage of .065. They used a "hot" spell — winning five of their final 20 games — to get over the .100 mark.

The losing, Campbell said, had to be taking its toll on Kosloff. He had been ultra-successful as a paper manufacturer. "And he must have been taking a beating from his associates and competitors about this terrible team that he had."

In the middle of another long losing streak, Campbell was with the 76ers in Los Angeles. "We got our brains beat out, as usual," he said.

Campbell and some of the traveling party had a few drinks after the game, and Bill headed to his hotel room. That's when the night, from Campbell's perspective, became memorable.

After a few hours sleep, the phone rang in Campbell's hotel room. It was 4 a.m., Pacific Coast Time, and the caller was Kosloff, the 76ers' owner. Kosloff had momentarily forgot about the time change when he made the call.

"Hello, Bill. Oh, geeze, were you asleep? Sorry to get you so early, but I had to talk to you."

"OK."

"Are you all right?" Kosloff asked.

"What do you mean," answered Campbell.

"You sound like you're going to die on the air," said Kosloff, who wasn't fooled by Campbell's artificial enthusiasm. "I'm really concerned about you from a health standpoint. I know it's tough broadcasting these games and we're getting killed, and I feel somewhat responsible."

Campbell said he will never forget the kindness displayed by Kosloff.

"That's the first and only time in my whole career that anybody ever said to me that they were really concerned about my heath," Campbell said. " I just thought it was a gracious, gracious thing to do. That was the nicest thing that any owner ever did for me. He said to me, 'If you'd like, come home and take a week off, or we'll fly Jo out to be with you for a week. Whatever you want to do. We'll have someone do some games for you and you just take some time off.' "

Campbell appreciated the gesture but respectfully declined.

"Kos," he told the owner, chuckling between words, "I may sound like I'm dying but I'm really not. I'm staying.' "

He would not abandon the ship, even if it was headed on a journey to nowhere.

———

Lamaine, now a longtime Channel 3 weatherman, said the season seemed as if it would never end.

"Most of the games were blowouts. I remember doing a game at Madison Square Garden — this was when the Knicks were in their heyday — and when the Sixers scored, a big cheer went up," he said. "It wasn't a sarcastic, derisive cheer. And then I figured out what was going on. The gamblers could get the Sixers and 25 points and a lot of them would take those odds. I had to explain on the air why there was some cheering. I didn't want to say *point spread* on the air so I just tried to dance around it."

That forgettable season also included the 76ers' first visit to the brand-new Omni, home of an Atlanta Hawks team that featured Pete Maravich and Lou Hudson.

Before the game, Lamaine approached the Atlanta public relations director and asked if he could line up a guest for his halftime show. Late in the half, Lamaine received some bad news. "The PR guy comes up to me and says, 'I don't have anybody for your halftime interview. The Braves are in spring training and the Falcons are all out of town,' " Lamaine said. "I told him it didn't have to be a sports celebrity. It could be anybody. He came back a minute later and said, 'OK, I have a guest for you. It's Jimmy Carter.' "

"Who," Lamaine replied, "is Jimmy Carter?"

Lamaine was told that Carter was the governor of Georgia.

"Nah, I remember reading history books and Lester Maddox has *always* been the governor of Georgia," Lamaine answered.

Lamaine was told that Carter won the election in 1972 and that Maddox was the state's lieutenant governor.

He wasn't one of Atlanta's famous athletes, but Carter would have to do.

"Well, if he's the governor of Georgia, he can't be too bad of an interview," Lamaine told the Hawks' PR director. "Tell him I'll meet him under the basket at halftime."

And sure enough, a small, smiling man came shuffling over at the intermission.

"He had red hair at he time — or at least light brown — and he said, 'Mr. Lamaine, I'm Jimmy Cah-ta.' I did the interview — unfortunately, Channel 29, which was doing the games at the time, did not tape the halftime, so I don't have a record of it — and then went back to our broadcast location at courtside," Lamaine said.

When he got there, Campbell had a puzzled expression.

"Who the hell was *that* you were interviewing?" Campbell asked.

"You're not going to believe it," Lamaine said. "but he's the governor of Georgia, Jimmy Carter."

"Jimmy who?" Campbell said.

"Jimmy Carter," Lamaine repeated, "the governor of Georgia."

And three years later, he was elected President of the United States.

"That," Lamaine said, "became the original 'Jimmy Who?' joke."

Lamaine worked for five years as Campbell's sidekick before expanding duties at WIP radio and at Channel 3 forced him to step down. Campbell "was not a very healthy man" during that time, Lamaine said. Campbell's Crohn's disease made him suffer. "There would be games where I knew he was in pain," Lamaine said. "After the game, we would go out but he wouldn't join us because he went back to his hotel room. But through it all, there were only one or two games that he missed — and one of them was for his daughter's wedding."

———

Campbell's broadcasting career also included a bizarre game in which viewers got to stare at the center-court circle. Players from the 76ers and Boston Celtics would whiz past center court, but the camera wouldn't follow them.

About 15 minutes into the Channel 48 broadcast at the Boston Garden on March 22, 1972, the Boston camera crew, director, and assistant director walked out of the booth and announced they were going on strike because of a dispute with Channel 27 in Worcester, Massachusetts. Channel 48 was using Channel 27's equipment and facilities to send the game back to Philadelphia.

One camera was locked into a position in which it could only film the center circle. One of the Celtics' statisticians tried to unlock the camera. "But after a couple of minutes, the technicians sent up this burly guy who told him to get off the camera," Lamaine said. "So the camera was frozen again and Philly called and told us, 'You might as well sign off.' "

After the game, "Bill got a little feisty and confronted one of the technicians. He said to him, 'Why didn't you tell us this was going on? You don't have a gripe against the Philly stations, and all you did was tick off the Philly people.' "

Especially the normally easygoing Campbell.

"They just told him it was something they had to do. I told Bill to leave him alone because we weren't getting anywhere," Lamaine said.

At least TV viewers were spared from watching another 76ers' loss. Boston prevailed, 113-106, in the 76ers' final "telecast" of the season.

"I've broadcast a lot of crazy things, but nothing like that ever happened," Campbell said of the walkout. "I've worked football games where the lights went out, and I once got hit in the mouth with a foul ball [courtesy of Clay Dalrymple] while announcing a baseball game. But never anything like that. They just pulled the plug on us and said they were going on strike."

———

In addition to Lamaine, Campbell broke in several other 76ers' announcers, including Doug Collins, Matt Goukas, Steve Mix, and Billy Cunningham, all of whom played for Philadelphia. Collins, Guokas, and Cunningham went on to become national broadcasters, while Mix has become a 76ers' broadcasting fixture. Mix officially began doing games in 1987, but he received his first taste of announcing when he was injured and unable to play for the 76ers in 1975.

Breaking in ballplayers-turned-broadcasters (including Tom Brookshier and Richie Ashburn) is one of his proudest accomplishments, Campbell said.

Collins actually got his broadcasting baptism during his rookie season with the 76ers. An injury sidelined Collins, whom the 76ers had selected with the draft's No. 1 overall pick in 1973. "Irv Kosloff was the owner and he came up to me one day and said, 'We've got to get something out of our No. 1 draft choice.' He said, 'Why don't you use Doug Collins as your color man?' I told him it was all right with me. Doug was very articulate. So I asked him and he said sure, he'd love to do it. And he did a pretty good job for a rookie in the league. He knew the game, knew a lot about it; he did pretty well," Campbell said. "About the fourth or fifth game, Gene Shue [the 76ers' coach] called a timeout and as he was getting the players around him, I saw him look over and take a look at me and then a look at Doug Collins. When the game was over, I went to the locker room and Gene said to me, 'What was Doug Collins doing with you?' I said he's been doing the color."

Shue was incensed.

"Doing the color?! I don't want a damn rookie doing color on any game that I'm coaching," Shue shouted.

"Oh, really."

"That's right."

"I'll tell you what, Gene," Campbell said. "Go to the owner and tell the owner that, because he's here at the request of the owner. And until the owner tells me to remove him, he's staying here."

"You have to remove him," Shue insisted.

"No I don't. The owner wants him on. He's paying him. Tell the owner."

Shue did. Two days later, Kosloff phoned Campbell.

"You better take him off," Kosloff said, apologetically. "The coach is really upset."

Campbell surmised that Shue was afraid that Collins would give away some of his coaching secrets. Campbell listened to orders. He told Collins he was off the air, that his broadcasting career was temporarily over.

A few years later, Shue had become more understanding; he permitted another one of his players, Mix, who was sidelined with a broken ankle, to join Campbell's broadcasts.

Bill Campbell (right) breaks in Steve Mix (center), a 76ers player who temporarily joined the club's broadcast team in 1975 while he was recovering from a broken ankle. At left is statistician Barry Abrams.

As a player, Mix was deadly on long-range jumpers. Campbell used to call that area "Mixville". The nickname spread and, eventually, Mix became known as the Mayor of Mixville.

The Mayor was thankful for the chance to work alongside Campbell for a few months in 1975.

"I floundered around for a while, but Soupy made it a lot fun; he was professional and I learned things about broadcasting from him," Mix said. "I saw all the preparation he did and I knew you couldn't just put the headset on. As a player, I didn't do a whole lot of prep work, but as a broadcaster…."

The preparation was necessary to live up to Campbell's standards.

Mix said Campbell was a perfectionist. "You can still hear it today in his [KYW commentaries], how prepared he is."

Mix said the 76ers' broadcast team pays Campbell the ultimate compliment every now and then while they're sitting in a hotel restaurant or a press dining room. Invariably, he said, "someone in our little group — whether it's [announcer] Marc Zumoff or Shawn Oleksiak, our producer — will break into Soupy imitations. It's tremendous. Bill was their guy growing up. If you wanted to go into broadcasting, he's one of the guys you wanted to emulate and sound like."

To borrow a Campbell-ism: That's unreal.

———

After hitting rock bottom and finishing 9-73 in 1972-73, the 76ers made dramatic strides. They hired Shue as their coach and drafted Collins out of Illinois State, starting their revival. In the next five seasons, their record improved each year — from 25-57, to 34-48, to 46-36, to 50-32, to 55-27.

George McGinnis joined the club in '75 and played an important part in the 76ers' rise. But no one played a bigger role than Julius Erving, who had electrified ABA crowds for five years before taking his above-the-rim act to Philadelphia. The 50-win season coincided with "The Doctor's" arrival.

Early in the 1976-77 season, Erving's first year with the 76ers, Campbell received a 10 a.m. phone call while in a Seattle hotel. The 76ers were playing the Seattle SuperSonics later that night.

Caller: "Bill, I'm from Philadelphia and I'm a season-ticket holder and I'm at every game, and my daughter is here in a Seattle hospital."

His eight-year-old daughter had cancer.

"My daughter *loves* Dr. J. She was a Dr. J fan when he was playing in the other league, and she's all excited that he's now with the Sixers. And I was wondering if you could do me a favor?"

"What is it?" Campbell asked.

"You're going to be here for a few days and do you think it would be possible for Julius Erving to speak to my daughter on the phone? I'm not asking for him to come visit her in the hospital but could you arrange for him to call her?"

Campbell told the caller that Erving had recently joined that team and that he didn't know him that well. "I've been introduced to him, but I doubt if I've had any long conversations with him yet. I'll ask him, but it's his choice."

The man thanked Campbell repeatedly and gave the announcer his daughter's information.

Campbell went down to the lobby, had breakfast, and then got on the team bus that was taking the 76ers to the arena for their shoot-around. Campbell sat next to Erving and told him the story.

"Here's the note and the girl's name and telephone number. If you want to do it, it's up to you."

"Do you think it's legitimate or do you think it's some nut?" Erving asked.

"I don't believe a guy would tell me about his daughter dying. My guess is that it's legitimate," Campbell said, "but, hey, it's a crazy world, Doc."

Erving took the note and stuck it in his sneaker.

"I thought that was the end of it. I didn't know what kind of guy he was," Campbell said.

At 5 o'clock that evening, as he prepared to leave for the arena to broadcast the game, Campbell answered the phone in his hotel room.

"Bill, what can I do for you? I don't care what it is. Would you like me to buy you a car? Anything you want, I'll do."

"Who is this?" Bill asked.

It was the sick girl's father.

"He told me, 'Do you know what Julius Erving did? He called my daughter and talked to her for a half hour. I couldn't believe it. At first, I thought it was somebody pretending to be to be him.' "

After the game that night, Campbell told Erving that the father had called to express his gratitude. "I told Doc that it was a really nice thing he did, and he said she was a really nice kid and he didn't mind at all. He said it was no problem. He passed it off like it was nothing."

When the 76ers returned to Philadelphia from their road trip, Campbell made it a point to visit with Fitz Dixon — who six months earlier has purchased the 76ers from Kosloff — to talk about Erving's kindness.

"I want to tell you a little story," Campbell said. "I think you'll enjoy hearing it because you just got this player who you're paying a lot of money, and this is the type of guy whom you've hired."

Dixon was thrilled.

"Fitz was a nice man, filled with philanthropic stuff himself," Campbell said. "He thought what Doc did was terrific."

Erving bristled when he learned that his good deed was making the rounds. He called Campbell over to his locker after the team's next game.

"I don't mind doing those things, Bill, but I do object to you telling the owner about them," Erving said. "I did that because you asked me to do it, and I don't need any credit for it."

"Doc, I'm sorry you feel that way, but I wanted him to know the nice thing you did and that was the only reason I told him," Campbell said.

"Well, anytime you want me to do anything in the future, I will do it," said Erving, who, along with Moses Malone, led the 76ers to the NBA title in 1983, "but let's just keep it between you and me."

"Agreed," Campbell said.

When the 76ers opened their 2005-06 season, Eving and some other former club luminaries — including Campbell — returned for a ceremony.

"I hadn't seen Doc in a long time," Campbell said. "My wife and his wife, Turquoise, became quite friendly. They called her Turk. Nice gal. We used to go to the games all the time and they had a special room in the Spectrum for the Sixers and the players and the press. And Jo used to go to every game. Jo and Turk would mingle in the press room and they looked forward to having dinner together all the time.

"I hadn't heard from Julius in a long time. We used to hear from them all the time at Christmas. And now he and Turk have separated and they've had a lot of domestic problems. I don't know what happened. But on opening night of this [2005-06] season, I had a five-minute conversation with Doc in the hallway, just the two of us. And as we were leaving, he said, 'Give my love to Jo.' Now how the hell he even remembered her name impressed me. I always liked him. A good guy. A really good guy. For a guy who was a star, one of the best players in the game, he was really a good fellow."

A very good Doc.

———

Campbell announced 76ers games for nine years before stepping down in 1980.

"I've seen enough airplanes and hotels," he said at the time.

He moved into the 76ers' front office, becoming the club's director of broadcasting, a position in which he coordinated radio, TV, and cable TV.

"This is basically at my request, because I had to get off the road," he told the *Daily News*. "I've been hospitalized four or five times the last couple of years, and in terms of my health, my family, and watching my grandchildren grow up, this is the right move to make."

One year later, after the team was sold by Dixon to Harold Katz in the summer of '81, Campbell was let go. It wasn't nearly as traumatic as when he was canned by the Phillies. In fact, it wasn't traumatic at all.

This time, Campbell *expected* to get the pink slip. A new owner was aboard and was putting together his own team of executives. Campbell understood the situation.

"You're going to have setbacks in this business," Campbell said. "If you become bitter, it can ruin your career. You stew in juice for a couple weeks and then you say, 'OK, let's go. Let's move on.' "

The 76ers' Dixon and Kosloff were caring owners, Campbell said. So was another Philadelphia sports owner, Leonard Tose. "Leonard," Campbell said, "was one of the most generous men around. He never saw a check that he didn't pick up. He was generous almost to a fault."

Tose was also eccentric. A chain-smoking, compulsive gambler, Tose liked to live life to the fullest. He was the Eagles owner when Campbell did a 1970's show on Channel 29 called "The Eagles Nest." The show was filmed from the station's studio, located in Jenkintown, a Philadelphia suburb.

One year, Campbell phoned Tose to see if he would be a guest before a season opener,

"Sure, Bill," Tose said, "But you know that I don't travel any-where if I can't get there by chopper."

"What do you mean?" Campbell asked.

"I don't go by car or limo, so if I can't get there by chopper, I don't go," Tose explained in a matter-of-fact tone.

Campbell started cracking up.

"Leonard, the studio is in Jenkintown. Where in the hell am I going to find a place for you to land a helicopter in Jenkintown?"

"Well, that's your problem. You figure it out."

"I'll get back to you, Leonard."

Campbell called the executives at Channel 29 and explained the situation.

"And through some politicians or somebody, the general manager of Channel 29 finds a place for Leonard to put the chopper down — a big plot of ground that's about two miles from the station," Campbell said. "So now it means somebody has to get a car and drive to this landing spot, pick up Leonard, and take him to the studio and then bring him back to the landing strip."

Campbell and Tose did the first part of their interview and then took a break for a commercial. During the pause, Campbell told Tose that he was heading to Philadelphia after the show because he was broadcasting the 76ers' game that night from the Spectrum.

"How are you getting there?" Tose asked.

"The same way I got here — driving my car," Campbell said.

Tose, a man who made millions in the trucking business, couldn't understand why anybody would drive in traffic when they could fly over it.

"He clicks his fingers and says to me, 'Give so-and-so your keys.' " Campbell recalled. "One of his little henchmen was there and he wanted him to take my car and drive it back for me. I said, 'No, that's OK, Leonard, I can drive.' And he says, 'No, no, no. You're going back in the chopper with me. Give him your keys.' You couldn't argue with Leonard. He was persistent. You couldn't say no. So I finally I gave the keys to one of Leonard's men."

They finished filming the Eagles show and then boarded the helicopter. Tose insisted that Campbell sit next to the pilot.

"It's 6 o'clock at night and we're flying over Center City and the people look like ants," Campbell said. "We're right over Walnut Street and Leonard says, 'See that big plot of ground over there across the street from Bookbinder's. Every night on my way home from Veterans Stadium I jump in the chopper, we put it down in front of Bookbinder's and I go in and have two martinis and get back in the chopper and go home.' "

Campbell was amused, but there was no way he wanted Tose's pilot to make a pit stop for a few drinks at Bookbinder's. He had a ballgame to broadcast. When the helicopter landed at Veterans Stadium, Campbell thanked Tose for the ride and started across the street to the Spectrum.

"No, no, no. My limo driver will take you, Bill," Tose said.

"Leonard, I can walk. It's only a block."

Tose wouldn't listen. He clicked a few buttons and up pulled his limo.

"So he says to his limo driver, 'Take Mr. Campbell to the Spectrum; he's got a game tonight.' And I'm feeling like a damn ass, but I get in the limo," Campbell said. "And the limo driver, a nice guy named John, drives out of Veterans Stadium, stops for a traffic light, makes a left-hand turn and goes one block and stops for another red light, and makes a right-hand turn. It took us like 10 minutes and I could have walked there in two!"

Ah, that Leonard Tose.

"A real piece of work," Campbell said.

After leaving the 76ers, Campbell hosted a sports talk show on WCAU radio and also broadcast Temple football and basketball games. He would get his baseball "fix" by filing reports on the Phillies.

Campbell had a grand time in 1983, covering an enigmatic Phillies team that featured Mike Schmidt, Steve Carlton, John Denny, and Al Holland. It was an aging team that made headlines because it included former players from Cincinnati's famed Big Red Machine: Pete Rose, Joe Morgan, and Tony Perez.

In 1950, Campbell covered the Whiz Kids.

In 1964, he announced games for the Was Kids.

In 1983, he reported on the Wheeze Kids.

When the Phillies surprisingly reached the World Series against the Baltimore Orioles in 1983, fortune was smiling on Bill because it enabled him to spend time with his sister, Polly, who was a religious superior at St. Joseph's Hospital outside of Baltimore.

Bill doesn't remember what surprised him more: the Phillies reaching the '83 World Series or the news that his sister — who would be known as Sister Immaculata — had decided to become a nun during the 1940s.

Campbell was serving in World War II when he received a letter from his dad, explaining that Polly was going into the convent. Campbell was incredulous. He wouldn't have been surprised if his other sister, Julie, was going to become a nun. In Bill's eyes, Julie was saintly: never raised her voice, never got into trouble.

But Polly? Polly was a rabble-rouser.

When Campbell came home on military leave, he went to visit Polly at the convent.

"What the hell are you doing?" he asked her.

Bill flashed back to that conversation with Polly when he talked with her before traveling to Baltimore to cover the '83 World Series. Campbell phoned her and said he would like to take her out to dinner. Polly insisted she eat with the nuns in the convent's dining room.

"I went down there and had dinner with 15 nuns," he said. "They were great. And during the dinner, I told her I was staying at the Lord Baltimore Hotel, and she said to me — and believe me, you did not say no to my sister — 'Leave your car here and take your suitcases and I'll have one of my nuns drive you to the hotel. And when you're ready to go home in a couple of days, we'll pick you up and take you back here to get your car.' "

Campbell, then 60, didn't argue with his persuasive sister, so Polly and three other nuns drove him to his hotel.

"Thank you very much, sisters," Bill said when they arrived at the hotel. "Have a good night and I'll see you later."

The nuns, feeling protective of Sister Immaculata's big brother, insisted that they walk Bill to his room.

"They said they wanted to come in with me and make sure I got in OK," Bill said. "So I troop into the lobby with four nuns. I get to the front desk and check in and we head to the elevator to take it up to my room. The worst thing was that, while standing at the registration desk, a big bus pulls in and it's the Phillies' bus; they're arriving a day before the game. I'm thinking, 'I gotta get to my room before these guys see me with a battery of nuns.' So I go to the elevator with the nuns and I know these guys see me. I see Pete Rose and the other guys. I go up the elevator with the nuns; they're walking me right up to my room to make sure I get to my room safely. They come into the room and look around and check out the beds and the furniture and the accommodations and finally they leave. They weren't out of the room 30 seconds when the phone rings."

The person on the other end used a syrupy female voice, "Did you get all your homework done, Sweety?"

Damn, that Pete Rose could bust your chops.

CHAPTER ELEVEN

A WIP pioneer

When WIP radio executives decided to heavily emphasize sports in 1987, Mike Craven, the station's general manager, had to have Bill Campbell.

Nearly a half century after he had worked as a WIP relief announcer in 1940, The Dean was coming home. He returned to the station and did a sports talk show.

"If you're thinking of doing sports in a sports town like Philadelphia — and if you believe localization is the key to a successful format — you couldn't get a guy with more credibility than Bill Campbell," Craven said.

Now part of an investment group that owns the *Village Voice* and other weekly newspapers, Craven said signing Campbell was key to WIP's transformation. "We thought the sports format would give us something unique to the market," he said. "We were carrying the Eagles at the time and we were vying for other teams, and getting Bill seemed like the sensible move to make. Bill was The Dean of sports — and still is. I grew up listening to Bill Campbell."

Which begs the question: Didn't everybody?

Campbell said he jumped from WCAU radio to WIP because he thought the station was committed to doing a more extensive job in sports. At the time, WIP wasn't yet an all-sports station — Bill "Wee Willie" Webber and Ken Garland still had morning music shows — but it was getting there. Piece by piece.

Campbell was the biggest piece.

After being hired by the station, Campbell told *The Inquirer* that listening was an integral part of a talk show host's success formula.

"I have certain strong opinions," he said, "but I'm not dogmatic. I don't lecture people. I'll disagree with people, but it's their 25 cents, and they deserve to be heard," he said. "I think talk show hosts can learn as much from listeners as they can learn from us."

By late in the summer of '88, after the arrival of former Eagle Tom Brookshier and Art Camiolo as two of the station's owners, WIP had gone all-sports. The new ownership group, headed by Spectacor and its main man, Ed Snider, came aboard about seven months after Campbell had been hired. "We had to decide who to keep and who to let go," Camiolo said. "With Bill, it was a no-brainer. He was the most respected guy in Philadelphia sports. If anything, he was the guy we used for an awful lot of believability."

By 1988, WIP was firmly targeting middle-age, sports-minded males, and Campbell was right in the middle of its lineup. There was "The Morning Sports Page," an hour-long talk-show featuring a parade of *Inquirer* sportswriters at 9 a.m. At 10 a.m., Joe Pellegrino, former TV sportscaster, hosted a show until 1 p.m. Campbell followed with a three-hour show. After that, fitness guru Pat Croce and Howard Eskin were on the air, followed by a 90-minute *Daily News* show. At night, there was some kind of play-by-play, whether it was a Flyers' game, a Big 5 basketball game, or some other pro or college game plucked off the satellite dish.

"Bill was a perfect fit for the station," Brookshier said. "I thought he was one of *the* Philadelphia people. Bill had been in town for so long and had been the premier sportscaster for so long, and if you didn't have him on the air, you were nuts."

Campbell was happy to be back on the same team with Brookshier. The feeling was mutual. Brookshier broke into radio business while doing a call-in sports show — a rarity in those days — with Campbell in the late 1950s. Brookshier was still playing defensive back for the Eagles at the time, and they did the shows from a city restaurant/bar every Monday night.

"When we did the shows back then," Brookshier recalled, "it was usually after a loss. It wasn't unusual for us to be in last place, and we'd be doing a show and someone at the bar would yell, 'You guys are bums!' But, surprisingly, the callers didn't rip the old Birds. Dutch [Van Brocklin] had just come over and the people really didn't get on us. It's not like today. Today, the team makes the playoffs and people still criticize them."

Julius Erving (left) and Bill Campbell do a show on WIP radio.
Campbell calls Erving one of the classiest athletes he has ever known.

After he retired from the Eagles, Brookshier worked alongside Campbell as an Eagles' broadcaster from 1962 to 1964. Brookshier would later become a fixture on CBS TV, working there for nearly 27 years and teaming with Pat Summerall to form the network's top NFL broadcast team. "And I probably wouldn't have done any of it if it wasn't for Bill," Brookshier said. "I didn't go to college and learn communications."

Campbell was his teacher. He helped him get acclimated to the business at WCAU radio and TV, and in the Eagles' broadcast booth. Now, it was Campbell who was working for Brookshier.

At WIP, which would become known for its wacky, off-the-wall personalities like Angelo Cataldi and Eskin, Campbell was a stabilizing force.

This was a time when it started to become popular for some radio hosts to shout their opinions. Their belief: The more shocking, the higher the ratings. Campbell would have none of it. He remained dignified, remained respectful of his listeners and made them feel like their point was as valid as his. To Campbell's thinking, it wasn't his show; it was the listeners'.

Cataldi called Campbell the best broadcaster in Philadelphia sports history and credited him with WIP's rise in popularity.

"I cannot tell you how much Bill has impacted my own career, and that of many others in Philadelphia," Catladi wrote in *The Great Philadelphia Sports Debate*, which he coauthored with Glen Macnow. "Bill was there when I started at WIP in 1990, and he had every right to show disdain at my sudden appearance within his domain. I had been a writer all my life, and I was presented with a full-time radio job in a plum time slot with almost no experience. On top of that, I was definitely not doing radio in Bill's style. I was shrill, caustic, often downright outrageous. Bill has never been any of those things.

"Instead of shunning me, however, Bill helped me. He answered every question with patience and class. He did for you, too, Glen. And for all of us at WIP. He could have tried to intimidate us with his incredible resume, but instead he took on the role of mentor and teacher. His very presence at WIP in those early days gave all of us more credibility than we deserved."

"Soupy," Brookshier said, "always spoke the truth. If something controversial happened, he never avoided it. If he was talking about the Eagles, he didn't come across as an Eagles fan; he was always straight down the pike and I admired him for that."

Cataldi, a former *Inquirer* reporter, said he was amazed at Campbell's work ethic.

"It was like no one's I had ever seen," he said. "Here was one of the greatest play-by-play guys in three sports....and he could have just coasted. But he was just the opposite. He would come in early, do a monologue every day and he was totally prepared — and it came through on the air. When I went from the newspaper to radio, I thought I could almost semi-retire. But after watching Bill and Tom Brookshier and the way they worked, I thought, 'Damn, I'm gonna have to work even *harder* over here.' "

The best thing about Campbell, Cataldi said, was "the way he could integrate things that happened 10, 20, 30, 40 years ago and bring them into current topics. He had a great perspective of past years and yet he would still be totally current with what was going on today. In my lifetime, he's the single most impressive broadcaster I have ever heard. He did three different sports so well, he was a talk show host, and the guy is a phenomenal writer and a total gentleman. And he has no ego. You just don't find that package anywhere."

Cataldi, who says "I'm still in awe when I'm with him," does have a major criticism of Campbell.

"I've heard him sing on WIP," he said, smiling. "He is not a good singer."

———•———

Campbell did a talk show at WIP until "retiring" (for a few minutes, anyway) in 1992.

Not too long after Campbell left the station, Joe Conklin became a part of the WIP Morning Show. Conklin did impressions of people from the Philadelphia sports scene, past and present: Bobby Clarke, Rich Kotite, Jim Fregosi, Ricky Watters, Mike Schmidt, Charles Barkley, and Jimmy Lynam. You name someone with a distinctive voice, Conklin did a masterful impression, spiced with dialogue that was often R-rated.

There was no voice that he did more often — or better — than Campbell's. He punctuated a lot of the dialogue with Campbell's trademark lines — "Unbe-lieeevable! Oh, baby! Unreal!"

In *The Great Philadelphia Sports Debate*, Cataldi noted that Conklin's characterizations sometimes "pushed boundaries of good taste that the real Bill would never have ventured near. I can't tell you how many times after a show we'd brace ourselves for a call from Bill, blasting us for disrespecting him. I can tell you how many times he actually made that call: none. In fact, Bill often told Joe that he had become more famous through Joe's impersonations than he had ever been during his long and varied career."

Conklin did a bit called "Bill and Stan's Meet Market," in which he imitated Campbell and veteran *Daily News* columnist Stan Hochman as they tried to match peculiar types who were searching for dates. He made Campbell almost a daily part of his routine and featured him in his irreverent Christmas CD. In Conklin's version of *Twas the Night*, "Campbell" lashed out at modern-day athletes.

> *"Twas the night before Christmas and the game doesn't matter.*
> *The players' only concern was that their wallets were fatter.*
> *Their guaranteed contracts were hung by their agents with care.*
> *In the hopes that a sneaker deal soon would be there...."*

Conklin never got tired of using The Dean to make a point. On WIP, he imitated Campbell singing about the then-sad-sack Eagles, to the tune of "You're 16 (You're Beautiful And You're Mine)."

"Well, you're a fraud of a team.
You come apart at the seams.
God help your sorry behind.
You'll be 0 and16. Why?
Because you're PITIFUL and you're mine.

You can't catch passes,
Your running's no threat.
You fall behind every chance you get.

You've got no talent,
The owner's a dork.
And everybody knows that the coach loves pork.

You've ruined all of our dreams and broken our hearts.
What you've done to this team is a crime.
0 and 16, you're PITIFUL,
But you're mine."

Not exactly "Fly Me to the Moon," which Campbell, a crooner whose voice has graced many church choirs over the years, used to sing around the ballpark or when he was out with media friends and club personnel after a game.

———•———

Growing up in Philadelphia, Conklin and his two older brothers, John and Jim, had imitated Campbell for years. "We all did him. Everyone in the neighborhood had a Bill Campbell impression, the 'Oh, baby!' " Conklin said. "Everyone did Bill. We idolized him. For some reason, Bill's voice is the easiest in the world for me, and whatever I do with him is funny. I'd say 80 percent of it is unscripted."

Conklin was the class clown at St. Helena's in the Olney section of Philadelphia and later at Cardinal Dougherty High, also in Olney. He amused his classmates with imitations of Campbell, Harry Kalas, and Bobby Clarke. Howard Cosell and Alfred Hitchcock also worked their way into his routine. Now he was actually getting paid to be WIP's class clown. Conklin worked part-time at WIP when Campbell was there, but their paths never crossed; Conklin didn't land a full-time gig at the station until 1994 — two years after Campbell was gone.

Late in 1994, with his impersonations quickly becoming WIP's most talked-about asset, Conklin felt uncomfortable when he saw Campbell at the station.

"He came in and was doing a voice-over or some commercial and I approached him and introduced myself," Conklin recalled.

For Conklin, it was a clumsy moment. He had heard whispers that Campbell was upset with his impersonations of him, that he thought they were done in poor taste.

"I was doing all these impersonations for years — never expecting I'd meet any of these people face to face," Conklin said. "So it was somewhat awkward when I met Bill. I had heard through the grapevine that he was a little miffed at some of the stuff that was coming out of my mouth."

Conklin put out his hand and introduced himself.

"I hear you're somewhat upset at my impression of you," Conklin said with a nervous laugh.

Campbell swung back his head and Conklin sensed that he was not on The Dean's good side.

Joe Conklin (right), the comedian who specializes in sports impersonations, introduced Bill to a new generation with his humorous (and sometimes risqué) impressions of Bill on WIP radio. Their relationship had a frosty start, but the two became good friends. Here, they are shown at Ponzio's Restaurant in Cherry Hill in 2006.

"Oh, it's not so much me," Campbell said, politely, as he shook Conklin's hand. "It's my daughter who's upset with it, Joe. And she's an attorney."

The message, Conklin felt, was clear: Watch your step, pal.

"I felt terrible because I grew up revering this guy and the last thing I wanted was Bill Campbell pissed at me," Conklin said. "He's an institution and he never had a bad word to say about anybody — until the words came out of my mouth. I could tell he was upset. I apologized and told him I didn't mean any disrespect. I told him I'm a comedian and that I've listened to him my whole life and that I don't mean to be offensive."

Conklin and Campbell didn't talk much for at least the next year.

"I think he stayed mad for a while because he would hear through his contemporaries, whether it was [former Eagles executive] Harry Gamble or somebody else, that I was making a fool out of him," Conklin said. "We had so many bits. We had him and Stan Hochman at go-go bars. We had them going down to Wildwood during senior week. We did a lot of different things and people were telling him some negative things."

But then Campbell began getting some positive feedback. A younger generation — fans who weren't around when he did the Phillies, Eagles, 76ers, or Warriors — began to appreciate Campbell's longevity and coolness.

"I was on the radio every day and I think I turned a new generation of people on to him and I think he kind of dug it," Conklin said. "Eventually, I'd see him at some banquet and I'd be doing him at the podium and we became friends. Within a couple years [from their first meeting] he came around and I've never met a nicer, more mannerly gentleman."

Conklin and Campbell started meeting for lunch or dinner every few months, usually at the Tavistock Country Club. They had a common bond: a love for sports — and that voice. That familiar, wonderful voice.

"He kind of reminds me of my dad a little," said Conklin, a feeling shared by thousands of listeners who only know Campbell from his intimate, friendly radio broadcasts over the years. "He's a class act all the way around. I shouldn't even be sitting with him. We go out and I'm overwhelmed that he'd even be sitting at the same table as me. A street-corner punk like myself sitting next to Bill Campbell. It's pretty amazing. We couldn't be more different. He's so dignified and classy and I'm so unpolished."

Campbell said before he ever heard Conklin's impersonations, he was getting some negative feedback.

"A lot of people told me that he was making fun of me," Campbell said. "But when I heard him, I didn't think he was ridiculing me. It was a plus, really. People got a kick out of it for the most part. Every time I would go to a banquet, they would say, 'Are you Joe Conklin or Bill Campbell?' "

At the Philadelphia Sportswriters banquet one year, a teenager heard Campbell talking and walked over to his table and asked for an autograph. Campbell obliged. The young fan looked at the signature and was dumbfounded.

"Oh, I thought you were Joe Conklin," he said.

"I'm sorry you're disappointed," Campbell said with a smirk.

If he hadn't been a sportscaster, Bill Campbell would have made a terrific columnist. When given the chance to write, he was entertaining, provocative, and informative.

He wasn't as wordy, flowery, or bombastic as some columnists. Campbell wrote in "Everyday Speak." He got right to the point, and he wrote for the readers, not other writers.

Take the start of the piece he wrote for *Philly Sport* while he was still working for WIP in 1990:

With 76ers coach Jim Lynam, what you see is what you get. Nothing contrived. No affectations. As my Monday afternoon broadcast partner, his passion for the game comes crackling across the telephone lines like a beacon. He treats his game with respect and affection, while reducing it to its simplest terms. Some coaches talk about their profession like it's calculus and trig combined, talking down to us as if there was no way we could possibly understand such a profound and complex subject.

Lynam puts it in the terms of the average guy and even enjoys a second-guess or two. One afternoon he even admitted that he made a mistake in a game that the 76ers lost in the final seconds when Mike Gminski's inbounds pass on the baseline was stolen by Isiah Thomas. "Shouldn't you have called a timeout?" demanded a somewhat agitated caller from Center City. "Yes," replied Lynam. "Given the same situation over again, I'm sure I would have handled it differently."

How long has it been since you've heard a coach say something like that?

Think hard. Coaches don't talk like that. There is usually some official in a convenient spot or a player who missed a signal or something. One of the charms of Jim Lynam is that he knows he is a good coach but not an infallible one.

Campbell's crisp writing style often went under-appreciated. It was overshadowed by his unique voice and the conversational way he interacted with the call-in folks and the listeners.

But his writing was at the center of his success. He would generally write a three-minute monologue on a timely issue, using it to spark reaction from his WIP listeners.

Those monologues helped give WIP credibility. So did the conversations that followed. There were disagreements, to be sure. But they were always done with a modicum of respect and fairness. Campbell gave his listeners their say. There was give and take. Conversation. This was talk-radio at its best. There was no ranting, no rage. Just two people having a friendly debate about whether Ruben Amaro Jr. or Wes Chamberlain should be one of the Phillies' outfielders.

"I was young in the business and it was a special time for me to work with him," said Joe Weachter, who produced some of Campbell's shows. "I usually just sat there in awe. He came in so prepared; he was such a radio professional. Every day he would start with his monologue and it was some of the best written stuff I've ever heard. And he almost commanded the callers' respect. You knew you were going to get an objective and honest response when you talked to him."

For five years, Campbell's conversations became a staple with WIP listeners. They felt a sense of loss, then, when Campbell announced on his June 19, 1992 show that he was retiring in the next month.

Callers spent the morning thanking Campbell and telling him how much he was going to be missed.

"You grow up in this town watching Steve Carlton and Mike Schmidt and you think players like that will be with you forever," Rob from Philadelphia said. "I remember the day I heard Steve Carlton was released by the Phillies and a shiver went down my spine. I have to tell you, when I heard you were leaving, I got the same feeling."

Throughout the show, a choked-up Campbell kept saying he was at a loss for words to thank the listeners for their kindness and their outpouring of affection.

"You don't realize the impact you have until something like this happens," Campbell said after the program ended that day. "It was difficult to get through the show."

It was time, Campbell said, to take a little break. His health wasn't at its best and the show was becoming a grind.

"People think you just get here and push a button and start talking," he said. "It takes a lot of preparation the night before and a lot of work in the morning before I go on."

But you made it sound so effortless, Bill.

Campbell's departure would leave a void at the station, said Jack Williams, the WIP president. He called Campbell a "consummate professional and a true gentleman in our business. Bill Campbell is that rare breed of talent, that one-of-a-kind original."

Stoney McLinn, the man who served as Campbell's mentor during his WIP days in the 1940s, would have been proud.

CHAPTER TWELVE

🎤

A premature farewell

Perhaps the best way to understand Bill Campbell's connection to Philadelphia is to listen to his two WIP farewell talk shows in 1992. On June 19, Bill announced he planned to retire from the station soon, bringing a flood of phone calls from well-wishers.

His farewell show, on July 10, turned into a two-hour lovefest that included calls from listeners, players, coaches, and media members — and left Campbell feeling humbled and embarrassed.

And loved. Very, very loved.

Bobby Clarke called. So did Reggie White and Steve Van Buren. And Paul Owens, Richie Ashburn, Harry Kalas, and Gene Hart. And numerous other Philadelphia icons.

But it was the listeners who made the most impassioned, heartfelt calls. Some callers, their voices cracking, had to stop in the middle of their conversations. They needed a few seconds to compose themselves. It was like they were saying goodbye to a friend — a favorite uncle, if you will — whom they had known their entire life.

Mike from Northeast Philadelphia:

"Bill, it's a great honor. You and I have been bantering back and forth the last couple of weeks. I've become a regular caller about my father and what he thinks about baseball players today and how you and him kind of have the same attitude. And you've told me I probably should have listened to my father — and you're probably right. I cut my teeth listening to Bill Campbell as a youngster...."

Mike's voice became choked with emotion.

"It's getting a little difficult here to talk, Bill. I really take my sports seriously. I'm glad I was able to grow up in an era when I had to learn about baseball [from Campbell]. When I turned on my black Zenith radio with the two orange dials that I'll never forget, you were there, buddy. And I really appreciate that.

"My adult life has been spent in the inner city, working with children. And I've always said, the true testament of a man is who he considers his friends. And today, Bill, you have had calls from the spectrum — from white people and black people — and I think if we had more Bill Campbells in this world, we'd probably have less problems going on...."

Throughout the show, Campbell, who was then 68, kept saying he was "inadequate" to describe his feelings of appreciation and kidded that "if I had known all these people were going to say all these nice things about me, I would have retired long ago."

The WIP switchboard didn't stop lighting up. Campbell could have done a 24-hour show and there still wouldn't have been enough time to get to all the calls.

Steve from South Philadelphia:

"I'm thinking of Father's Day in two days, and whenever I think of Father's Day, I think about Jim Bunning's Perfect Game on Father's Day, which this year is also on June 21, as it was in 1964. And when I think of you, I think of you as a father figure in the Philadelphia area. You're the guy who's going to be the good judge and good jury of who needs to be praised and who needs to be scolded and you're very fair that way. There's nothing sugary or anything like that about you; you get right to the point. I don't know you and I've never met you, but just by listening to you I feel very close to you — and I know I'm getting, as someone said before, a voice of reason. In other words, with this [Charles] Barkley trade, I don't know if it's good or bad, but I want to hear what you have to say about it. What you have to say about it, whatever it is, is going to make sense to me."

Mike from Pleasantville:

"I'm 37 and you were talking about Father's Day and listening to the Phillies. My earlier recollections of being with my father was when we used to work at Liberty Bell Park, always running over to the car where we had the radio on and listening and hearing your voice. Like one caller said, hearing Marichal strike out the side or something like that. Part of that stuck with me as a youth and going through the years and listening to the Sixers and you. The common thread was you, Bill. When I heard you were retiring, I thought, OH, BABY. That's UNREAL! You've given Philadelphia so much that we can never repay what you've given us."

Responded Campbell: "That's a nice thing to say, but let me tell you right here, at the risk of sounding corny, I could never, *never* give the sports fans of Philadelphia as much as they've given me. They've given me a reason for being. They've given me a whole life. You can't put any kind of a value on that; you can't put any kind of a dollar value on that. I am in your debt. I am in the debt of everybody who calls this show, and everybody for almost five decades who has allowed me to come into their homes and their cars and their offices and their stores and their shops and wherever. That is a rare, rare privilege that is extended to very, very few people."

On his way to Thomas Jefferson University Hospital to have an infected elbow treated, Ed Rendell, then the mayor of Philadelphia, stopped by the WIP studio and presented Bill with the city's highest honor, a replica Liberty Bell. The inscription read: *Presented to Bill Campbell by the people of the city of Philadelphia. July 10, 1992.*

Rendell told listeners what Campbell has meant to the city.

"The reason I came by, I heard one of the writers 10 minutes ago say how insignificant sports reporting is. In the grand scheme of things, yes; in a sense, that's right, Bill. But in a sense, it isn't," Rendell said. "Since your announcement, one of the things that you've proba-bly gotten an appreciation of, is how much of a role you've played in peoples' lives. In shut-ins' lives, in people who are sick, in people who are older —even young kids growing up who are just getting into the fantasy of loving sports. And in sports fanatics like myself.

"...When Frank Rizzo died, people asked me, what's the signifi-cance? I said, for the people of the city, whether they loved him or hated him, Frank Rizzo was an enormous part of their daily lives for

30 years….And for the people of this city, you have been a part of our lives for so long and we want to recognize all you've done," Rendell continued. "….Bill, it is with the gratitude of not only millions of Philadelphians, but millions of people in the Delaware Valley and South Jersey and Atlantic City and Lancaster and places like that, whose lives you've been a part of for decades and decades and decades. Not that you're going away, but we will never forget you, and never forget what joy and happiness you brought us."

Some of the callers' comments were nostalgic, some were filled with humor. Many included feelings that aren't usually addressed in public by grown men.

Steve Sabol from NFL Films:

"Bill, I was at the Chadds Ford Museum last week, the Andrew Wyeth [display], and there's a big picture of an old sea captain; he's got an old pipe and the weathered face and underneath, there's a little inscription, and it says, 'You'll never see his like again.' And when I thought of calling you up this morning, that's exactly the image that came to my mind. For the years I've listened to you, the sincerity, the knowledge, the enthusiasm that you brought to your profession, it's left all of the sports fans here — and people like myself, whose business is sports — with an enormous legacy. You should be very proud of it."

Ed from Reading:

"I want to thank you for many a great moment in the sports field. Many, many great moments that I listened to you. You were the Matthew, Mark, Luke, and John of the sports world….I enjoyed every moment that you broadcast, even when you had the ticker-tape ballgames, you made them sound great."

John from Center City:

"I'm a longtime listener and this is my first time calling you. Anytime I wanted to call, I didn't think I could put it into words....I was born in 1955, and one of my fondest memories of growing up was sitting on the porch with this old radio, listening to you, with the guttural, excited voice. And your home run calls still stick to my ribs. When Richie Allen would hit the ball over the roof....I remember one time, I had a transistor radio tucked under my bed, and I'll never forget you calling a Frank Robinson home run. 'That baby was hit on the ROOOOOF!!!!' Anyway, yours was the original home-run call."

John Chaney, then the Temple basketball coach:

"Bill, I've been on the road recruiting.....and when they told me you were getting on a horse or a mule and riding off into the sunset and getting away from this business, I said I've got to get back home and talk with him and tell him a few things that were on my mind.....I was talking to Jimmy Lynam and I told him I have to hang up and get my thoughts together. And he said, 'You mean you're going to write something down?' I said, no, when you want to tell a guy that you love him, you don't have to come up with a script. The only thing you need is the theme and you're ready to rattle off.

"Bill, I hope Temple is going to be in line, along with all the other colleges, to one day try to bestow upon you a doctorate because you've been very special. You've not been a handmaiden to buffoons. You've worked hard to do it right and to get it right. And what I've always admired about you is that no one has convinced you that all the [Jim] Romes in sports should suddenly become right. I just want you to know that's very special in my heart. You've worked this thing with all kinds of honesty and you've just been right for all people."

———

In between all the love, Campbell delivered a zinger at the Phillies.

"The thing the Phillies did yesterday, which I found a little bit distasteful, was to come out and play a game in their practice jerseys.

Hey, boys, this is the major leagues. This is the National League of professional baseball. This isn't a softball team. That was bush, absolutely bush.

"So you're trying to break a losing streak and all that nonsense. You dress like major leaguers. That was terrible to go out there and play a game on television and before a crowd of people paying their money....and they play in their practice jerseys. Are you kidding me? If you're going to play in your practice jerseys, then don't charge anybody. Let 'em all in and see the game for nothing. I mean, what's going on here?"

Back to the callers....

Jim Solano, football agent:

"I had to call you to thank you in two ways — first as a fan. I'll never forget the 1960 Eagles' championship game that you broadcast. I was sitting by my radio listening to that game and what a thrill I had and I will always remember it. I also wanted to thank you as a professional. In my 23 years as an agent, you've been extremely objective and always fair in treatment of myself and my players. Even though sometimes you didn't agree with what we were doing, you were always fair and objective and you never had an axe to grind. I just can't say enough. You are without peer, as far as I'm concerned."

Walt from Northeast Philadelphia:

"You're one of the few people on WIP that I listen to, because as you mentioned before, the constant never-ending complaining and negativism. I don't like it."

The reply was vintage Campbell. Quick on his feet. Professional. He defended his colleagues but, at the same time, gracefully shared his opinion.

"I didn't mean it as an attempt to criticize anybody else," Bill said. "If we all did the same thing in the same way, this would be a real big bore and nobody would be listening. Everybody has to do their own thing. That's their privilege, just as it's my privilege to do it the way I want to do it. I've been very grateful because nobody has ever told me how I should broadcast. There's a great, great variety of opinion out there, Walt, and everybody is entitled to it and entitled to broadcast the way they see fit."

Walt didn't back down.

"I don't like all the complaining and criticizing all the time and all the back-biting."

Replied Campbell: "I think there's an awful lot of negativity that's crept into the business and crept into sports. I wish it wasn't so, but that's the way it is. Everybody's a critic and that's the way it's going to be."

Al Meltzer, then a broadcaster at Channel 10:

"I couldn't be happier for you — for a lot of reasons. Not the least of which is, you've been able to call the shot, and as you know, in this business, that's darn near impossible. You're a legend and you've lasted a long time. People like you will never happen again, Bill, because things have changed so much in the industry. One guy this long in one town is probably something that is just going to be a part of history.

"I will miss your voice of reason. Usually around shaving time, I catch your opening act to hear what you have to say for the day and, more often than not, I kind of nod, yeah, yeah, he's got a point. And it's not because of your age, it's because of your perspective. You're able to look at things a lot differently because you've been down the road. You are a voice of reason. You don't just fire from the hip all the time and I really appreciate that. I think people who listened to the station and heard that probably got a better idea of what was really happening in sports than anything else during the day."

Lee from a payphone near Hammonton:

"I have to thank my own father for telling me to listen to Bill Campbell. He just retired this year, and one of the best parts of his work day was walking over to Burger King with his transistor radio and listening to you."

Mark from Upper Darby:

"I guess you're feeling all the love that the city of Philadelphia feels for you today, and I just want to give you some more. I'm a 26-year-old medical student and I haven't had the chance to listen to you as much during the day as I used to, but my memories of you go back to the 1970 Sixers games on Channel 48 that you used to broadcast. I remember every 'Oh, baby!' and 'Unreal!' that you used to say and they're very important to me. It's a sad day [that Bill is leaving]…. We're very lucky in the city in regard to the announcers we have; it goes from Harry Kalas and Richie Ashburn and Gene Hart all the way through you. Your professionalism is something that all young people in the city should pattern themselves after….I hope I can carry that professionalism into my career."

Richie Ashburn, then a Phillies broadcaster:

"Bill, the person I worry about is Jo. She cannot handle you that long for that many hours in the day."

Bill Campbell's thought-provoking monologues on WIP radio formed the foundation of his entertaining talk show from 1987 to 1992.

Paul Owens, then a Phillies executive:

"Bill, I've enjoyed the program immensely and I know the fans have. All I can say is, the 37 or 38 years we've known each other real well, you've always been a class guy; you have a great feel for the human element, and every sports crisis I've seen, you've talked about. [You have] that charisma and you did your homework. Basically, I love you because you've always understood the chemistry of a team or a lack of it."

John from South Philadelphia:

"As they say, nothing great lasts forever. You're a legend in this city — as big as any superstar we've ever had — and I'm going to miss you."

Jim Murray, former Eagles general manager:

"I'm calling as Jim Murray, the Eagles fan....who had a favorite chair listening to Bill Campbell do those games. Bill, to me, you're a perfect prayer. I know you're not going away. I know you're on the back nine like the rest of us, but you're not at 18. But you just hang in there and know you are a guy who has affected a lot of lives, and all for the good."

Frank from Avalon:

"I missed your monologue this morning and, boy, it's like missing church. I just feel badly about that. But what I feel would be just wonderful is if you could call one inning of a Phillies game. Just one inning so that all the young people could find out what a call really was. It would be outstanding. I have so many memories of Bill Campbell calling the Phillies. I'm 68, so I've been around for a while. I go way back...Young people should learn how a game should be called. And I'm going to call the Phils' office and put that [suggestion] to them."

(Shortly thereafter, Bill *did* join Ashburn and do two innings of a Phillies broadcast.)

Eric Gregg, then a National League umpire:

"I'm gonna miss you. As an official coming from the other side, I listen to your show all the time, and other shows also. We come with a different perspective, and to finally turn on a show where I don't hear officials getting *hammered* day in and day out — and that really means a lot to me and other officials. To see a guy like you come on and be fair and honest, that's all we ask."

Larry Litwin, secretary of the Philadelphia Sportswriters' Association and a former KYW reporter:

"Your producer asked if I go way back with you. I'll just bring back a couple of memories. You're the first TV anchor I ever remember watching over at Channel 10, and I also used to make a trip over to the Robin Roberts Show on City Avenue, and you co-hosted that show with Robby. Another recollection I have is that no one could ever call a touchdown like you could, with the Eagles and some of the college games you did. Nobody ever will, I don't think, because there was a way you had of controlling your voice...As a kid growing up and then getting into the business and doing play by play, I tried to emulate you. I tried and I just couldn't come close."

Bill Lyon, then an Inquirer *columnist:*

"You've always been a gentleman and a consummate professional, and I don't think a human being can do any more than that."

Tom Brookshier, Bill's former broadcast partner:

"You're leaving at the top....and if there's been a father in the business to me, it's been you, Bill."

Ray from Juniata Park:

"As a child in 1963, I moved from New York City to Philadelphia and always wanted to be a radio announcer from Day One. I grew up listening to the great Mel Allen and those great calls he used to make for the Yankees. And then moving to Philadelphia — which was a bit of change for a guy who thought as a child that everyone played the season to play the Yankees in the World Series — and not having a very good team and not a lot of history that I was aware of.

"But there was an announcer that made me feel very good, like Mel Allen made me feel. I used to love this announcer making the home-run calls where he was so excited that it would make me excited, to the point where I took the old 54 bus up Lehigh Avenue to become a Phillie's fan. And that gentleman was Bill Campbell."

Joseph from South Philadelphia:

"This is a little bit of a sad day for me because I've been following you since 1960 and…it's going to be hard to get up in the morning and know you're not going to be on any more…Bill, can I have just one special moment with you? On a nice summer night, there's about 14 fellows on the corner of Moyamensing and McKean Street in South Philly, and we're all sitting down and you're broadcasting the game and Wes Covington was at bat. We've talked about it time after time. It was an ordinary ballgame, but after he hit that ball and you described that home run, all of us felt like it was a World Series game."

Channel 6 sportscaster Gary Papa:

"Scott [Palmer] and I came to this town in '81, and we heard about Bill Campbell and The Dean and all that. I like to call you *The Professor* because you taught guys like Scott and me — and I'm sure as lot of other younger-now-middle-aged-broadcasters — the way to do it. Like Julius [Erving] taught certain ballplayers and Charles [Barkley] taught other ballplayers and the greats of sports taught other athletes how to act. Professionalism and accuracy and just a perspective about all this stuff. We can get all beat down by the bad side of sports, but somehow you had an ability to tell what it *really* means. Few people have that type of insight. It's not so much we're going to miss you tomorrow or the next day, but when a real big sports story comes up in the next month or two, I'm going to be sitting there wondering, 'What does Bill Campbell think?' And I'm not going to know. And that's where I'm going to miss you, Bill. I'm going to feel very sad about that."

Lee Thomas, then the Phillies' general manager:

"I've been here just about four years and…I appreciate the support and fairness you've given to myself and the Phillies, even though we've had some tough times."

Jim from North Philadelphia:

"I'm shocked to hear that you're leaving, and the one thing I must say — and I want the people who are listening to understand that this has nothing to do with racism — you are the only radio reporter in this city who has ever given recognition to the former black players…. and we appreciate it and we're certainly going to miss you."

Cal from Cherry Hill:

"I'm an original Bill Campbell listener on WIP. During World War II, you were known as The Kid with Stoney McLinn. And you were phenomenal then and you are phenomenal now."

Ed Harvey, Bill's sidekick at WCAU when they announced the Eagles' 1960 championship season:

"I want to leave you with the one sentence that Jack Whitaker said to me when I retired: Have yourself a great back nine."

Jody McDonald, then a WIP talk-show host:

"When I first came here to Philadelphia, they said, 'You'll be following Bill Campbell,' and I said, 'Oh, OK. I think I've heard of this guy Bill Campbell.' Unfortunately, I didn't get to grow up here in Philadelphia and I didn't get to listen to you do baseball and basketball and the Eagles. I know what the Voice of Philadelphia is. I knew it was Bill Campbell. I just didn't have the pleasure of listening to him. I certainly have over the last two years, and you've made my transition here to Philadelphia an easy one…and like everyone else who's come on here today, I've learned a lot from The Dean and that's meant a lot to me. About the best way to put in perspective what Bill Campbell has done, is to look at the sport that I know both you and I love more than any else, and that's baseball. Baseball's greatest honor is to be placed into the Hall of Fame, and stars come and go...but the one who have longevity, the ones who can stick around for 10, 12, 15, 20 years, they become Hall of Famers. And your longevity is a testament to what you've meant to the world of broadcasting and to here in Philadelphia."

Jim Lynam, then the 76ers' general manager:

"You did it with class and you did it with dignity."

Scott Palmer, then a Channel 6 sportscaster:

"When I first started working at Channel 6, I emulated yourself and also Bob Bradley, another dean who retired a couple years ago. You both enjoyed longevity because of who you were and the way you did your business. You have also preached patience, as well as thoughtfulness, and that isn't something that is done by everyone in this town. This is a very quick town to judge. There needs to be a matter of perspective and you have always given us that, and for that we are thankful."

Bobby Clarke, then the Flyers' senior vice president:

"We know it's only semi-retirement, but it means more time at Tavistock." (Which is where Bill does most of his golfing.)

Harry Gamble, then president of the Philadelphia Eagles and Campbell's neighbor in Haddonfield:

"I wonder who's going to look after you now, because the last couple of times that you and I have gotten together for football games, you've ended up in the hospital...Kidney stones, chest pains..."
    Replied Bill: "It's your football team that causes all this. It's your fault, Harry, it's your team!"

Flyers broadcaster Gene Hart (Bill describes him as "Big Mound of Sound"):

"Good morning, young guy. Bill. As I'm in my 60s, too, thoughts have come into my mind on how and in what matter I would like to see my career come to a final point. And you gave me the idea Tuesday. I couldn't ask for a better ending than to have somebody in hockey with the prestige and stature of Tommy Lasorda, giving me a call one morning after a loss and saying, 'Hey, you did it well.' [Lasorda, the Dodgers' manager, had phoned Bill.]

"I thought this years ago about our business. There's an army of people, male and female, who can do a professional job about a sports event. But I always thought among that whole host, there's just a very few select people who are able to rise to the level of a great game or a great sports story or a great incident. And you are one of the blessed few....That's a standard you've left for all of us....Unfortunately, as you and I know, ethics and accuracy and reason are maybe lost adjectives that have come to many people in our game, many of whom will make more money in one year than you may have in part of a lifetime, but who cannot carry your microphone."

Jon Gurevitch, then a 76ers' broadcaster:

"A few years ago, you invited me to be a regular guest on your show, and at the time, I was still a fairly new broadcaster in Philadelphia... I think having me on your show in a lot of ways helped legitimize me as a broadcaster to what can be a very tough Philadelphia audience. To be on with Bill Campbell, and to be considered by you to be a legitimate source of information and comments, was a great boost to me personally and I really appreciate you believing in me."

Daily News *columnist Bill Conlin:*

"There's two things I don't do in life: I don't do windows, and I don't do columns the day after I come back from Wimbledon. But for you, I made an exception....Every word was from the heart."

Sportswriter Jayson Stark, then with The Philadelphia Inquirer:

"You're a big reason I'm involved in sports today. I would not have the same love for sports that I have if it was not for you, because I was one of the lucky ones who grew up listening to you and later had the honor of working with you. One thing I don't understand, what's a young guy like you doing retiring?"

Bill's "retirement," of course, was short-lived. He soon did pre-game and halftime shows during Eagles' games on WYSP radio. "Now that I'm on a classic rock station, my grandchildren, who've never paid much attention to what I do, think I'm a star," Campbell said at the time.

Campbell then took his talents to KYW Newsradio and continued his sports commentaries, but he later admitted he missed the give-and-take with his talk-radio listeners.

Before his last show at WIP, Bill was followed by numerous local camera crews. When he arrived at the studio and got out of his Buick, he was greeted by Channel 3 cameras and reporter Ukee Washington.

Eagles quarterback Randall Cunningham (left) and Bill Campbell converse while on a WIP radio show in 1988. Campbell was the Eagles play-by-play broadcaster from 1956 to 1964.

The cameraman got sidetracked, however, because he noticed a tall, attractive WIP secretary as she walked toward Bill with her long legs and a short smile. They walked hand in hand toward the station as some of the passing cars beeped their horns with delight.

"Bill," one motorist shouted as he drove past the couple, "retirement looks pretty good from here!"

At the beginning of his final show, Bill thanked the morning guys — Angelo Cataldi, Al Morganti, and Tony Bruno — for all their kind words. "I thought you were talking about somebody else," he said, "but I want you to know I really appreciate it."

As his show started, Campbell talked about the party that the station held in his honor at Downey's the previous night. He ribbed WIP talk show host Howard Eskin, a man with whom he had some verbal on-air spars in the past, for the "generous" gifts he had given him. "Three Wilson TC3 golf balls, which I'm sure he got for nothing. And inscribed on each golf ball, 'Howard Eskin, The King.' Unbelievable! Absolutely unbelievable!"

Campbell told listeners that, as per their request, producer Joe Weachter was going to play snippets of Bill's 1960 Eagles-Packers NFL championship game broadcast throughout the show.

"I didn't even think I had any tape, but I did find a cassette in my junk closet at home and I brought it in," he said.

Toward the end of the show, Jack Williams, WIP's president, told Campbell, "You're respected by your peers, you're respected by your fans and you're respected by your coworkers. I don't know how you can do any better than that."

Williams talked about Campbell's fairness, his dignity, and his devotion to his family.

"A couple of years ago, Bill, you told me you didn't know how much longer you wanted to do this thing, but that when you went out, you wanted to go out a winner. Well, Bill, when Webster does the next dictionary, when they put the word *winner* in there, they should put your picture beside it."

Campbell was nearly speechless.

"I've always prided myself in my ability to put some words together," he said, "and I find myself totally inadequate to respond to that except to say that I really appreciate it, Jack."

In his sign off, Bill thanked his coworkers and his listeners.

"The last thing I'd like to say, above all, I owe a great debt of gratitude to all of you."

And here, the words became difficult. You found yourself listening to the broadcast and thinking, *Come on, Bill. Come on. You can do it, pal. Swallow hard. We need to hear what your heart is telling your head.*

Bill regained his composure.

"I owe a great debt of gratitude that I can never really repay," he said, his voice cracking with emotion. "For without you allowing me to visit with you everyday — without you, I don't know what I might have done.

"Good day, good sports, and God bless you."

CHAPTER THIRTEEN

Remembering Whitey

Richie "Whitey" Ashburn was probably the most beloved figure in Philadelphia sports history. He was the speedy centerfielder and base-stealing king who helped the Phillies — known as the Whiz Kids because of their youth and exuberance — capture the 1950 National League pennant. As an announcer, Ashburn became a folk hero. His dry sense of humor, candidness, and folksy, down-home delivery made him the king of the Phillies' broadcast booth.

Yet, when Ashburn first joined the Phillies, there were doubts if he would last. To some, his flat Midwestern drawl made him sound like an outsider when he joined the broadcast team in 1963, which also happened to be Bill Campbell's initial season as a Phillies announcer.

Unlike Ashburn, Campbell was a media veteran. He had done play-by-play for the Eagles, Warriors, Penn and Penn State football, and Big 5 basketball; he had served as a Channel 10 sports anchor, along with a 17-year stint as WCAU's sports director. By 1963, Campbell was already in his third decade as a broadcaster.

Like a protective big brother, Campbell took Ashburn under his wing. He had known Ashburn since he was a player with the Phillies. Back then, they had a friendly working relationship. Now, they were broadcasting teammates.

"Dad always attributed a lot of his success to Bill because Bill guided him," said Richard Ashburn, the son of the late Phillies announcer. "Certainly, Dad was knowledgeable and witty, but he didn't know the first thing about broadcasting. Bill nurtured him. I remember as a kid, people saying that my dad wouldn't make it in broadcasting. He didn't have that booming voice, but in his nice quiet way, he succeeded, and Bill realized what he had to offer and brought out the best in him."

And he taught Ashburn not to feel compelled to comment on every pitch or every situation. Sometimes, less banter is more effective, Campbell told him.

"I used to tell him, 'Unless you have something to say that affects the play or enlightens the fans, don't be afraid to say nothing,' " Campbell said. "And if you listen to Ashburn throughout his career, he would sometimes go an inning, or longer, without talking, and you'd wonder if he was there. But the result of that was, when he did say something, people remembered what he said. The thing I object to — and I object to it now just as much as I did back then — is that there are too many people in the booth. To me, there is no sport in the history of the world that requires three men to describe it. There ain't no way. All those guys do is keep fighting for airtime. They keep interrupting each other and it's absolutely ridiculous."

Campbell, who frequently hits the mute button when watching a sports event today, and Ashburn didn't have that problem.

"The first time I worked with Whitey, I told him not to be afraid to be quiet," Campbell said.

It was easy for Ashburn to keep a low-key demeanor.

"That was Rich's nature, anyway," said his wife, Herbie Ashburn. "He thought he was insulting the public's intelligence if he described every little thing. If anyone wanted his opinion, he would give it, but he didn't say much unless he had something to say. He had a real sense for what to do and what not to do."

Richard Ashburn said he would listen to the Phillies' broadcasts "and I was probably the only one around who knew Dad was in the booth. There would be many innings where he wouldn't say anything, but I could hear the *ti-ti-ti* in the background."

The soft, barely audible noise was coming from Ashburn as he contentedly puffed on his pipe. *Ti-ti-ti.*

"I don't think anyone else would have heard it, but that's how I knew he was still in the booth," Richard Ashburn said.

Campbell remembers the first game he did with Ashburn, spring training in 1963 in Clearwater, Florida.

"It was the first time Whitey was up in a press box or a radio booth. Ever," Campbell said. "I'll never forget what he said. He sat down with us and we're getting ready to go on the air and he said,

'It looks like an easy game from up here, boys.' They used to have a sign with those words in the press box at Veterans Stadium, but that's where it originated."

The text on the plaque, which now hangs from the Citizens Bank Park press box, reads:

Rich "Whitey" Ashburn
Broadcast Booth
"This game's easy, Harry."

Campbell and Ashburn came from vastly different backgrounds. Campbell grew up in the big city. Ashburn grew up milking cows. Yet, they had an instant chemistry in the broadcast booth. Bill served as the straight man, setting up his partner for one of his deliciously dry one-liners. Unlike By Saam, they talked about more than what was happening in front of them. Saam was the man in the booth who didn't alter

The Phillies' new 1963 broadcast team consisted of veteran By Saam (left, inside the booth) and newcomers Richie Ashburn (seated in the center) and Bill Campbell (right). Behind Ashburn and Campbell is Joe Scott, owner of the Philadelphia distributorship of Ballantine beer, at spring training in Clearwater, Florida, and Campbell believes it was the first time Ashburn was ever in a broadcast booth.

the script. He was professional and his voice was oh-so-commanding. Saam's straight-laced style matched perfectly with the tandem of Campbell and Ashburn, who gave the listeners humorous anecdotes with their behind-the-scenes stories about the players and the teams.

"I walked into a situation where Byrum had been there a long time and he was a good guy and I learned a lot from him — preparation and things like that," Campbell said. "But Byrum was not very humorous; he was dedicated to doing things by the book, and he didn't have time to worry about making Richie feel at home. And I was new and Richie was new and we just kind of hit it off right away, much like Harry Kalas and Richie hit it off when they became broadcasting partners."

Not everyone appreciated the levity that the Campbell-Ashburn duo brought to the booth.

Len Cella, sports editor of the *News of Delaware County*, wrote in his June 20, 1963 column that Campbell and Ashburn's "bantering back and forth during slow periods on the air is all right, I guess, but it's overdone at times. If Campbell has any faults, it's his habit of repeating himself, sometimes two and three times in succession."

Cella also wrote that "Bill Campbell of Broomall is the best announcer in the city when he reports the Eagles' football games. But Campbell is still feeling his way around in his first year with the Phillies, as is former Havertown resident Richie Ashburn…

"Although Ashburn's voice is the kind one has to get used to, there's no doubt he is teaching Philadelphia fans more about the game. The former Phils centerfielder can tell us the player's viewpoint in particular situations and has an uncanny knack of predicting strategy of pitchers, hitters, and managers. Despite his double negatives like He can't hardly find the plate, Richie is learning to speak English better."

In the July 5, 1963 edition of *The Philadelphia Inquirer*, a listener wrote a letter to the editor that was given the headline "Corny Commentators."

To the Editor of The Inquirer:
There is a fairly well-founded theory that vaudeville was killed by corny jokes. I am afraid that the Phillies' games on television are about to be killed off by the same lethal dose of corn-oil, dispensed in this case by the

comedy team of Bill Campbell and Richie Ashburn. Veteran sports announc-
er By Saam must think he has been trapped by Amateur Hour.

Campbell's asides to Ashburn are guaranteed to make you turn the
knob on the television set and gulp a few brands of Brand-X. As for the old
Phillies centerfielder, he is still hitting foul balls.

Can't we ever get announcers who will stick to the game?
FUSSY FAN
Philadelphia, Pa.

Three days later, a fan wrote that, "We here in Reading agree
with Fussy 100 percent. Never in our lives have we heard a group of
commentators, such as Saam, Campbell and, Ashburn. They scream
into the microphone when the Phils win and they love to belittle the
opposition in an unsportsmanlike manner."

Another fan wrote that Campbell, Ashburn, and Saam are too
slow to give the home-plate umpire's calls. "Too often, the ball and
strike calls have to wait until these fellows tell of an incident that happened one, five, or 10 years ago."

For the next six weeks, *The Inquirer* was besieged with letters
from fans who defended Campbell and Ashburn. Among the readers'
comments:

"….Bill Campbell is bringing him [Ashburn] along slowly into the
broadcasting game. The little comedy between them makes for a
more relaxed broadcast. I doubt if 'Fussy Fan' would sit through a
single game or doubleheader without an occasional laugh — or
maybe he is just the type who could do just that."

"The fan who wrote in complaining about the Campbell-
Ashburn comedy team certainly has a short memory." The reader referred to one of the former Phils announcers as "absolutely
colorless" and claimed that "we need color, not reminiscing of
the old days of the Athletics."

"Watching a baseball game, with its mound conferences, warm-
ups, lineup changes and just plain stalling is, at best, a tedious
affair; at worst, it's downright dull. Listen to the wry witticisms
of an outstanding personality on a game which he played so

well for 15 years is not dull at all; in fact, it helps to enhances the game's interest."

"The humorous analysis of the situations which so frequently occur in baseball by an outstanding veteran sportscaster cannot be classified as 'corn.' If the 'Fussy Fan' prefers to listen to By Saam's monotone of statistics, then let him. I'm sure that most Philly fans are pleased, as I am, by the addition of Bill Campbell and Richie Ashburn."

"I have always enjoyed By Saam, and the addition of Bill Campbell and Richie Ashburn gives me more pleasure."

"….Some people make me weary, and I refer specifically to the letter you have chosen to title 'Corny Commentators.' The people complained so much, [announcer] Gene Kelly left; next, they got on the neck of [announcer] Frank Sims until he was gone. Personally, I think Bill Campbell, accompanied by Richie Ashburn's wry humor, makes a very welcome addition to some of the ball games that fans have been forced to see because of

John Quinn's poor trades....I'm glad I'm not the 'Mrs.' of 'A Fussy Fan' — he'd be too hard to please."

———•·•———

Bill and Jo took a mini vacation in Avalon, New Jersey, in September of 1997. Bill always loved the Shore, perhaps because it conjured memories of the summers he used to spend with his doting aunts in Atlantic City, or perhaps because it gave him a chance to recharge from his hectic schedule.

At around 6 a.m. on this September morning, Bill and his wife were soundly asleep when they were startled by a ringing phone in their Golden Inn hotel room. Groggily, Bill picked the phone off his nightstand.

"Hello."

On the other end was Mark Helms, executive editor at the station where Bill was now working, KYW Newsradio.

"Bill, are you standing up or sitting down?" Helms said.

"Mark, I'm in bed. I just opened my eyes."

"Well, I have bad news for you."

"What happened?"

"Richie Ashburn was just found dead in his hotel room in New York."

Campbell, for one of the few times in his life, went silent. Ashburn had seemed indestructible to him. He was always playing squash or tennis, always keeping himself in great shape. Bill had known Ashburn had a diabetes problem, but he hadn't thought that his health was in any severe danger.

"When I got the news, I could not believe it," Campbell said. "I could not believe it."

Campbell did a radio piece on Ashburn for KYW. Shortly thereafter, virtually every TV crew from Philadelphia and the Jersey Shore descended upon the Golden Inn and did interviews with Campbell in the hotel lobby.

News crews went to Campbell because he and Ashburn seemed connected. "I had known Richie since he started with the Phillies in 1948," Campbell said. "In fact, he and his wife, Herbie, used to rent a house near us; we were living in Havertown at that time and then we moved to Broomall, and they lived in that area. We'd go out to dinner and do stuff."

Ashburn was 70 when he died, and the medical examiner in New York said the cause of death was a heart attack, with diabetes a contributing factor.

"It was a terrific shock because if ever there was a guy I was associated with whom I thought might live forever, it was Ashburn," Campbell said.

A few years earlier, Campbell accidentally discovered that Ashburn was a diabetic and that it was affecting his eyes.

Campbell had some suspicions that his former broadcasting buddy was having sight problems. "I had noticed in watching the games on television that he was losing balls that were hit to the outfield," he said. "But unless you were a broadcaster, you may have not noticed; it probably wouldn't have been noticed by the average fan. But I noticed he was losing some balls and it was obvious to me that he was having some sort of trouble."

The next time Campbell went to the Vet, he sat with Ashburn in the press dining room.

"He brought the subject up," Campbell said. "He told me he thought this would be his last year in the booth."

Ashburn mentioned a contractual problem he was having, and then he asked Bill about his daughter.

"By the way, what kind of problem is Chrissie having with her eyes?" Ashburn asked.

Campbell was surprised at the question.

"He had known Chrissie since she was a little girl, and I said, 'What do you mean?' " Campbell said.

Ashburn explained that he was having an eye problem of his own and that he had bumped into Chrissie in the Wills Eye Hospital waiting room. They talked briefly, but their conversation was interrupted as they were pulled apart for separate eye examinations.

Campbell said his daughter was suffering from something called a pseudo-optic tumor. "It looks like a tumor, but it isn't a tumor," he said to Ashburn.

Ashburn then told Campbell that he was a diabetic and that the condition was starting to affect his eyesight.

Campbell didn't think it was serious.

"I knew other people who had the problem and lived for a long, long time," he said. "And he kind of portrayed it as a run-of-the-mill thing, like Bobby Clarke and his diabetes."

After her father's death, Karen Ashburn Hall said her dad had suffered from diabetes for six or seven years; she said her grandfather, Rich's dad, also suffered from diabetes and that his last years were terrible.

She told *The Inquirer* that her dad dreaded his fate and that he was "taken at a good time" because he was spared the suffering.

"The diabetes had apparently affected his heart, and up until that time, I didn't know [the severity] of his problem," Campbell said. "I was suspicious that the diabetes was affecting his eyesight and maybe, this is my own speculation, that's why he was telling me he may not be back the next year as a broadcaster. Maybe he didn't feel like he could make it. Apparently, the diabetes led to his heart attack."

Ashburn is still with Campbell. Spend an afternoon with him on the golf course — as Dave Eynon and Charlie Rizzi have been doing for numerous years — and Ashburn's name invariably becomes part of the conversation. He loves to retell the story where Ashburn was trying to stretch a double into a triple and, as he slid into third base, umpire Jocko Conlan yelled "safe" but put his thumb in the air to signify that he was "out."

"Whitey is dusting himself off and staying on the base and Jocko says, 'What are you waiting for? Get off the base.' And Whitey says, 'What do you mean? You called me safe.' Jocko tells him, 'Only you heard me call you safe, but 32,000 people saw me call you out. Get your ass out of here.' "

There were numerous on-the-air stories that Campbell would coax from Ashburn — the way he built up his speed by chasing rabbits through cornfields as a youngster ("I used to catch the fat ones," he explained); the down-the-stretch drama of the Phillies' 1950 Whiz Kids; his days with the woeful 1962 New York Mets ("I was MVP for the worst team in baseball history; that ain't saying much."); the time he hit a poor woman in the head with a foul ball and, as she was being carted off on a stretcher, plunked her with *another* foul.

One of Campbell's favorite Ashburn stories centered around his contract dispute with Phillies general manager Roy Hamey. At the time, Ashburn was one of baseball's best leadoff hitters and arguably its premier defensive centerfielder.

"Richie came from this little town called Tilden, Nebraska, and he used to say that at that time, everybody in town was on a party line," Campbell said, smiling at the memory. "If you wanted to have a private phone line in those days, you had to pay extra for it. Richie said everybody had a party line, so everybody could get on and listen to your conversation anytime they wanted to."

It was especially fun to listen when Ashburn, the town's hero and a man who has a Tilden baseball field named in his honor, was negotiating with the Phillies' tight-fisted general manager.

Hamey would call and the two would get into a verbal sparring match. Back and forth they went, with Hamey unaware that his X-rated comments were being heard by the townsfolk.

"Richie says Hamey used to use horrible language, and Richie used to holler back at him," Campbell said. "There were no agents back in those days and they used to have screaming matches on the phone.

He said Hamey used to say to him, 'You little white-haired, little blonde son-of-a-bitch, you're lucky I'm giving you this.' That kind of crap."

Campbell's smile grew longer than one of the Ballantine Blasts he used to describe.

"And Richie said he would go to the store the next day and people would say"— and here, Campbell's voice imitated a church-choir sweet old lady — 'How dare that man talk to you like that!' "

Tilden loved Whitey. So did Soupy. Always did, always will. Spend eight years together, live in the same road hotels and you form a bond that won't go away — even when that friend is no longer here.

"We did a lot of games. We did 162 games together each year and that's more time than you spend with your wife, more time than you spend with your family," Campbell said. "It's a lot of time to talk to each other and you get pretty close to one another."

Every time he watches a Phillies game on television, Campbell's mind invariably drifts back to his partner, the pipe-smoking man who wore colorful caps and liked to give birthday wishes to listeners; the man whom *The Inquirer's* Terry Bitman once called "the Will Rogers of sports broadcasting — droll, homespun, opinionated, and self-deprecating."

Ashburn was ultra-popular as a player; he did, after all, win two batting titles and he usually was among the league leaders in stolen bases, walks, runs, and putouts. Amazingly, he became even more popular as an announcer, going from adored player to folk hero.

Bill Campbell played a part in that transformation.

You can bet the house on that, Soupy.

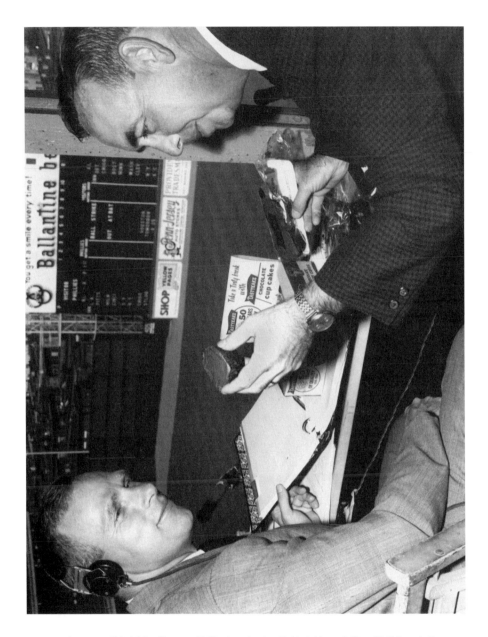

A distinctive Philadelphia flavor — Phillies broadcasters Richie Ashburn (left) and Bill Campbell, Tastykakes, and the backdrop of charming Connie Mack Stadium, with its mammoth Ballantine scoreboard.

CHAPTER FOURTEEN

Family life

Willie Nelson's "On the Road Again" could have been the theme of Bill Campbell's broadcasting career during the time his daughter, Chrissie, was growing up.

Unlike Nelson, however, Campbell hated the road. Hated eating in restaurants, waiting in airports, killing time in hotels. He was a homebody at heart. Maybe he despised the road because it reminded him of the unsettling days after his parents separated and he and his dad lived in different hotels and apartments.

Or maybe he just missed the comfort of being near his wife and daughter.

After getting married in 1947, Bill and Jo lived in a Philadelphia apartment on Walnut Street for six months, then moved in with her parents in the Parkside section of Camden. This was the same semidetached house where Jo had lived before she was married.

"We moved there to save money and pay for a car we had bought," she said, referring to their 1947 maroon Ford.

Two years later, in 1949, Jo and Bill moved into new apartments on Park Boulevard in Camden, not far from her parents' home. "Our apartment wasn't air-conditioned, so I would sometimes go over to the WCAU studio with Bill just so I could sit in his air-conditioned office," Jo said.

Three years after Bill and Jo moved into their Camden apartment, Christine Anne Campbell was born at Presbyterian Hospital in Philadelphia.

Bill, who had been smoking Salems in the lobby as he waited for news on his child's birth, walked into the hospital room after the delivery. He was thrilled that his wife was doing fine.

Jo's pregnancy was both exciting and scary.

Scary because Bill was worried about Jo's health.

"Knowing my mother had died in childbirth and that my dad's mother had died in childbirth, it's something that stays in your mind," Bill said.

He was worried that his wife might suffer the same fate. The thought also concerned Jo.

"She said to me later, 'Don't think that thought didn't occur in my mind,' " Bill said. "And I know it sure as hell occurred to me. Fortunately, we broke the chain."

After their baby was born was born, Bill visited with his wife in her hospital room.

Jo looked at her husband.

"I'm afraid I disappointed you; it's a girl," she said.

"Disappointed? Oh, no!" Bill scolded. "How can I be disappointed? We have a child and that's all I wanted."

Decades later, the little girl became an accomplished attorney. And Jo had a confession to make about the day Chris was born.

"Bill doesn't know it, but I said to God, 'We waited five years for her. If we're only going to have one, please make it a girl!' " she said, giggling at the memory. "So I got my way."

Shortly after Chris was born, the Campbells paid $17,500 for their first house, a two-story brick Colonial with a one-car garage in Havertown, Pennsylvania.

City people all their lives, the Campbells were giving it a try in the suburbs.

The Campbells lived in Havertown for five years and then moved to a bigger home in Broomall (cost: $30,000) in 1958.

With Bill on the road a great deal of time — especially after he took the Phillies' job in 1963 — Chris was raised primarily by her mother. Jo didn't mind. Bill was happy so she was happy. And when he was home, he fussed over his little girl and tried to make her a part of his world; he would sometimes have her sit beside him when he broadcast the Phillies' or Warriors' home games.

"Dad would always sit with his leg jiggling as he did the game," Chris said. "His leg would go and he'd pick the skin on his thumb. It was just this nervous habit. His thumbs would be bleeding by the end of the game. That was just his intensity.

Bill gives a putting lesson to his daughter, Chris, while his wife, Jo,
watches the instruction in their Broomall home in 1959.

"And after a while, you didn't want to sit next to him!"

She was kidding. She loved being with her dad, loved watching how he crafted his broadcast. He made her feel like a big shot when he took her on a flight to Boston, where they stayed in a hotel after she accompanied him to the Celtics-Warriors game that he was announcing.

"Chris was the apple of his eye," Jo said.

Still, it wasn't easy when he went on an extended road trip and left his family behind.

"I just made up my mind that this is the way it was going to be," Jo said. "I just had to make the best of it, so I took the bull by the horns and took over. But she wasn't hard to raise; she was no trouble. It was just one child and there were plenty of kids in the neighborhood who were friendly with her and she loved being there. My only regret was, whenever she was sick, he seemed to be out of town. I had to handle it myself and that frightened me. But I had my sister and mother to consult, and we got through it."

Chris never felt slighted that her dad was on the road so much. It was just a normal part of growing up.

"That was his job and I was used to it," she said. "To me, it surprised me when I started to realize in grade school that every kid's dad wasn't on TV. It really did!"

She let out a hearty laugh.

"I mean, it was normal in my house. The radio was on and Dad was on it. When TV was becoming more and more popular and everyone had televisions, Dad was on. If it was dinner time and Dad wasn't home, he was on television. So I knew who he was and what he did, and I must have had some appreciation that this was a rather cool job — though I wouldn't have put it in those terms back then. And when he was home, he was *home*. We spent a lot of time together, the three of us. We were very close. And my mother was the kind of person who was always so organized. She is so reliable and so steady that he knew he could leave; if it had to be two or three weeks at a time with the Phillies and there was a flood in the basement or I had the chickenpox, he could rely on her to handle it."

When Chris reached her teenage years, Bill felt pained that she was going to a big event and he was, say, stuck in St. Louis announcing a Phillies game.

"The moments I remember him missing were really later. They were things like proms," said Chris, who bears a striking resemblance to her dad. "I remember going to proms and he was not there to see me go. He'd always call me. He'd always ask Mom, 'When is her date coming?' And if he was coming at 6, Dad would call at 5:30. A couple of times he sent me flowers. It really ate at him to miss those moments. But I knew it bothered him. It wasn't like he was away and ignoring it, so he always made himself and his presence known in his thoughts.... And God bless him, we had all kinds of musicals and things at my school and I loved to sing — and still do — and he tried to make as many shows as he could. He would fly all night to get somewhere if I was in a play the next day.

"I just understood that this was the demand of his job. The tradeoff, for instance during the baseball years, was that he was going to be home all winter. So by the end of October, he was home."

There was another bonus in having a dad who announced Phillies games: spring training in Florida. When Bill took the Phillies job, the Campbells couldn't spend summer weeks at the Jersey Shore in Stone Harbor, like they did when Chris was younger. That was OK, because the family got to take a unique vacation every winter, when Chris and Jo would join Bill for two weeks in Clearwater, Florida, where the Phils prepared for the season.

"We'd all cry when he left for spring training, but we would join him in a couple of weeks. I would sit down with my teachers ahead of time and they'd give me the lesson plans for the time I'd be away," Chris said. "How are you going to complain that your dad has to be away when you get to head to Florida in the winter?"

———•———

No one understands Bill and Jo's marriage better than their daughter.

"They've been married since 1947 and they're quite human. They have their flaws. They've had their battles," Chris said. "I know they've had their moments when each has been ready to chuck it in and say, 'I can't take one more day with this person.' "

She flashed a smile and you could feel the pride in her voice.

"But I don't think they even know this beautiful romance they have been living. They would not put it in those terms, but I can. And particularly for someone whose own marriage didn't last."

Chris and her husband were divorced in 1993 after a 21-year marriage.

"To look at them and see the connection — they still finish each others' sentences. When they walk out the door, they always reach for the other one's hand. It's instinctive. They have a wonderful partnership, and what he doesn't do well or doesn't handle well, she does. And vice versa. She has been the mother that my dad never had; she's been the love of his life. She's been his best fan" — Jo has kept a detailed scrapbook of Bill's accomplishments since the 1940s — "and she's also his critic. But she is the most loyal person to those whom she loves, and my dad needed that and found that in her."

Jo and Bill have become happier people because they keep each other in line, Chris said. Jo is the pennypincher, Bill is a spender. "If you can't go first class, stay home" is one of his favorite sayings. Jo and Bill balance each other. They've leaned on each other during medical problems and during disappointments — such as their draining, unsuccessful attempt to adopt a child in the 1960's. But the good times have far outweighed the bad, and their perspectives have provided a wonderful chemistry that has made their relationship so special.

"My mom is a rather black-and-white person. I'm a person who lives in gray," Chris said. "With my mom, it's either right or wrong; it's good or bad. My father has tempered that in her, and when she gets a little judgmental or a little ornery and her Italian background comes out in her, he's the one who can say to her, 'You know what, you think about that again.' And she will rely on his judgment."

In 1997, in her 70s, Jo was diagnosed with breast cancer and underwent a lumpectomy.

"I was with Dad in the hospital when the surgeon told us, and I saw his face go gray," Chris said. "And I remember stupidly thinking, 'Well, I have to see them through this.' "

It was Bill who took charge. He told the surgeon he would tell his wife about her condition. The doctor and Chris left the hospital room and Bill gently broke the news.

The Campbells returned to their Haddonfield rancher, where they have lived since 1977, and, a short time later, Bill took his wife for radiation treatments and trips to the oncologist every day for about a week. The doctor then suggested that Jo drive herself to the appointments. The doctor wanted her to have some independence and "wanted to show her she wasn't at death's door," Bill said.

Early in the treatment schedule, Chris went to her parents' home and explained to her father that she would take some time off from her lawyer duties to help chauffeur her mom to appointments.

"I took for granted that I would be required and needed," Chris said, "And my dad just sort of looked at me and said, 'We appreciate it, but Mom and I will see this through. And if we need you, we'll tell you. But you have to go to work. You have your life and you take care of your kids.' And this circle — they just drew this circle around each other. I'm not sure they ever expressed to the other one how scared they were. It was just, 'We have to do this now.' "

For years, it was Jo who had taken care of Bill as he fought a battle with ulcers and Crohn's disease. Now it was Bill's turn to look after his wife.

During their marriage, Jo has catered to Bill, lined up his daily medication, stocked the refrigerator with food that he is allowed to eat, nagged him about what he is permitted to order when they go to a restaurant.

"She would gently oversee things for him, and she's been doing it forever," Chris said. "He doesn't even understand it. We see it from the outside. And I think my father saw my mother's illness as an opportunity to take care of her and he took advantage of it. As a child of these people, what a lesson that was for me. It was, 'Give us the space to say what we need to say to each other and hold each others' hands and get through this.' "

Jo was declared cancer-free in 2002.

———·——

Earlier in his career, Campbell had opportunities to pursue network jobs. He frowned on the idea because it would mean moving to

New York and uprooting his family. Or taking a daily train ride to New York and spending more time away from Jo and Chris.

Bill was a Philadelphian, plain and simple.

"I didn't like New York," he said. "I didn't like the influence of New York. Every time I had to go up there to do something, I never enjoyed it. Maybe I thought it was too big. I couldn't wait to get out of there."

He did do a few things for New York after Red Barber, his idol, became the CBS sports director and asked him to contribute to a college football roundup for the network. Barber would anchor it from the studio. Sometimes Bill would have to be in the New York studio, other times he would broadcast from Philadelphia, where he would report on Penn's game or the Army-Navy matchup. Vin Scully would report from another game in another part of the country.

The CBS folks frequently told Bill his voice belonged on the network. He never had a concrete offer, but the implication was that there were jobs that he could have if he pursued them.

Begrudgingly, he applied for one of them. CBS had a national scoreboard show for college football, and Jack Dolph, who used to be the program director at Campbell's station, Channel 10, asked Bill to audition. Dolph was now CBS' sports director.

"Jack, I don't really want to do it, but I appreciate you thinking of me," Campbell told him.

Dolph kept persisting. Bill caved in.

At the end of his audition, Dolph approached Campbell.

"You're a lock. You're going to get this job," he said.

Three days later, Dolph phoned Campbell. "Of all the guys who auditioned for the job, you had the best audition," he said. "But you're not going to get it."

It had nothing to do with Campbell's voice, nothing to do with his delivery, nothing to do with his ability to ad-lib.

It had everything to do with his hair.

"We just found out the sponsor is Vitalis," Dolph said, "and you're losing your hair, so...."

The network's loss was Philadelphia's gain. It was also a gain for his family. They would have Bill closer to home.

"Bill had many opportunities to go to the network, but he'd always say, 'I'm a Philadelphian and a Philadelphia sportscaster," said Julie Rooney, Bill's sister. "The main thing in Bill's life is his marriage, and I remember him saying to me, 'Almost everybody I ever knew from Philadelphia who left to go to the network, their marriage didn't make it.' "

Bill and Jo were strict parents. They were determined not to spoil their only child. There were always questions about where Chris was going and what she was doing when she went out for the night. And there were curfews. Lots and lots of curfews.

"I knew if I was out and called, I'd be fine. If I told the truth, I'd be fine," Chris said. "If I screwed up and lied or just tried to pull it over on him, I'd be dead meat. I actually had a healthy fear of that. I did not want to be in a position to have Dad yell because I'd hear it and the whole neighborhood would hear it, too.

"That voice carried!"

The vocal chords had gained power from his years on radio and TV.

"You did not want to have Dad yell at you," Chris said. "It was like hearing God Almighty yell at you."

Chris looks back on her father's rough upbringing — "a childhood right out of Dickens, just aimless and rootless," she said — and she wonders how he became such a great father.

"He didn't always have the best lesson on how to parent and how to father, but he figured it out," she said. "He's one of the most solid people I have ever met. He knows exactly who he is. His faith has been tremendously important to him throughout his life. He doesn't argue with anyone who doesn't agree; he just goes about his business. I think that somewhere along the way, he was fortunate enough to find a path that he could happily and comfortably travel, and he just stayed on it. And no matter what disappointments he has had, or heartbreaks, or challenges, he's always gotten himself back on the path. And he was fortunate. My mother is a very maternal person. I think he found in my mom so much of what he missed growing up, without a strong female presence in his life."

As she was growing up, Chris wasn't all that interested in sports.

"I often felt bad for Dad. I know he didn't feel bad and I'm glad he had me, but he should have had a son who was sports fan," she said with a laugh. "Guys would come over to pick me up and if he was home it was hard to get them out the door again because they were so thrilled to meet him. I took being his daughter for granted. And if he said, 'Let's go to the game tonight,' it was like, 'Oh, God. We're going to sit in the press box.' That was not the most thrilling thing for me growing up. I certainly appreciated what he did and how well he did it, but it's really only since I had my kids and we took them to the ballpark and went to some wonderful games.....and I got some perspective. Now I'm a great football fan. I love the Eagles. When it's summer it's like, 'Please get the football season started.'"

While Chris wasn't a die-hard sports fan growing up, she still became identified with her father. When she transferred from Villanova to St. Joseph's at the start of her sophomore year, Bill helped her move into her dorm.

"My dad arrives with me, which means I now have like six guys helping me take my stuff to my room," Chris said with a smile. "Not because of me but because they want to talk with him."

Later that night, after going to orientation, Chris returned to her room and was greeted by a huge homemade sign on the door:

"Oh,Baby! Bill Campbell's Daughter Just Moved In!"

Chris laughed at the memory.

"And of course, that's who I was for a long time on campus," she said. "I was 'Oh-baby-Bill-Campbell's-daughter-and-she-just-transferred-from-Villanova-to-St.-Joe's, yes!'"

Bill Campbell is at his best when he's telling a story. Pick a subject — any subject — and Campbell seems comfortable. Whether it's the Eagles' special-teams' woes, United States politics, or the war in Iraq, the man can talk for hours. With authority.

Yet, when his daughter was going through a painful separation and, ultimately, a divorce, Campbell held back his thoughts.

The world-class conversationalist didn't want to interfere.

Six months after Chris' husband left, she felt her world was falling apart. Her two children, Kate and Kevin, were distraught, and Chris was strapped with financial burdens she didn't expect to carry.

Angered and scared, she sat with her parents at their kitchen table in Haddonfield.

"I was just stuck and feeling miserable for myself," she said.

As Chris and her mother sobbed, Bill eyed the situation and didn't know if he should give his viewpoint.

Bill had been reticent to criticize anybody in the marriage breakup. "I think he was just trying to step back and let the dust settle, and maybe we'd work it out," Chris said. "He wanted to stay out of it as best he could and be a presence when he was needed."

On this day, with tears falling from the two women in his life, Bill felt needed. He was tired of biting his tongue.

"All right, I'm going to tell you something," he said.

Startled, Chris snapped to attention and sat back in her chair.

"This guy is misleading you and you must stop crying and look at your life and decide to move on," he said. "You can stay stuck here in miserable and waste your time and waste your education, or you can *do* something. It's up to you."

Chris took a deep breath and stopped crying.

"It doesn't mean I never cried again," she said. "But these words of wisdom, coming from a person whose opinion I respected and who knew my ex and knew me, I can't explain exactly why but it turned the tide. Something clicked."

The outburst gave Chris the direction she needed. Her father always knew how to cut to the chase.

"His assessment of the situation — 'It stinks but it's not the end of the world, you can get through it' — gave me the first little piece of confidence that maybe he's right. It will be OK," she said. "And I never forgot that and I've told him years later. As I look back, that was a turning point for me. And, of course, he pooh-poohs it, but he shouldn't. It was very important to me."

In a way, Bill became a surrogate father to his grandchildren, Kate and Kevin, who were 15 and 13, respectively, when their parents were divorced in 1993. The children lived with Chris, and their father wasn't around that much to visit.

Pop-Pop — Bill — filled the void.

"My dad is a very, very solid and grounded person," Chris said, "and when things go badly in life, while I know my mother is always there for me, the person who will never fall apart is Dad for me and Pop-Pop for my kids. My dad, in his own way, put me back on my feet again and really prodded me to get back into the world. And I owe a great deal to him."

Though a lawyer, Chris' real passion is singing. She is a song leader and soloist at a Cherry Hill, New Jersey, church where her dad is a lector. "When we're doing the same Mass, we say, 'You have the A-team here, Father. You don't want to mess up,' " Chris said.

Chris pulled out a photo of the grandmother she never met, Nan, who died while giving birth to Bill. Nan was seven years old in the photo and she was flanked by her younger sisters, Mae and Marge — the aunts with whom Bill stayed in Atlantic City during the summers of his teenage years.

"I always wondered where my voice came from," Chris said. "And when my aunt sent me this photo, she sent a description of her sister, Nan, as she remembered her. She said she had a beautiful singing voice."

How wonderfully sweet, Chris thought, to learn that her singing ability came from the mom that her dad never knew....and the grandmother that she never knew. "I was so glad to find out there's some connection because I had no idea what she was like," Chris said.

———————

Chris is extremely perceptive, especially when analyzing why her dad has outlasted everyone in his competitive media field.

One of the reasons, she said, is his ability to make people feel comfortable — even those who have had a reputation for not getting along with others.

Norm Van Brocklin, Gene Mauch and Richie Allen (who became known as Dick Allen later in his career) are three prime examples.

They were not media darlings. They could be gruff, uncommunicative, and aloof. But around Campbell, they were borderline gregarious.

Campbell was always open to others' ideas and thoughts, always curious, always ready to spice a conversation with humor. That led to a comfort level that few media members have enjoyed with sports figures.

"Soupy," said Allen, the Phillies' bad boy of the 1960s, "is good people. Always an honest guy. I love Soup."

Campbell looked past perceived shortcomings of athletes, managers, and coaches. Instead, he found the good in people.

"I really believe none of us are perfect; we all have faults," he said. "You overlook that stuff. I'm sure people had to overlook things in me that probably annoyed the hell out of them. Some people were kind enough to do that. I always tried to look at the positive side. I was raised pretty much in a boarding school and the nuns and priests used to preach to look for good things in people. I always tried to do that, especially with Mauch. Mauch used to irritate the hell out of people with some of the things he did and said. But I had an opportunity, in Gene's case, to spend some quiet time with him in the car, when nobody else was around. I think those are the occasions, when you go one on one with somebody and he's not trying to impress anybody, that you really learn about a person. And we talked about the team and the players and why you would do certain things with certain guys. It was very interesting."

Mauch felt comfortable with Campbell. So did Van Brocklin.

"When he came here, Van Brocklin had a reputation of being a real tough guy to handle," Campbell said. "He had been in a big quarterback controversy with Bob Waterfield and Billy Wade in Los Angeles."

But Van Brocklin took a quick liking to Campbell.

"My father was not intimidated by a Dutch Van Brocklin or a Gene Mauch," Chris Campbell said. "And his determination to learn from them was greater than any reluctance he may have had to try to break their shell. I think my dad is a pretty likable person and I think he had a way, with his own humor and own style, of breaking down people's shyness or their inhibitions about talking. And I think they came to understand that if he saw them at a moment that wasn't their best, or if they might have confided that they made a mistake or did something wrong, he was not the type of media person who would get on the air the next day and exploit it."

There's a fine line between constructive criticism and blasting someone to make yourself sound important. Campbell has walked that line with skill, grace, and compassion.

That's why folks like Van Brocklin, Mauch, and Allen opened up to him. That's why Richie Ashburn, his former broadcast partner, once called Campbell "the best interviewer I have ever seen."

"He developed a way of being so professional, and yet warm and real," Chris said. "So the guy who would usually be reluctant to talk with people would find a comfort level with Dad."

As a result, it was all of us — the listeners and viewers — who benefited.

———•———

In addition to being a part of some of the most memorable events in the region's sports history — Chamberlain's 100-point game, the Eagles' 1960 title and their two failed Super Bowl attempts, the Phillies' collapse in 1964 and their championship in 1980 — Campbell has stories on virtually every team that ever performed for Philadelphia.

Chris and Jo were constantly asking Bill to chronicle his seven-decade sports journey.

"Whenever we're in the company of people and he starts telling stories, they're all quiet and listening and then one of them will say, 'Bill, you really ought to write a book. You have so many stories to tell,' " Jo said. "But for the longest time, he didn't think it was worthwhile."

"I'd say to him, 'You really have to start to write this down, Dad,' " Chris said. "You go to a restaurant with my father— first of all, you never make it through a meal without someone stopping, which is lovely — and he's always having conversations with people. He enjoys it. He doesn't resent it or anything. And I have truly seen waiters hang out late and keep pouring water at his table so they can hear the rest of the story he has begun to tell. God blessed him with a memory that most of us would kill for. These stories are very much intact in his memory."

With that in mind, Chris bought her dad a Dictaphone, files, and legal pads as a birthday present in the early 1990s.

Her goal: To get her dad to put down his memoirs and to start writing a book.

"He had begun doing these editorials on KYW, and they're little gems every day," Chris said. "I don't even get to hear most of them, but people will stop me and say, 'Did you hear your dad yesterday? He made the best point.' "

The more Chris thought about it, the more she wanted her father to write about his experiences.

"I told him, 'Dad, if you can't do it for Mom or me, do it for [his grandchildren] Kate and Kevin and do it for the babies [great-granddaughters Erin and Meghan] because they're going to want to know all of these fascinating times that you lived through. And of course, his response was, 'It wasn't so fascinating.' "

Chris' voice rose, like her father's when he was describing a Richie Allen rooftop homer.

"Yeah, it was!" she said.

In 2005, Bill finally agreed with his daughter and wife. He decided to collaborate on a book.

———

His family has been the center of Bill's universe. It extends to his sister, Julie, a widow whom Bill takes to the hospital every few weeks for treatments related to esophagus cancer.

"I can't tell you how many people have told me, 'Boy, are you lucky to have Bill.' And I always tell them, 'And Jo, too.' His wife is just as giving as he is," Julie said. Bill and Jo always include Julie in social events that revolve around their Catholic church, St. Pius X in Cherry Hill.

The church, Julie said, has kept Bill on a straight road throughout his life.

Chris agreed. She said her father's difficult childhood — the death of his mother when he was born, the separation of his father and stepmother, the constant changing of schools and homes — was made more bearable because of his faith and sports.

From conversations she has had with her dad and with relatives, Chris said, she thinks religion helped shape Bill's life.

"The church has always been very important to him," Chris said. "And contrary to all the horrible things we're reading about, the priests were very good to him. The nuns were a source of comfort to him. I think they took pity on him. He was a bright kid; he had great coordination and was active and could play any sport. I think between the church and sports, that saved him. He often said, 'If I didn't have to get up and go be an altar boy in the morning, get to school, and then have a game or a catch somewhere in the afternoon, I would have been in jail.' "

Campbell attends Mass at St. Pius X almost every day. His dedication to the church goes back to when he was a youngster and one of his role models was his mom's brother, "Brick," a former St. Joseph's Prep football player who got Bill interested in sports. Brick eventually left for the seminary and became a priest. Bill considered him his unofficial big brother.

Years later, it became a tradition: Father William Graham, S.J. — Brick — would stay at the Campbells' home for a few days after Christmas. "Every New Year's Day, we'd have neighbors and friends over and Brick would say Mass for us in the living room or right at the dining room table," Campbell said. "When we were living in Broomall and then in Haddonfield, we'd have 30 or 35 people packed in here and then Jo would order a big brunch and that's how we celebrated New Year's. It was a great way to welcome in the year."

Campbell finds comfort in attending Mass.

"Religion does play a big part in his life," said Monsignor William Brennan, the pastor at St. Pius X. "And he uses it everyday. Just the way he treats people and looks at people. He doesn't try to cut anyone apart. There was an article in the paper the other day and Bill was talking [fondly] about Harry Kalas. You'd think he'd pick on Kalas because he took his job, but that's not Bill. He doesn't hold grudges."

Three days a week, Bill is a reader during a Mass at St. Pius X. Before he reads from the Bible, he frequently checks out the pronunciation guide so he doesn't stumble over the words.

"He calls it my bestseller," Monsignor Brennan said. "It's like his cheat sheet."

Father Brennan and Campbell have developed a good-natured rapport over the years. The pastor explains to Campbell that being a lector will help prepare him for a career as a broadcaster.

"I tell him this will move him along," Monsignor Brennan said, smiling. "He might make it some day."

Finding a niche on news radio

To a lot of listeners, the best part about Bill Campbell's WIP radio show was the three- or four-minute monologue that he did at the start of each shift. It was clever, topical, and crisply written, with punchy lines that made you stop and pay attention. The subject could have been Jim Fregosi's robot managing or Buddy Ryan's love for the spotlight; it could have been the 76ers' need to acquire bench scoring or the Flyers' futility on the power play. Whatever the subject, you came away from Campbell's commentary feeling informed, feeling in touch with one of the most pressing issues on the Philadelphia sports scene.

About two months after Campbell left WIP and moved over to all-news KYW radio in September of 1992, it was an easy transition. In essence, it was an extension of his WIP monologues, except that they were shorter — they ran for a minute — to fit KYW's tight format. Campbell was hard-hitting but fair — not an easy balance to keep — and his dry humor and sarcasm made his words sing.

Take the start of this commentary early in the 2005 NFL season:

Andy Reid is a very good football coach, but not much of a media communicator. We would feel very safe as a nation if he ran the CIA.

Touche.

Some in the media call his weekly press conferences 'no-news' conferences.

Double touché.

He signed a kicker to replace David Akers, then failed to activate him. Akers strained a hamstring in Game 2, tore it in Game 3. But Reid called the injuries unrelated.

The sarcasm was so thick you needed a steak knife to cut through it.

After stepping down from WIP in 1992, Campbell did some Eagles pregame and halftime shows on WYSP, but he missed being in the middle of the Philadelphia sports scene. There would be a controversial issue that struck a nerve and Campbell needed to express his feelings on the matter.

"I'd get up certain mornings and there was something I wanted to say, but I didn't have the forum for it," he said.

KYW became his forum.

In 1992, Mark Helms, KYW's program director at the time, met Campbell at a South Jersey restaurant to see if he was interested in joining the station. "I expected to meet someone who had an ego and was boastful," Helms said, "but Bill was so down-to-earth, just a regular guy. He certainly had a lot of stories to tell, but he didn't act like we owed him a job. He was very respectful and you felt good meeting him and good hiring him because he was such a good guy."

Until that afternoon, Helms had never met Campbell. "But I felt like I had known him my whole life," he said. "When I was 10 years old, I can still remember sitting in my parents' car listening to Bill do the Eagles' championship game in 1960. I can still remember the excitement in his voice, and I remember him doing the Phillies games for all those years."

Helms and Roy Shapiro, who was then KYW's vice president and general manger, were responsible for bringing Campbell to the station.

"Bill is Philadelphia and Philadelphia sports, and we believe KYW is Philadelphia," said Shapiro, who retired from the station at the start of 2004, "so it seemed like a natural fit."

Hiring Campbell was "a win-win situation," Helms said. Bill could work a less-hectic schedule than at WIP, but still be involved with broadcasting. "He wanted to remain on the air, and we wanted someone who could add punch to our lineup," Helms said. "We both came out winners. With Bill, you get instant credibility and the recognition factor."

Bill Campbell makes last-second changes to a commentary he is about to narrate at KYW Newsradio's Cherry Hill office in 2005. The office closed a short time later and Campbell began filing his commentaries from his Haddonfield home.

You get a man who attended a record-breaking 1929 World Series game, covered a 1947 World Series epic in which Cookie Lavagetto broke up a ninth-inning no-hitter with a game-winning, two-out double, and reported on the 2005 World Series, when the Chicago White Sox won their first championship since 1917.

You get a man who has covered the Eagles — or did reports on the team — for every decade since the 1940s; a man who was reporting on the National Basketball Association when it was born in 1946.

You get a man who has been on the scene so long that he used to lend his WCAU office to Edward R. Murrow whenever the legendary CBS newsman — the subject of the critically acclaimed 2005 movie, *Good Night, and Good Luck* — was in Philadelphia to file stories from the city.

"Bill was a well-recognized figure in Philadelphia and we agreed that if we could find the right format for him, he'd be a great plus for KYW," Helms said. "We agreed on three commentaries a week, which fit Bill's schedule and certainly helped us. And the rest is history."

At the start of 2006, Campbell was 82 years old — though he looked 20 years younger — and except for some eye problems that made it difficult for him to drive at night, he was showing no signs of slowing down. He was in his 14th year at KYW, which, ironically enough, was now owned by CBS Radio. Campbell started working for CBS seven decades earlier, so, yes, his career had gone full circle.

His three weekly sports commentaries have helped him feel young.

"It's been great for me because it keeps me involved; it makes me use my noodle," he said. "It makes me current and it makes me write. It's like writing three columns a week; that's what it amounts to. Even such an accomplished guy as Bill Lyon said, 'I don't know how you do it.' "

Lyon, the brilliant former columnist for *The Philadelphia Inquirer*, had recently retired. "And he's considerably younger than I am," Campbell said with a smile. "I don't think there are too many guys who are still broadcasting at my age."

After undergoing laser surgery early in 2006 to try to correct a vision problem, Campbell said he had no immediate plans to retire.

The KYW gig, Campbell said, has forced him to stay on top of the Philadelphia sports world, "and it makes me go to the games. I don't go as much as I used to, but if I could ever get over this eye problem at night, I would go more frequently. But I'm scared to death to drive at night. If it's somewhat familiar territory, I can still drive. But when I get on the bridge in traffic, you better not be near me because I'm dangerous."

Campbell let out a robust laugh.

The eye problems didn't affect his close-up sight. He was still a vociferous reader; he still scoured several newspapers each day and almost always had a political book on his night table. The reading kept his commentaries current, kept him as the voice of reason on the region's sports scene.

When Eagles' starting linebacker Jeremiah Trotter and Atlanta backup cornerback Kevin Mathis were ejected for getting into a pregame skirmish before the Falcons' season-opening 14-10 win in 2005, Campbell put the developments into perspective in his KYW commentary.

Reading the words he had written on a yellow legal pad, Campbell filed this report:

While the Phillies pitched rookies, the Eagles' veterans stumbled.
A soapopera of a summer with an offbeat training camp carried over

to opening night, with the Eagles losing a key player before the national anthem.

Followed by some lack of focus, an appearance of not being ready to play. Completely uncharacteristic of an Andy Reid team.

Having said that, may I add this: Ejecting the players for a pregame hassle was a little much. Beyond the pale.

Break it up. Get them off the field. Fine them, if you choose, for disorderly conduct. But let's focus on the game.

It's opening night in the Georgia Dome; the adrenalin is pumping. The players' pregame nonsense was childish. But officials should be people of judgment and maturity.

And this was a scene that called for exercising both.

This is Bill Campbell, KYW Newsradio.

Terrell Owens' off-the-field antics stole headlines and air time in 2005. Begrudgingly, Campbell made the self-centered receiver a part of several of his commentaries.

Nov. 7, 2005

Football is the ultimate team game, as displayed by Penn State. Doormats of the Big 10 last year, now within a victory of the league title.

Nine and one this season, just seconds from perfection. Achieved through strength of character and amazing determination.

The good of "The Team" is what the Terrell Owens thing is all about. And why it has finally come to a head after festering much too long.

This Eagles' season of great expectations has become an inconsistent mess. Had something not been done about the reckless T.O., the rest of the season would have been anticlimactic.

For almost all of us, no matter our talent, someone signs the checks. And that very act of signature commands respect. Those are the rules of the game.

That someone as classless as Terrell Owens could accuse ANYONE of lacking in class — his own team, no less — could not go unchallenged. No matter the cost.

This is Bill Campbell, KYW Newsradio.

Nov. 9, 2005

I wish I could say these will be my last words on Terrell Owens. But that wouldn't be accurate.

He and his dogmatic agent were back at it yesterday — again on that coveted lawn in Moorestown — with T.O. reading that transparently phony apology.

Suddenly, it has penetrated — "Gee, these Eagles must be serious, they're taking my football away. What do I do now?"

Our time would be better spent talking about the Phillies' Ryan Howard, the National League rookie of the year. Or the future of Jim Thome, a really class act.

Or what the Flyers are accomplishing with Peter Forsberg and Simon Gagne. Or the Sixers. Or Villanova's lofty perch in the preseason basketball rankings.

Anything but T.O., who now says he's sorry while his agent trashes the media and then says, "Next Question."

This is Bill Campbell, KYW Newsradio.

Nov. 25, 2005

For some time, billionaire owners of sports teams have been trying to get on an even footing with the millionaire players. That's what the Eagles-T.O. fuss was really all about.

The baseball owners ignored the steroids issue until Congress got into the act. Basketball came up with a dress code and hockey lost a full season arguing about a salary cap.

In the NFL collective bargaining agreement, there is a clause about conduct detrimental to the team. The Eagles decided to exercise it on T.O.

Before forming an opinion, ask yourself what the reaction might be where you work if YOU parked in the boss' spot, told him to shut up, complained about your contract, and promised to become disruptive, among other transgressions. How long do you think you'd survive?

On the same day that T.O. was run out of town, a class act by the name of Jim Thome left agreeably. No hard feelings anywhere.

It's a shame Thome had to SHARE the headlines. He deserved a headline all his own.

This is Bill Campbell, KYW Newsradio.

———————

When Phillies general Ed Wade was fired by David Montgomery shortly after the 2005 season, Campbell offered a unique spin — and took a subtle jab at the Phils for his own dismissal many moons ago.

Has anyone considered that it could easily have been the Phillies in that historic 18-inning playoff game last Sunday?

And if it had been — especially if they had won — would Ed Wade still be the general manager?

Interesting questions.

David Montgomery is an honorable guy. This had to be a traumatic decision. He and Ed Wade were friends.

A general manager must know not only the on-the-field stuff, but he has to have a clue for the business side, the attendance and, for sure, media relations.

That, more than anything else, seems to have been Wade's problem. He was considered condescending by many on the beat and was so portrayed in the media.

That the media influenced fan opinion goes without saying, leaving Montgomery with just one objective: the best interest of the Phillies.

Ironically, the axe fell during the best season of Ed Wade's term. It's a cruel business and I speak from experience.

This is Bill Campbell, KYW Newsradio.

———————

Campbell's best pieces are the ones in which he draws from his vast experiences. As an example, here is his commentary from November 11, 2005:

Will you indulge me a personal memory?

Sportswriter Kevin Mulligan touched a memory nerve in his Daily News *column on Wednesday.*

He runs a little feature entitled "Whatever Happened To" and inserts a sports name from yesteryear with a brief biographical sketch.

This week, it was Steve Donches, a former St. Joe's basketball player. I've been wondering about him for years. I broadcast that historic St. Joe-Villanova game in 1966 at the Palestra.

Donches won the game with perhaps the longest shot at the buzzer in Big 5 history: 71-69, Hawks.

Underlying the memory, my wife and I had invited Jack Ramsay and Jack Kraft, the coaches, and their wives for dinner after the game. The first Sunday afternoon Big 5 game at the Palestra.

It was the most thrilling game I ever broadcast, even more so than Wilt Chamberlain's 100 points. Now it is startling to realize that was almost 40 years ago and that Steve Donches in a grandfather.

Thanks for the memory, Kevin.

This is Bill Campbell, KYW Newsradio.

In seven decades, Campbell has covered Eagles home games at Municipal Stadium, Shibe Park/Connie Mack, Franklin Field, Veterans Stadium and, now, Lincoln Financial Field. He has covered 18 Eagles head coaches — from Earle "Greasy" Neale to Andy Reid. He has covered quarterbacks from Tommy Thompson, who excelled despite losing the central vision in one eye as a child, to Donovan McNabb, and virtually everyone in between. He has reported on Steve Van Buren and Timmy Brown, Tom Woodeshick and Wilbert Montgomery, Ricky Watters and Brian Westbrook.

All those years, all those games, have given him a wonderfully unique perspective when comparing players from different eras. On September 21, 2005, he demonstrated that perspective:

David Akers' injury and the arrival of The Eagles Encyclopedia *triggered some old memories. The book, by Ray Didinger and Bob Lyons, is hot off the press.*

No true Eagles fan should be without it.

Akers' injury got me thinking about another kicker of yesteryear, a very underrated Eagle named Bobby Walston.

He is the Eagles' all-time leading scorer; he was also the tight end, the last Eagle to lead the league in scoring. And a key player during the 1960 championship season.

He might have been the smallest tight end in football, but he was such a good athlete that Norm Van Brocklin said Walston would play till he was 60. Unfortunately, he died at age 59.

He once played a game with a broken jaw. When he broke his arm, he continued to kick with his arm in a harness.

David Akers is that kind of competitor.

This is Bill Campbell, KYW Newsradio.

In mid-September of 2005, he also went down memory lane:

Once upon a time, a couple of generations ago, a man named Gus Dorias introduced the forward pass to football.

It revolutionized the game. Players like Sammy Baugh and Sid Luckman and others became household names.

On Monday night in Atlanta, the Eagles threw the ball 45 times, ran it just 14 times against a blitzing defense. Maybe it's time for Andy Reid to re-introduce the run. Especially if your quarterback is Donovan McNabb, whose health may not be 100 percent.

As for where the Phillies will finish, I have no idea. Nor does Ed Wade or Charlie Manuel or Billy Wagner. Somehow, I have to believe that Wagner could make the difference.

Because they could come that close. Who thought they would win those two clutch games with two rookie pitchers starting? Has there ever been a more unpredictable team?

Are we seeing the rebirth of the Phillies or the collapse of the Braves? Stay tuned.

This is Bill Campbell, KYW Newradio.

Oct. 7, 2005

There was a time when I thought that Ed Snider was a major prob-
lem in Philadelphia sports.

That was maybe 40 years ago. Snider was with the Eagles then. I
was broadcasting their games, among other things.

Now as I drive though and around the sports complex in South
Philadelphia, I think about Ed Snider in a very different light.

I see the Spectrum and the big, cavernous [Wachovia] Center and
the two impressive stadiums — all of which might never have happened if
not for the vision and courage of Ed Snider.

He got the whole thing started. He brought big-league hockey here.
Created the Flyers, who are now back in business.

As is Ed Snider.

He has been involved with three of our four major sports teams —
and our overall sports image has been better for his presence.

His only immediate need? Probably a victory tonight over the Devils.
This is Bill Campbell, KYW Newsradio.

Maybe it was all his years of experience that made him cau-
tious, or maybe it was just because he grew up with the city's mostly
sad-sack sports franchises. Whatever the reason, Campbell did not
feel confident when the Eagles faced the Tampa Bay Buccaneers in the
2003 NFC championship game.

Few gave the Bucs a chance. The Eagles were playing the final
game in Veterans Stadium's history and would receive an unparalleled
emotional charge from their pumped-up fans. And besides, Tampa can't
play in cold weather, went another theory. In their sorry history, the Bucs
were 1-21 when they played with the temperature under 40 degrees.

Campbell, in his KYW commentary a few days before the game,
looked beyond those theories and issued a warning: Do not assume
the Eagles are headed to the Super Bowl in San Diego.

I can't be the only one around here who remembers Connie Mack Stadium, who can recall feeling so privileged to walk into Veterans Stadium in 1971 and enter our new palace of sports. That's why it's a bit hard to digest this business of how to eliminate it: by implosion or piece by piece. And why some of us wince when we hear it called "The Dump." And there is also the attitude of so many, proclaiming that all the Eagles have to do in this last football game at the Vet is show up on this path to San Diego; that Tampa Bay again will slump at The Dump. Maybe. But, please, this is only the semifinal. For the record, if the Eagles show up without their "A" game Sunday, they could lose.

He was right. Tampa ignored the 26-degree temperature, a super-charged home crowd, and the fact that it had been 0-6 in post-season road games in its history.

Final: Tampa Bay 27, Eagles 10.

———·———

Like Campbell, Bill Roswell was fascinated by radio at a young age. As a 14-year-old living in Cherry Hill, New Jersey, in 1964, he received a 21-in-one electronics kit for Christmas. The kit's best feature was a tiny radio that had to be assembled.

The radio could pick up only one station — WCAU. Roswell would put on his earphones at night and listen as Campbell, By Saam, and Richie Ashburn described the Phillies' games. Like thousands of other listeners, the ups and downs of the season fascinated Roswell. So did the broadcasters. Their friendly voices gave him a feeling of comfort, a feeling that life was good.

Even when the Phillies weren't.

"Bill was always such a great storyteller," said Roswell, now the managing editor at KYW.

Campbell's storytelling, even though his segment ran for just a minute, became a KYW staple. "He makes you think when you hear him," Roswell said.

The station took pride in having announcers who weren't looking for fame, weren't on ego trips. All the personalities were the same. All exuded professionalism. While other radio stations' hosts looked to shock listeners with their banter, KYW's announcers were white-bread bland. By design.

"At KYW," Roswell said in a matter-of-fact tone, "the news is the star."

The format worked. The station was usually the highest-rated in Philadelphia and among the most-listened-to news stations in the nation.

Campbell's commentaries are aired on Monday, Wednesday, and Friday at 9:45 a.m., 11:15 a.m., 12:45 p.m., 2:15 p.m., and 3:45 p.m.

Well, at least most of the time they can be heard at those times.

"Sometimes I get blotted out by such conspicuous figures like President Bush or Ariel Sharon. Or people like Judge Alito or Senator Specter or Ted Kennedy," he said with mock amazement. "How dare those guys! Who do they think they're fooling with!"

Campbell was the closest thing the station had to a star. But he wasn't a star in a Howard Stern or Angelo Cataldi way. He was a star because of his longevity and, quite simply, because his perspective and hard work made him so widely respected.

That kind of star, KYW executives figured, would fit with their ultra-successful format. The addition of Campbell was met without jealousy from any of KYW's longtime sports broadcasters.

"Bill is an icon. Having a guy like Bill Campbell, with his pedigree, how could anyone complain?" asked Harry Donahue, who has worked for KYW since 1973 and started doing sports for the station in 1978.

There aren't many inflated egos in the radio business, Donahue said. "If this was TV, maybe somebody would have complained," he said with a smile, "but not on radio. Bill was a welcome addition."

It was Donahue who indirectly played a part in Campbell's hiring. Donahue had been doing sports commentaries for KYW, but "it got to be too much" because of his workload in other areas, he said. "I wanted to come off the commentaries because I was so busy, and I remember telling someone at the station that Bill Campbell would be great doing them."

"They don't come any better or more professional than Bill Campbell," said Shapiro, the retired KYW executive. "And Bill knows every nook and cranny about the listening audience."

And he never took shortcuts. If a major sports story broke after he had already written his commentary, Campbell did the professional thing: He rewrote his piece and filed another broadcast. Like the March morning in 2006 when an icon named John Chaney surprisingly resigned as Temple's men's basketball coach.

Campbell brought "an authoritative perspective because he's seen everything under the sun," said Roswell, who has worked at KYW since 1980. "He's experienced things that no one else has. He can talk about Donovan McNabb and about Norm Van Brocklin. That was then and this is now. Or the whole T.O. mess. He has believability. He's somebody people have listened to for…"

Roswell searched for the right time frame.

"For forever!" he decided.

"The listeners know him; they trust him and they believe him. They may not always agree with him, but I think he has their respect."

It was Roswell who unknowingly extended Campbell's career in the summer of 2005. KYW was closing its South Jersey bureau in Cherry Hill — where Campbell, after a short drive from his Haddonfield home, would do his three weekly broadcasts into a microphone and an engineer sitting in the station's Philadelphia studio would record it and put it on the air.

The tiny Cherry Hill studio, which he shared with Ed Kasuba, KYW's South Jersey bureau chief, was located within a high-rise of business offices on Route 70. The studio wasn't glamorous, but it was comfortable — and it was convenient for Bill because it was close to his home. In a rather plain office, which included a coffee maker and a small TV and had a wall with colorful old press credentials hanging from their strings, Bill would practice his commentary in front of an oversized wall clock that looked like it belonged in an elementary school. When he had it down to 60 to 65 seconds, he was ready to record. With his left hand cocked behind his left ear, Campbell would then read his commentary, fax the copy — always handwritten on legal paper, and "pauses" signified by his half-inch vertical marks — over to KYW's Center City offices. After it was over, he'd head over to the 9 a.m. Mass at St. Pius X in Cherry Hill. Bill liked the routine and was disappointed when it was disrupted.

Late in the summer of 2005, KYW closed its Cherry Hill bureau. Steve Butler, the station's program director, told Campbell he wanted him to continue his reports; he explained that all he needed was a computer and that he would send Roswell to his home to set things up. The beauty of it, Butler told Campbell, was that he could file the reports from home. Heck, he could do it in his pajamas if he wished.

Campbell didn't like the idea. Not the pajama part. The part about filing reports through his computer. He was intimidated by the new technology.

"I thought this was the end for me," he said. "There's no way, at my age, that I wanted to try to do this. I thought, 'You know, I've been doing this for a long time and maybe it's time. Maybe I've overstayed my leave and this is a good way to end it.' I came close to saying to Steve Butler, 'Tell Bill Roswell not to waste his time because there ain't no way I'm going to learn how to do it.' "

It didn't help matters that, a few years earlier, Campbell had taken a computer course at Camden County College and found it a waste of time.

"I got nothing out of it," he said. "It isn't like when you're young and listening to a professor lecturing and you take notes, and some of the stuff stays with you. It's not that way when you're older. It went right over my head and I got nothing out of it. It wasn't the teacher. There were 10 or 12 people in the class, mostly women, and they seemed to be absorbing this stuff. But I was out of it."

His fears were eased when the patient Roswell, a model of professionalism, made four trips to Campbell's home and gave him one-hour tutorial sessions on how to record and send his commentary through the computer.

"He let me sit by the computer and screw it up, and then he taught me how to fix the screwups," Campbell said. "And all of a sudden, it didn't seem quite so impossible for a dope like me to learn this. I do it all by myself now and I owe it all to Bill Roswell."

And so, to borrow a By Saam-ism, Bill Campbell's remarkable broadcasting career kept rolling along....edging closer to his eighth decade in the business.

CHAPTER SIXTEEN

The Hall of Fame calls

When Bill Campbell received a phone call from Dean O'Keefe, an executive with the Naismith Memorial Basketball Hall of Fame in Springfield, Massachusetts, he figured someone was playing a joke.

At first, he thought it was Ed Kasuba, one of his KYW Newsradio colleagues, who was trying to trick him.

Then it dawned on him. This wasn't the work of Kasuba; it was the work of comedian Joe Conklin, the impressionist who was the king of practical jokes.

Damn, that Conklin. Didn't he have something better to do?

But the more O'Keefe talked, the more his story seemed credible. He told Campbell he had tracked down his phone number from the *Daily News'* Phil Jasner, who had won the Hall of Fame's print-journalism award the previous year. He explained details about the award ceremony and mentioned some of the past winners.

Suddenly, Bill Campbell realized this wasn't a joke.

He was going to the Basketball Hall of Fame in 2005, the winner of the Curt Gowdy Award for electronic media.

"I couldn't believe it. I was totally shocked," he said.

"Some people know they're a candidate, but Bill never even knew he was being considered," O'Keefe said. "He had no idea why I was calling."

In previous years, Campbell had been inducted into the Philadelphia and Pennsylvania Sports Halls of Fame, along with the Broadcast Pioneers of Philadelphia Hall of Fame.

Campbell was humbled and appreciative to be selected, "but it was never one of my great ambitions to be a member of a hall of fame," he said. "I'm grateful, don't misunderstand. But I've never been completely overwhelmed by halls of fame."

Fame didn't mean anything to him. His life revolved around his family, his church, his friends, his sports, his community. The awards? They were nice, but he enjoyed them more for the chance to be reunited with old acquaintances than for the awards themselves.

But even the unassuming Campbell got an extra measure of satisfaction from his latest honor. This award, because it was on a national stage, had more prestige than any of his previous hall-of-fame selections. What made it particularly rewarding was that the award was named after Gowdy, the former Boston Red Sox and national announcer who was one of Campbell's highly respected contemporaries when he did Phillies' games.

It also put Campbell among pretty select company. Some of the previous winners of the electronic media award were Dick Enberg, Chick Hearn, Johnny Most, Billy Packer, Marv Albert, Bob Costas, Dick Vitale, Dick Stockton, and Jim Nantz.

As the days passed and Bill thought about his acceptance speech, he kept going back to that 1962 night in Hershey. The game he had called "a farce" now seemed like a very special part of the broadcaster's resume.

Wilt Chamberlain's 100-point performance, he said, was one of the major reasons he was selected to go to Springfield.

"There's no question about it," he said. "I'm associated with that game, and I'll always be grateful to Wilt. Thank God he scored 100."

In a way, Wilt had placed the diminutive Campbell on his wide shoulders and carried him into the Hall.

"I did a lot of NBA games, a lot of college games, a lot of Big 5 games," Campbell said, "but I think the Wilt Chamberlain thing probably helped a great deal."

Funny thing is, Campbell's broadcast of that 100-point game would not have been shared with millions of fans if not for the generosity of a listener.

The day after Chamberlain reached triple digits, Campbell was sitting in his WCAU office when a fan called and told him he had recorded the final quarter of the game. "He said to me, 'I know you probably have a professionally made tape of the game, but I have the last quarter if you want it,' " Campbell said. "He had an amateur recorder, which, in those days, was not very good. He said he had the last quarter and he wanted me to have it as a gift."

Campbell smiled at the memory.

"I thought to myself, 'Where do you live? I'll come right over and get it!' It was like a gift from Santa Claus."

Campbell said WCAU had not taped the game, so he was grateful for the fan's kindness.

"He sent it to me, and it was pretty scratchy, a homemade job. But I gave it to the sound guys at the station and they cleaned it up and got some disturbances out of it and it made it presentable," Campbell said. "And for a long time, that was the only tape in existence, as far as I know. Gary Pomerantz in his book [*Wilt, 1962*] says somebody else had another tape that he got somewhere, but I don't know anything about that one. The tape that was sent to me was the only tape I knew was available — or thought was available — for a long, long time. When Wilt was elected to the Hall of Fame, he called me from L.A. and said, 'Do you have the tape of the 100-point game?' I said, 'Yeah, I have the last quarter. He told me to send it to the Hall of Fame because they have nothing. I sent a dub of it to them and, for a while, it you called the NBA office and asked for somebody, they'd put you on hold and they'd played the greatest moments in NBA history — and that was one of them because I heard it on the phone."

Back in 1962, when Chamberlain had his 100-point game, radio stations didn't tape every broadcast.

"Now they tape everything; they tape when you go to the bathroom," Campbell kidded. "It wasn't a common procedure back then, but I should have done it. I mean, 100 points."

Then again, Campbell had no way of knowing that history was going to be made that night.

"He had 69 points after three quarters and it was obvious he was going for 100," Campbell said. "And as a broadcaster, the thing that was ever-most in my mind was to keep the mathematics straight, to make sure that when he got 100, that he really had it. When he did it, oh, how the crowd poured out of the stands. How they finished that game, I'll never know."

In fact, it wasn't until 2005 — 43 years after the historic event — that Campbell realized the game had been completed.

"All these years, I thought they never finished the last 46 seconds of that game. I had been telling everybody that the game was never finished," Campbell said. "I was doing a TV show with Lou Tilley and he had a tape of the game and, sure enough, I heard myself broadcasting the last 46 seconds."

Before the 63-year-old Chamberlain's death in 1999 of congestive heart failure, Campbell went to many banquets with the man they called Dippy. "It's amazing how many times people would come up to Wilt at the head table and, you know how people like to pop off, tell him how they'd never forget that night he scored 100," Campbell said. "I heard one guy tell him, 'Wilt, I was there in the Garden the night you scored 100 and it was the greatest thing I've ever seen.' And another time, a guy says, 'Wilt, I was right there in Convention Hall when you got 100.' "

The game, of course, wasn't played at Madison Square Garden or Convention Hall; it was held in Hershey. But Wilt never bothered correcting the admirers.

"I asked him why he never said anything to them, and Wilt smiled," Campbell said. "He said it was the umpteenth time that it's happened to him. I believe him because I know I saw it at least twice."

While Chamberlain's 100-point game was Campbell's most famous basketball broadcast, it wasn't his most memorable. That distinction belongs to Game 6 of the 1980 NBA Finals, when Lakers 20-year-old rookie point guard Earvin "Magic" Johnson, spending time at center because of Kareem Abdul-Jabbar's injured ankle, collected 42 points, 15 rebounds, and seven assists in a title-clinching 123-107 win over the 76ers at the Spectrum.

"One of the greatest performances I have ever seen," Campbell said. "Magic did everything. He brought the ball up, set screens, rebounded the ball; he played all five positions. I enjoyed doing that game even though the hero was on the other team."

———

Campbell found out he was the Basketball Hall of Fame's electronic media winner when he received a phone call in June of 2005. Less than two months later, he and his wife, Jo, and their daughter,

Chris, headed to Springfield for the September 8 ceremony. Bill turned 82 the previous day.

"They're coming to my birthday party," Campbell cracked. "I still can't get over the surprise. It never once entered my mind that I'd be eligible for a basketball award, but I guess I've done enough games — and thank God for Wilt Chamberlain!"

His daughter, Chris Campbell, beamed at the national recognition her father was receiving.

"My dad takes tremendous pride in his work, but he has very little ego," she said. "He is a genuinely humble person, and I think he's genuinely surprised that, at his age, he's being recognized for this.

"When I heard about it," she added, laughing, "I thought, 'Well, Cooperstown and the NFL Hall of Fame should be following soon.' "

The induction ceremony went without a hitch. Campbell and *Sports Illustrated's* Jack McCallum were honored as the media winners, and five people were inducted into the Basketball Hall of Fame: Jim Calhoun, coach of Connecticut's 2004 NCAA championship men's team; Jim Boeheim, who led Syracuse's men's team to the 2003 NCAA title; Hubie Brown, a two-time NBA coach of the year; Brazilian women's star Hortencia Marcari; and the late Sue Gunter, who was the third-winningest women's coach in NCAA history.

Campbell was his typical unflappable self as he gave his thank-you speech, ad-libbing the piece.

O'Keefe, the man who had phoned Campbell and informed him that he was going to enter the broadcasters' wing of the Hall of Fame, said Campbell's "genuineness" left an impression with him.

"Sometimes you get winners who are jaded," O'Keefe said. "With Bill, you could see he was genuinely excited. He was like a kid in a candy store and not like someone who thought it was just another event to go to."

Jo Campbell said the award "came out of the blue because he hasn't done basketball in such a long time." Jo oozed with pride during the Hall of Fame festivities. She had been by Bill's side — and had been his No. 1 supporter — since the very start, so in a way, this was her award, too. Had it really been 43 years since Bill broadcast Chamberlain's 100-point game? Had it really been 59 years since Bill proposed to her as they were watching *Finian's Rainbow* in a Philadelphia theatre?

A deeply sentimental person, Jo liked to surprise Bill by writing him a poem on special occasions. She didn't do it the day Bill went into the Hall of Fame; eight years earlier, however, she showed her love in words as they celebrated their 50th wedding anniversary in 1997:

> *Can it really be 50 years*
> *Since we stood side by side?*
> *The up-and-coming sportscaster*
> *And his blushing child bride?*

A little more than 100 heartfelt lines later, Jo came to a realization:

> *He was on the road half the time*
> *NOW I know how we survived!*
> *It isn't fifty years at all…*
> *It's only twenty-five!*

Bill and his wife, Jo, proudly pose for a photo on the day Bill was honored by the Naismith Memorial Basketball Hall of Fame in Springfield, Massachusetts, in 2005.

If Jo had written a poem about Wilt Chamberlain, it may have started like this:

He liked to party and stay out late,
The opposite of an early riser.
He scored in triple digits once,
And bragged he was a womanizer.

Decades after his 100-point performance, Chamberlain became known for making some outrageous statements. The most bizarre was his claim that he had slept with more than 20,000 women.

During his playing days, however, Chamberlain wasn't nearly as outlandish in his dealings with Campbell.

"Every encounter I ever had with him was OK," Campbell said. "He had a reputation as a prima donna and all that, but he went out and played every minute of every game — and [Warriors coach] Frank McGuire let him do it. Whatever he wanted to do, he did. I'm sure if he lived in New York and played in Philadelphia, he missed a lot of practices or came and sat around in practice like Allen Iverson does now. It seems like every time you look up, Iverson is at practice but he doesn't work out. But he plays 45, 48 minutes every night. Wilt played 48 minutes every game that year. He told Frank McGuire that's what he wanted to do and Frank let him do it."

Campbell says he doesn't recall Chamberlain being a remarkable interview. "I don't remember any unpleasant instances," he said, "but he wasn't around that much; he got there in time for the game and the shoot-around. He played the game, took a shower and he was gone."

Chamberlain wasn't nearly as colorful, Campbell said, as the Warriors' owner, Eddie Gottlieb.

Gottlieb, who was inducted in the Basketball Hall of Fame in 1972, was one of the NBA's pioneers. At one time, he served as the Warriors' owner, general manager, coach, and chief ticket seller. Nicknamed "The Mogul," Gottlieb helped establish the Basketball Association of America, the forerunner of the NBA. He served as chairman of the NBA Rules Committee for a quarter century, and he played a role in nearly every NBA innovation, such as the 24-second clock.

Back in the early 1950s, Campbell would share a room with Warriors head coach George Senesky when the team was on the road. Gottlieb usually remained in Philadelphia. Lucky him. He didn't have to sit next to Senesky on flights. Campbell did, and he jokes that he still has Senesky's fingernail marks in his arm. Senesky, who had a fear of flying, would grab onto Campbell during different points of the flight.

It was not a big traveling contingent.

"Money was very tight in those days," Campbell said. "We had a 10-man team and George and I made it a 12-man traveling party. If one of our players got hurt, he was in the hands of the home trainer. It was just 12 of us; the press didn't even travel with us in those days."

When the Warriors were on the road, Gottlieb would keep track of the team from Campbell's radio broadcasts. After one game, he called Campbell in a huff. Campbell had told listeners that the Hawks' Bob Pettit had been cold from the foul line. No sooner had Campbell uttered the words, Pettit made several free throws in a row to send the Warriors to a defeat.

Gottlieb blamed Campbell.

"If you would have just kept your mouth shut and not made such a big deal about the guy missing all these foul shots, we might have won," Gottlieb said.

Campbell smiled as he remembered the phone call.

"And he meant it; he really thought I was the reason we lost," he said. "He called me a couple of times to chew me out."

Senesky received more irate phone calls than Campbell. Many more.

"He'd chew him out about the lineup he was using, about the substitutions that he put in. You name it," Campbell said.

"But I really liked Eddie. He was a really good guy and an unbelievable character. Eddie could walk into any arena in America and he could tell you, within a couple hundred, what the exact attendance total was that night. He had a brilliant mathematical mind. He made up the schedule for the entire league on a notebook in his pocket. He did what computers do now. He not only made up the local schedule but the *league's* schedule. And we used to travel to places like Moline, Illinios, Davenport, Iowa. We went to some ungodly cities."

Gottlieb, who served as the NBA's lone schedule-maker for more than 30 years, organized and coached a professional team representing the South Philadelphia Hebrew Association (known as the SPHAS) in 1919. The birth of the SPHAS is one of the few pieces of Philadelphia sports history that Campbell missed. Campbell was born four years later and he recalls the SPHAS dominating the Eastern Pro League and the American Basketball League from the late 1920s to the mid-1940s.

The SPHAS games, with Dave Zinkoff serving as the public-address announcer, were actually secondary to the dances that followed. "People went for the dances more than the games. Nobody paid much attention to the SPHAS as a formal pro franchise," Campbell said. "It was more of a social event than anything else."

In his pro basketball broadcasting career, Campbell covered the SPHAS, Warriors, and 76ers. Of all the basketball people he met during those seven decades, no one made a more lasting impression than Gottlieb, a man whom former NBA Commissioner Larry O'Brien called "Mr. Basketball."

Hail, Soupy! 76ers president Pat Croce raises his arms to salute Bill during festivities in 2000, when the club held "Bill Campbell Night" and honored the broadcaster for his years of service.

Campbell seconds that label.

"Eddie was one of the most colorful, brightest guys I've ever been around," Campbell said.

Gottlieb owned a Negro League baseball team in Philadelphia and had hoped to become one of the Phillies' owners, Campbell said. But a deal was never consummated. If it was, it may have been the Phillies, not the Brooklyn Dodgers and Jackie Robinson, who broke baseball's color barrier.

———

In 1996, as part of a celebration for the league's 50th anniversary, the NBA announced the 50 greatest players of all time. Campbell has seen all of them play. In person.

Campbell's all-time 10-player NBA team includes two players —Joe Fulks and Kobe Bryant — who are not on the panel's list of the 50 greatest players. Bryant had recently graduated from Lower Merion High and had yet to play in the NBA when the league released the team, so he wasn't eligible for the list. Fulks was just overlooked.

When you consider Campbell has covered the NBA since its inception in 1946, his opinion carries more credibility than the NBA's top-50 voters, many of whom weren't even born when the league originated.

Campbell's first team is composed of Chamberlain, Michael Jordan, Fulks, Larry Bird, and Magic Johnson, while his second team consists of Elgin Baylor, Oscar Robertson, Jerry West, Paul Arizin and Bryant.

Mention any of the players on the NBA's all-time, 50 top-player list and Campbell can give you a description of their style of play and can talk, authoritatively, about their strengths and weaknesses.

Perhaps just as impressively — and certainly more charming — he can also provide colorful anecdotes about most of the players.

Take the Boston Celtics' Bob Cousy, for instance.

The Cooz was one of the greatest passers and playmakers in NBA history. Known as "The Houdini of the Hardwood" because of his spinning, razzle-dazzle dribbling and his no-look and behind-the-back passes — he was the Magic Johnson of his day — Cousy was a 13-time all-star during the 1950s and 1960s.

During that era, Campbell was preparing to broadcast a Warriors game against Cousy's Celtics from Convention Hall when Eagles general manager Vince McNally approached him at courtside. At the time, Campbell was also the Eagles' broadcaster, so he and McNally had been friendly.

Twenty minutes before the game, McNally tapped Campbell on the shoulder.

"I want you to do me a big favor, Bill," McNally said. "I'm a Bob Cousy admirer and I've never had the pleasure of meeting him. I wonder if you would introduce me to him."

"Sure," Campbell said.

At the time, the Celtics were going through their layup drills. Cousy, Bill Russell, Tommy Heinsohn, and the rest of the dynasty were coached by Arnold "Red" Auerbach.

"The Celtics were right in front of us, and Cooz was a real good guy," Campbell said. "So the next time he went by, I put my arm out and stopped him. I said, 'The guy standing behind me, Bob, is Vince McNally, and he's the general manager of the Eagles and he asked to meet you. The next time you come around in your drill, would you stop and shake hands with him?' And Cousy said sure. So he went up and laid the ball in and the next time he came around, he stopped and I introduced the two of them. Vince was very grateful and Bob was fine — and all of a sudden, this *enraged* Red Auerbach, who had been sitting on the bench, comes tearing up to me and says, *'What the hell are you doing with my team?!' What are you doing?!!!* How *dare* you interrupt my team's layup drill! And he proceeded to chew the living hell out of me. It never would have happened today, but Red was in complete control and his layup drill was important to him, and I interrupted it and he wouldn't let me forget it."

After the game, Auerbach again addressed Campbell.

"I went into the locker room. The Celtics had won the game and he was all calmed down, and he said to me, very calmly, 'I'm sorry I laid into you, but don't ever do that,' " Campbell said. "I said, 'Red, I had no idea [it was going to bother you].' I told him that the guy who asked me to do it was a friend of mind, and he's also the general manager of the Philadelphia Eagles. It wasn't just some fan from out of the stands. It was a guy of some reputation."

Campbell laughed as he recalled Auerbach's reaction.

"And Red said, 'I don't give a damn who the hell it was, don't ever interrupt my layup drill.' "

Campbell didn't hold it against Auerbach; he figured the coach was just looking after his future Hall of Fame player. Paying attention to detail, after all, made Auerbach a Hall of Fame coach.

Just like it made Bill Campbell a Hall of Fame broadcaster.

CHAPTER SEVENTEEN

"Good Night, Good Sports"

As Bill Campbell looks back on his still-flourishing career, he recalls fondly the 1960 NFL championship game between the Eagles and Green Bay Packers as his No. 1 thrill. The fact that the game wasn't on local TV (it was shown nationally but blacked out in Philadelphia) made his radio broadcast even more special. Anybody who was an Eagles fan — including many of the 67,325 spectators who attended the game and listened to Bill's broadcast on transistor radios — was tuned into his exhilarating play-by-play account.

It didn't have to be an NFL championship for listeners to feel an intimacy with Campbell's broadcasts, to feel as if he was sitting across your kitchen table discussing the ups and downs of your favorite team. That feeling was also conveyed when he broadcast middle-of-the-season Phillies, 76ers, or Eagles games. It is more difficult for today's broadcasters to develop an intimacy with their listeners, simply because there are so many more options, so many more sports channels and stations, so many more games to choose.

Today, there is an over-saturation of sports, and sports coverage. When Campbell did the games, sports didn't have a big-business edge to them. The games were more pure, the athletes more accessible, the times more innocent.

The sports industry was more fun and less cutthroat in the days when Campbell ended his WCAU sportscasts with "Good Night, Good Sports." There was a sense of adventure, a sense of camaraderie that isn't as prevalent today.

Take the September 3 afternoon in 1947, when Campbell was filing reports on the Philadelphia A's for WCAU radio, a CBS affiliate. A right-hander named Bill McCahan was pitching a no-hitter for the Athletics against the Washington Senators.

In the eighth inning, Campbell got a phone call from Red Barber, the sports director for CBS radio who was calling from the New York studio.

"Do you have a car with you?" Barber asked.

"Yeah."

"If he pitches a no-hitter, can you bring him down to the 'CAU studio because I would love to do an interview with him at 6:30?" Barber said.

McCahan, a 26-year-old from Duke who was a Philadelphia native, finished his gem. He became the fifth rookie in American League history to pitch a no-hitter, blanking the Senators, 3-0, before a sparse crowd at Shibe Park.

Campbell phoned Barber and gave him the news. Barber sounded excited.

"Drive him to the studio and tell him there's 50 bucks in it for him," Barber said.

Campbell complied.

"Fifty bucks in those days was a lot of dough," he said. "Guys would jump through a hoop for 50 bucks."

In the clubhouse after the game, Campbell recalled A's second baseman Pete Suder moaning about the lack of attendance that day and taking delight that they missed watching a little piece of history.

"It serves these goddamn fans right for not coming out to see the game," Campbell remembers Suder saying.

After the post-game celebration, Campbell told McCahan that Barber wanted him to be on CBS radio, coast to coast.

"Now today, you have a remote and you do the interview right there in the clubhouse after the game," Campbell said. "You didn't do it like that then. You didn't have the facilities. So I went over to McCahan after everybody was done interviewing him and I said, 'Red Barber is doing his show on CBS and he wanted me to ask if you would get in the car with me and drive down to 'CAU?' "

It was McCahan's moment of fame. He finished his career in 1949 with a 16-14 lifetime record.

"McCahan was a disciple of Jack Coombs," Campbell said, referring to the former Athletics pitcher who once won 80 games over a three-year span and later became the respected baseball coach at

Duke, "and he looked like he was going to be a helluva pitcher, but he never did much after that year."

McCahan was thrilled to do the five-minute interview.

"He said, 'Sure, no problem,' " Campbell said. "Players did things like that in those days."

Ah, those were the days. The days when the athletes, fans and the media generally made the same salaries. They lived in the same neighborhoods, drove similar cars, traveled in the same circle of friends.

Money changed all that.

The multimillionaire athletes became walking corporations. Many developed an air of combativeness with the media. Most became guarded when they did interviews.

Back in the '40s, '50s and '60s, covering teams was a lot more enjoyable for the media — and the athletes — than today. Unlike today, the athletes weren't besieged by several dozen reporters at a fairly meaningless regular-season game. Back then, the athletes seemed to find pleasure with the coverage.

"I used to go down to the Warwick Hotel every Friday afternoon because a visiting baseball team was always staying there," said Campbell, who worked for WCAU radio at the time. This was the start of the golden age of baseball, the 1950s. "Joe DiMaggio, Ted Williams, Bob Feller, Johnny Pesky, Dom DiMaggio. Anybody you can think of. If you asked them to stop over and do my radio show on the way to the ballpark, they'd say sure. Most of the time we paid them nothing. I think we later paid them $25 so they could use it for a cab to get to the ballpark, and I don't ever remember a guy turning me down. Can you imagine trying to do that now? You'd have to go through an agent and negotiate. It was a different age back then."

It was an age when reporters had to hustle to get their reports on the air. Campbell remembers covering a famous afternoon World Series game at Brooklyn's cozy Ebbets Field in 1947, taking the subway back to CBS' New York studio and telling WCAU (now WPHT) radio listeners that pinch-hitter Cookie Lavagetto had hit a double with two outs in the ninth inning to ruin Bill Bevens' no-hitter and give the Dodgers a 2-1 win over the Yankees.

So what if he had to fight through a crowded subway to file his report? That was part of the adventure, part of what it meant to be a hard-scrabble reporter who worked six or seven days each week.

Things weren't quite as adventurous in the '60s. Technology advancements made it possible for interviews to be done at the ballpark. When Sandy Koufax pitched a no-hitter to beat the Phillies at Connie Mack Stadium on June 4, 1964, Campbell didn't have to drive him to a studio.

He did the post-game interview in the dugout.

"I could have stayed up in the press box and done it from there, but that was a bad way to do it because the player can't find the headsets in the dugout and there's no one there to help him," Campbell said. "I did the star-of-the-game show back then and I used to call down to the batboy in the seventh or eighth inning and ask him to tell so-and-so that I'd like to talk with him after the game. I can't ever remember being turned down. Willie Mays, Sandy Koufax, you name him. They all came on."

Campbell would broadcast the ninth inning and then take a crowded elevator down to the field to do his post-game show.

After Koufax pitched his 1964 no-hitter to beat Chris Short and the first-place Phillies, 3-0, the Los Angeles Dodgers' lefthander waited patiently for Campbell to meet him in the dugout. Koufax had faced the minimum number of batters — Richie Allen reached on a fourth-inning walk but catcher Doug Camilli threw him out when he tried to steal second — and had struck out 12, including every batter at least once except for Cookie Rojas. He whiffed pinch-hitter Bobby Wine to end the 1-hour and 55-minute contest.

"He was dying to get into the locker room and get a shower and all, and I had one of the batboys get him a beer or something while he waited," Campbell said. "When I got down there, I told him I really appreciated it and he said, 'No problem.' We'd give them 25 bucks in cash as the star-of-the-game guest and they loved to get it."

In general, athletes were less self-centered when compared to their 21st-century counterparts. Perhaps it's because they don't need the 25 bucks anymore. Perhaps it's the strain of the media coverage. In the '60s, you may have had a half-dozen reporters covering a Phillies game, for instance. Now you might have 100, many of whom come in different waves and unknowingly repeat the same questions that were asked a few minutes ago.

Now you have talk-radio hosts and Internet writers who are quick to criticize even though they rarely make an appearance at an event.

"Players resent it. They really do," Campbell said. "I have found that if you show your face once in a while and they know who you are, they'll accept criticism a little bit. But if you never come and they don't know where this is coming from, they say, 'Who is this guy saying this? I don't even know who he is. What does he know?' And then they get their back up."

Athletes weren't as skeptical about the media when Campbell started his career. Nor were they as defensive.

"I'll bet in my whole career I can't remember more than two or three occasions when a player has come up to me and was really teed off about something I said on the air," Campbell said. "I remember [the Phillies'] Turk Farrell got mad at me one time; he was near the end of his career and he was knocked out of a game one day and somebody told him — it's always *somebody told them* because they didn't hear it, so their wives or *somebody told them* — that I said they were hitting line drives off him. He said, 'What are you talking about? They were off the end of the bat,' that kind of thing."

That "chewing out," as Campbell called it, seems oh-so-innocent when compared to the age of The Pampered Athlete, when a Barry Bonds goes into an expletive-laced tirade because he doesn't like a reporter's question.

Another time, Campbell received a phone call from Sara White, whose husband, Reggie, was a star defensive end with the Eagles. She was upset with something Campbell had said about White on his WIP talk show.

"She thought I was unfair to Reggie," Campbell said. "I don't remember the specific complaint. I was polite to her and, as far as I was concerned, that was the end of it. The next day, I got a call from Ron Howard, the Eagles' PR guy, and he asked if I could do him a favor. He said Reggie wanted me to have a discussion with him after practice. I said, 'Ron, are you serious?' My immediate reaction was, 'Tell Reggie White if he wants to talk with me, he knows where to find me.' But then I reconsidered and figured if I could smooth things over, fine."

A date was set. Campbell went to practice and, after it was over, he waited in the locker room for White.

"Reggie, you wanted to see me?" Campbell asked.

"Give me a couple of minutes, Bill," White said.

White walked away from his locker. "He went into the trainers' room. The all-sanctimonious trainers room, where the sinners [media] are not allowed," Campbell said with a laugh.

White was gone for nearly 25 minutes. "Finally he comes out and walks right past me and goes into the shower room," Campbell said. "And he was in the shower for 15 minutes and he came out and went down the other end of the room and dried off. Now I've been sitting in the locker room for almost an hour; it's getting to be kind of ridiculous. And he's chatting with the guys and players and all that, and I finally went over to him and said, 'Hey, Reg, did you want to see me?' He said, 'Oh yeah.' I said, 'Well, I've been here now about an hour or so and I can't wait much longer. What's on your mind that you'd like to talk about?' He said he couldn't remember. I said, 'Reggie, my time is as important as your time. I've got to go to work. If you've got something to say to me, say it now because I'm leaving.' He didn't say anything. Nothing. It was ridiculous."

Campbell didn't hold a grudge. He overlooked the incident and developed a rapport with White.

When Campbell retired from WIP in 1992, several athletes phoned the station to thank him for his professionalism and to offer their congratulations.

White was one of the callers.

—•—

Campbell is more than a proverbial walking encyclopedia for anything connected to Philadelphia sports. Much more.

And he doesn't just have the memory of a main event — the time he watched Babe Ruth slam a homer out of Shibe Park and onto 20th Street, or when he witnessed Army's famed "Mr. Inside" and "Mr. Outside," Doc Blanchard and Glenn Davis, run wild in Philly — but he has countless behind-the-scenes anecdotes that give the Philadelphia sports world so much color, so much texture.

There are hundreds of examples, including his tales about the Eagles' Frank "Bucko" Kilroy and Philadelphia boxer Joey Giardello.

Kilroy — who, as a scouting consultant, helped the New England Patriots win three of four Super Bowls from 2002 to 2005 — was a standout Eagles defensive tackle in the 1940s and '50s with a reputation for being a dirty player. Kilroy was featured in a 1955 *Life* magazine story that focused on the violence of pro football.

Campbell said Kilroy's wife helped her husband clean up his act.

"One day I'm in the press gate at Connie Mack Stadium to broadcast an Eagles game, and walking in front of me was Bert Bell, who was then the commissioner of the league," Campbell said. "As we walked through the gate, a lady came running over. We didn't know who she was and she said, 'Commissioner?' And he said, 'yes.' And she said, 'I'm Mrs. Kilroy, Bucko's wife.' "

"Nice to meet you, Mrs. Kilroy," Bell said.

"I just came over here to tell you that you cost me a fur coat," she said.

"And how did I do that?"

"You fined Bucko so much money, and that money was supposed to buy me a fur coat."

That gave Bell an idea, Campbell said.

"Bert very quickly said, 'Mrs. Kilroy, I'll tell you what I'm going to do. If you keep Bucko fine-less and tell him he's got to play the game the right way and he goes through the whole year without a problem, the National Football League will buy you the best fur coat you have ever seen.' "

Campbell chuckled.

"They had no more trouble with Bucko. He didn't have another fine the rest of the way," he said.

Mrs. Kilroy got her fur coast.

As for Giardello, he was preparing to fight highly regarded Gil Turner in 1953. In those days, CBS televised Wednesday night fights to the nation and, when the telecast ended, Campbell would do a local show on Channel 10. On this night, Campbell interviewed Giardello and Turner, a pair of Philly fighters, and hyped their upcoming welterweight fight.

"After they did the show, I didn't have checks to give to the guys and I was really embarrassed," Campbell said. "Somebody in our accounting department forgot about them, so I told them I would bring their checks. The day of the fight, I go into Gil Turner's dressing room and they're taping him up and I give his manger his check. Then I go over to Giardello's dressing room — I had known him a little bit — and I said, 'Joe, I'm sorry I didn't have the check the other day.' He said, 'Don't worry about it. No big deal.' "

Giardello wanted to talk about his fight with Turner, who took a 36-1 record, including 27 knockouts, into their bout.

"I see I'm the underdog, huh?"

"It looks that way," Campbell said, mindful that Turner was a 3-1 favorite.

"Where are you sitting?" Giardello asked.

Campbell gave Giardello the location of his ringside seat.

"You know what I'm going to do?" Giardello said. "Just for you — and you can tell anybody you want — I'm going to knock this kid on his ass and you know what I'm going to do? I'm going to knock him right on your lap."

Campbell smiled.

At one point, with 7,377 fans watching at the Philadelphia Arena, Giardello knocked Turner through the ropes.

"A couple of feet from where I was sitting," Campbell said in an amazed tone.

Campbell still doesn't know what impressed him more: Giardello's unanimous decision or the fact that he had almost put Turner on his lap, just like he had promised.

Ten years later, after an upset of the legendary Sugar Ray Robinson, Giardello would become the world middleweight champion. After beating Dick Tiger for the title, Giardello held the crown for nearly two years, and one of his decisions — a win over Rubin "Hurricane" Carter— was scrutinized in the 1999 movie *The Hurricane*. Giardello sued the film's producers, claiming he was defamed and that the facts of the fight were fictionalized.

Giardello eventually settled out of court — for a lot more than the $50 check that Campbell delivered to him in 1953.

Baseball was Campbell's favorite sport to cover. Track and field was his worst. Especially the Penn Relays.

"This will probably offend some people who think the Penn Relays are the end-all — and they are to a lot of people — but I was never a track-and-field participant and never had much interest in the Penn Relays," Campbell said.

He smiled.

"And my boss at 'CAU knew that and insisted that I cover them. It was like punishment. They're very difficult to cover for a radio guy. Maybe not for a newspaper guy who is assigned to cover a certain event. But there are so many events, and it's difficult to do on radio when you have to cover the whole spectrum. It drove me crazy."

Not all media members despised the Relays.

"Ted Husing loved it," Campbell said. "Ted was one of the great all-time sportscasters, the dean of sports at CBS for many, many years."

Husing is the guy who indirectly got Campbell interested in a radio career. It was his Husing's description of the thrilling 1937 Davis Cup match that transfixed Campbell, then 13 years old, and steered him toward a broadcasting career.

Now Campbell was one of Husing's colleagues, and they would usually compare notes during the several days that they covered the Penn Relays at Franklin Field.

"Penn thought so much of him that they built him a special platform to broadcast the mile run," Campbell recalled. "In those days, there were some great milers, and they built this platform and sat it right near the finish line, with a swivel chair so Ted could follow the runners. Two or three days before the final mile run, Ted became ill and had to stay in New York, where he lived. I was told I was going to do the mile run."

As Campbell broadcast the event, he felt he was doing a credible job — until the third lap.

"As I went to spin around and follow the runners, I fell off the chair and fell to the ground. On the full CBS network!" Campbell said with a laugh. "I scrambled back up and, on the air, I just said that I slipped off Ted's platform. Ted called me three or four days later and said, 'What the hell happened?' I told him and that didn't endear me to the Penn Relays."

———

Franklin Field was also the site of perhaps the saddest moment of Bill's broadcasting career. It was where Bert Bell, the man who revolutionized the NFL, died while watching the two teams he had once owned, the Eagles and Pittsburgh Steelers.

Campbell had become friends with Bell, the former Eagles owner/coach who had become the NFL's commissioner. Bell, who negotiated the league's first national TV contracts and helped the NFL become part of Americana, grew up in a prominent Philadelphia family, and was the son of John Cromwell Bell, Pennsylvania's attorney general. Bert Bell's brother, John, was a justice to the Pennsylvania Supreme Court and he also served as the state's attorney general and, briefly, as its governor.

Bert Bell didn't make his mark in politics. Football was his passion and, as commissioner, he protected the sport like it was his baby. If he heard an announcer making what he perceived as a critical comment about the league or one of its teams, Bell would summon the broadcaster for a meeting.

Campbell was summoned many times.

Still, Campbell had a great rapport with Bell, who had married Broadway actress Frances Upton. Bill and Jo became friendly with Bell and his wife.

"Bert was a character," Campbell said. "He was the black sheep of his family and he fell in love with a gal named Frances Upton, who was a Ziegfeld Follies gal. And on one New Year's Eve, in the President Hotel in Atlantic City, he got completely ossified. And he took a glass and filled it up with Scotch and proposed to Frances. And she said, 'I wouldn't marry you if you were the last guy on the face of the earth.' She said the only way I will ever marry you is if you give up drinking for the rest of your life. And with that, he took this glass of Scotch and drank it, chug-a-lug, and fell on the floor. He passed out. He later married Frances and never had another drink again for the rest of his life. True story. And

Bill, with a little help from his five-year-old daughter, Chris, broadcasts a Philadelphia Warriors game in 1957.

Frances was waited on hand and foot and they raised three children, and their daughter wound up as the producer in Hollywood."

Before Campbell broadcast the Eagles-Pittsburgh Steelers game on October 11, 1959, he met with Bell, who was one of the few people who referred to Bill as "Willie."

"Bert, you haven't been a guest on our broadcast this year and I really think it's time you go on," Campbell said.

"Willie, you know I can't climb all those steps to the press box," Bell said. "That's why I haven't been able to do it. That's a long haul for me."

Bell, the NFL's commissioner since 1946, finally told Campbell he would do his best to get to the press box at the end of the game.

"He said to me, 'I'll tell you what I'll do. I'll try to start up there at the beginning of the fourth quarter, and I'll sit and rest, and maybe by the end of the game, I can get there,' Campbell recalled Bell saying. 'I won't promise I'll get there, but I'll do the best I can.' "

With two minutes left in the game, in the stadium where he began his football career as a Penn quarterback in 1919, Bell died of a heart attack at around the same time that Eagles receiver Tommy McDonald scored a touchdown.

McDonald later said part of the crowd was cheering the TD, and fans on the other side of the stadium were yelling and scrambling as they tried to get Bell some assistance.

Campbell went into the locker room after the Eagles' 28-24 win and was unaware that Bell, 64, had been stricken,

"I could tell something unusual had happened because there was a cluster of people all around the corner of where the Eagles dressed," he said. "My wife was down there and a lot of other people. Everybody was in tears and all upset. My wife came over and told me what had happened, that Bert had died in the stands."

Campbell remembers Bell as a fun-loving person — and a man who fought his wife's pleas to convert him to Catholicism.

Bell lost the fight.

"Frances was a devout Catholic and Bert was not, although he always claimed that he lit more candles than the pope. And he said he spent more money on candles than anybody in the history of the Catholic Church," Campbell said. "For years, Frances tried to convert him to the Catholic faith and he would have none of it. Finally, years later, we're sitting at home in Broomall and the phone rings."

It was Bert's wife.

"She says to me, 'Bill, are you doing anything important tomorrow? And I said, 'not really.' She said, 'Would you and Jo come over to St. Margaret's Church in Narberth at noon?' I thought it was an unusual request and I asked her why, and she said that Bert was going to put on a white suit. And then she said bye and hung up. I couldn't figure it out."

She meant that Bert was going to join the Catholic Church.

"Their whole married life, Frances had been trying to have him baptized," Campbell said.

Bill and Jo went to the church the next day. Bert was dressed in his white suit, ready for the big event.

"We get to the church and Bert's going to be baptized. He obviously had been taking instructions, which none of us knew at the time," Campbell said. "He's walking up the steps of St. Margaret's Church, and Joe Donoghue, who is the treasurer of the Eagles and is going to be Bert's godfather, says to him, 'Bert, you don't have your teeth!' And Bert, who must have been in his 60s, says, 'Did you ever see a baby baptized with teeth?!' "

Campbell laughed loudly.

Bell hated wearing his dentures. This was the perfect time to leave them home.

———————

They say the measure of a person is how much of an impact he or she has on others. That makes Bill Campbell arguably the most influential person in Philadelphia history.

Think about how many lives he has touched in his seven decades. Think about how many hours of pleasure he has given to listeners and viewers. Think about how many dinnertime conversations he has triggered with his thought-provoking commentaries.

To appreciate Campbell's impact, consider his plight after he was called for jury duty in the early 2000s.

Campbell was one of 50 candidates to serve on a jury in front of Theodore "Ted" Davis, a New Jersey Superior Court judge. "The lady in charge of herding us all around told us if she didn't call our name, we were dismissed," Campbell said.

When he didn't hear his name, Campbell was relieved. "I thought, 'This is great, I can get out of here,' " Campbell recalled. "So I got up out of the jury box and I went to walk out of the courtroom, and just as I put my hand on the doorknob to get out, the judge sitting on the bench says, 'Mr. Campbell.' I said to myself, 'Oh, man. I'm not out of here yet.' "

Judge Davis was making Campbell squirm.

"And he says, 'Would you please approach the bench.' I'm thinking to myself, 'What is this?' " Campbell said. "So I walked over and he says, 'Would you like to go on the stand and testify about the condition of the Phillies?' And I said, 'Is that a request or an order, sir?' "

"Get out of here!" Davis said with a smile.

Whether Campbell is in a courtroom, playing a round of golf (his one-time 12-handicap has climbed to 20), picking up groceries at the store, or getting something to eat at a restaurant (linguini with clam sauce is his favorite), people gravitate toward him. Some want to talk about his latest commentary, some want to get his spin on the Phillies, Eagles, 76ers, or Flyers.

Some just want to go down memory lane.

"I can't tell you how many times people stop me and say they were on 'Timeout,'" said Campbell, referring to the Saturday morning radio quiz show he did starting in 1948. The WCAU show had pro athletes and coaches as guests — they did it for free, Campbell said — and it had primarily teenage boys as contestants. "A month doesn't go by when someone will tell me they were on that show. These are guys that are now in their 60s and 70s and are lawyers and doctors and whatever. They all tell me they won a prize on the show."

Campbell loves to reminisce with fans, loves his early radio days.

Radio, in fact, has always been his favorite medium. Even in the days when he did TV, he had a special feeling for radio broadcasts.

"There's something about radio; as a broadcaster, you felt more involved in the game," he said. "With TV, you have to worry about the camera angle and how you look at all that. I just enjoy radio. It gives you a chance to be more descriptive. I think you learn more about the game from radio — and you're more intimately involved in the game. Even today, I'd rather listen to a game on the radio."

Football, he said, was his most difficult sport to broadcast. "It's the greatest challenge because you have to worry about 44 different people and it demands more concentration than the other sports," he said.

Harry Gamble remembers listening to Campbell do some of his earlier broadcasts. Back then, Gamble was a fan. He later became the Eagles president and one of Campbell's closest friends. The two live near each other in tree-lined Haddonfield.

In 2003, Gamble, who now serves as a consultant to the NFL commissioner for American football in Russia, saluted Bill at his 80th birthday party at the Tavistock Country Club.

Gamble wrote the eloquent words, but he spoke for the entire region when he delivered them.

"Today, we are honoring a special person, a friend to me as well as everyone in this room. For athletes of yesteryear, it is wonderful to come to our 'dream of dreams' and remember moments from the past. Our heroes cannot come back in time and perform again, but we can recall them in our

minds, remembering the thrilling moments they gave us, and no one does this better than Bill Campbell.

Bill was a pioneer in broadcasting. He was — and is — a tireless worker who has devoted his life to his profession. You have left an indelible mark on the Delaware Valley as an unparalleled performer in your field.

But in addition, you are a great human being. It is with much humility that I say thank you, Bill, for all that you have given to us..."

He has given us more than any broadcaster in Philadelphia history. He has given us joy (the Eagles' 1960 title) and sorrow (the Phils' 1964 foldup), thrills (Wilt's 100-point game), and agony (the 9-73 76ers). He has given us corny commercials: *"You get a smile, everytime, with Ballantine. Wow, what a beer!"* And descriptions that still leave goose bumps: *"Big string-bean right-hander comes sidearm to Allen. And there sheeeeee GOES! A TREMENDOUS drive. Way, way, WAY up on the roof in center field. A home run. Ohhhhh, baby!"*

But mostly, William Thomas Campbell Jr. has given us objectivity — always with excitement in his voice, always with the Philadelphia fans foremost in his mind.

"They are," he said, "the most passionate and knowledgeable fans in the country. They demand that you play hard."

———

Harvey Pollack, the Hall of Fame statistician, estimates that Campbell has broadcast more than 1,200 games with the Warriors and 76ers; 1,600 Phillies games; 250 Eagles games, plus another 150 college football games; 250 college basketball games, and 50 minor-league baseball games. Add it together and you have 3,500 contests, with a majority of them losses for the home teams.

That's a lot of games, a lot of time away from home, a lot of hotel food.

It's also a lot of special memories.

"I've loved every minute of it," said Campbell, temporarily forgetting about the 9-73 Sixers and the Phillies' 1964 collapse. "I wouldn't have wanted any other job. It keeps you young."

Broadcasting is more difficult today, Campbell said, than when he broke into the business seven decades ago. (Actually, his career has spanned eight decades if you count when he was a high-school student and did a nonpaid radio show for WTEL in 1939.) Media saturation has made fans much more knowledgeable. So has the Internet.

"People know a lot more about the athletes than they ever did," Campbell said. "The sportscaster really has to put in time and do homework" to come up with a unique story.

Campbell loved working alongside former pro athletes such as Rich Ashburn and Tom Brookshier, among many others. They were pros in the booth, he said. But he is troubled by the influx of former jocks into the media.

"It's changed things dramatically," he said, "and not for the better. I don't mean to generalize, because some guys do prepare and have made real contributions. On the other hand, most of the players who have come into the business have crossed the line between being a good analyst and being an entertainer. That's TV's fault in a way. The rewards are high; they cross the line and they became show biz. They're entertainers. It's happened to a lot of guys and I regret that. You hear them telling jokes and talking about all the parties. It makes you want to turn it off, which I do a lot."

Campbell has literally interviewed thousands of athletes in his decades as a broadcaster, including a staggering 57 people who have made it into the Baseball Hall of Fame. He has watched, in person, 111 players who have reached the Hall.

Asked to put together his all-time baseball team of players that he has seen in person, Campbell came up with the following:

Rightfielder: Babe Ruth.
Centerfielder: Willie Mays.
Leftfielder: Ted Williams.
Third baseman: Mike Schmidt.
Shortstop: Marty Marion.
Second baseman: Bill Mazeroski.
First baseman: Jimmie Foxx.
Catcher: Mickey Cochrane.
Right-handed pitcher: Bob Feller.
Left-handed pitcher: Sandy Koufax.

Campbell ranks Norm Van Brocklin as his favorite athlete of all time, followed, in order, by Robin Roberts, Julius Erving, Steve Van Buren, and Bobby Shantz.

All were special in their own way, Campbell said.

"Robby was — and still is today — the epitome of class. I could say that about all these guys," he said. "Dr. J has had his controversial moments since he retired, but I was around him for quite a while and, to me, as far as being cooperative, he was excellent. And Van Buren was a guy who showed more humility than any athlete I have ever known."

Campbell said Van Buren — a Hall of Fame running back who, though he retired before the 1952 season, still holds several Eagles offensive records — was a man of his convictions.

"In those days, Stetson hats were a very big deal. Almost every man wore a Stetson hat; even young men wore Stetson hats," Campbell said. "And the advertising manager from Stetson came to Steve and said, 'We would like you to do a commercial for us.' And Steve said, 'I don't know. I don't think I want to do it.' The guy said, 'Is it a matter of money? Because we could probably negotiate.' And Steve says, 'No, I don't wear a hat.' And he meant it. That defined his personality. That was an honest definition of his personality. Steve didn't want to do anything that wasn't him."

Sort of like the anti-Terrell Owens or Joe Horn.

———

Harry Donahue, the veteran KYW sportscaster, has a unique perspective of Bill Campbell's broadcasting career.

Growing up in the Olney section of Philadelphia, Donahue remembers listening to Campbell broadcast the Guy Rodgers-led Temple team in the NCAA men's basketball Final Four in 1958, and St. Joseph's in the Final Four in 1961, when the Hawks faced an Ohio State team that included John Havlicek, Jerry Lucas, Larry Siegfried, and Bobby Knight. (The NCAA would force St. Joe's to relinquish its third-place finish because of a gambling scandal.) He remembers listening to Campbell's reverent commentary when 93-year-old Connie Mack died in 1956, and being spellbound by Campbell's broadcast of the Eagles' 1960 NFL championship win over the Green Bay Packers, a game that Donahue recorded on an old reel-to-reel tape.

Years later, Donahue worked alongside Campbell broadcasting Temple basketball games when the Mark Macon-driven Owls were one the nation's premier teams in the 1987-88 season. And Donahue now frequently introduces Bill's commentaries on KYW Newsradio.

"I've gone full-circle with Bill, from listening to him as a kid and admiring his work to now working with him," Donahue said.

Donahue cherishes some of the stories that Campbell has shared with him over the years.

"There was the time he and Bill Bransome were doing the Eagles games in the '50s and they drive up to cover their game against the Giants in New York," Donahue said. "They get to the Polo Grounds with the engineer and the place is locked up. They were at the wrong stadium! Back then, the Giants also played home games at Yankee Stadium, so they hurried over to Yankee Stadium and they just made it before the kickoff.

"Something like that, of course, could never happen today" during the Information Age.

Then there was the time Campbell was filing college football reports for CBS radio. Red Barber was the moderator. Vin Scully, then an intern for the network, was doing Harvard reports from Boston, while Campbell was giving updates on Penn from Philadelphia.

"The weather is bad in both cities, and Red Barber keeps going back and forth to get game reports from both places," Donahue said. "Whenever he goes to Bill, he says [on the air] that the rain is coming down and the wind is blowing terribly and he's having a tough time reading his notes, and then they switch to Scully and he never referred to the weather at all. He just gives a perfect report on what's happening on the field."

Two days later, Barber phoned Campbell and gave him a critique of his performance.

"You know, the weather conditions were the same in both places, and the kid in Boston never made excuses," Barber told him. "Maybe you can take a lesson from the kid."

Campbell never again complained on the air about how the weather was affecting his job. Oh, he reported the conditions, he just didn't complain about them.

Donahue said Campbell's rapid-style broadcasting delivery and his endearing, perfectly timed inflections make him so unique.

"Bill," Donahue said, "is my hero. This isn't meant as a putdown to anybody in today's market, but there's only one Bill Campbell. Maybe because I grew up in the radio age and he left such an impression. I can still hear him now, '*Van Brocklin, looking, looking, LOOKING....*' He put the game in your mind with a vivid description. Nobody compares to him. You were listening to him, but you could see what he was talking about. '*Sideline left, openfield to the right.*' They were his words and I feel guilty for using them on Temple games now, but it's a vivid description of where the ball is being snapped and how much room they have on each side.

"I still remember so many of his calls. I'll never forget the championship game. '*Bednarik....he's not going to let Taylor get up!*' When you listened to Bill, it was like watching television because he was so descriptive. And when he did baseball, he made everything exciting. A routine ground ball seemed like a home run because he put so much excitement into it."

"When you think of Bill Campbell, you think of Philadelphia sports," longtime Phillies public relations executive Larry Shenk said. "Bill was never an offensive person; he was opinionated, but he didn't rub people the wrong way; he just took people for who they were."

When Shenk was attending high school in Myerstown, Pennsylvania, in the mid 1950s, he wrote Campbell a letter, asking him about the business. "I wanted to be a broadcaster," Shenk said, "and I asked him for advice. He wrote me a letter and said, 'Broadcasters have to do a lot of reading, so make sure you read.' "

———

Maybe the best way to understand Bill Campbell, the broadcaster, is to understand Bill Campbell, the man.

"He's not a gossiper," said his sister, Julie. "He looks for the good in people."

Sometimes, he has to search hard. But he finds it. That attitude has permeated his broadcasts and made him a lovable figure. It is a characteristic that can be traced to Bill's early days, when a priest shared a poem with him. The words had a profound effect.

Campbell keeps a worn-out copy of the poem — "The Man in the Glass" — in his wallet, and he uses it during most of his public-speaking appearances.

In March of 2006, shortly before he performed his annual solo of "When Irish Eyes Are Smiling" at a St. Patrick's Day party at the Tavistock Country Club, Bill recited the poem at a Rotary Club speech in Ardmore, Pennsylvania. Campbell made the appearance as a favor to his friend and former coworker, Herb Clarke, an Ardmore Rotary Club member who was the longtime weatherman on Channel 10.

Campbell also used parts of the poem to make a point in his KYW commentary that dealt with former Flyer Rick Tocchet's alleged gambling. On the air, Campbell said he thinks of the poem "whenever I read about some alleged misconduct or violation committed by one of our modern athletes."

There are many variations of the poem, written by Dale Wimbrow in 1934 and also known as "The Guy in The Glass." This is the version Campbell carries:

When you get what you want in your struggle for gain,
And the world makes you king for a day,
Just go to the mirror and look at yourself:
And see what the man has to say.

It isn't your father or mother or wife,
Whose judgment upon you must pass.
The one whose verdict counts most in your life:
Is the one staring back in the glass.

He's the one you must satisfy beyond all the rest,
For he's with you right up to the end...
And you have passed your most difficult test:
If the man in the glass is your friend.

You may be the one who got a good break
Then think you're a wonderful guy.
But the man in the glass says you're only a fake:
If you can't look him straight in the eye.

You may fool the whole world down the pathway of years...
And get pats on the back as you pass.
But your final reward will be heartaches and tears:
If you've cheated the Man in the Glass!

The poem, Campbell said, is how he has tried to live his life, and it helps explain his grounded perspective.

"I like to use it at communion breakfasts and banquets that I do," he said, "because it seems to register with people."

It registers with people just like Campbell: the guy with the reddened cheeks who is constantly being approached by fans who want his slant on Philadelphia sports, the silver-haired guy who instantly comes to mind whenever you hear the words "Oh, baby!" and "un-be-lieeeevable," the guy whose gravelly, excited voice is tattooed to a lot of our souls.

FINAL WORD

I read recently that Mike Wallace retired from "60 Minutes" at the age of 88. Which means that I only have 5 1/2 years to finish my act. Did anyone ever write a book about Mike Wallace? Someone should have. He had a much more varied and distinguished career than me — and on a national stage.

So, how come this book? My wife, daughter, and some friends are somewhat responsible. They have listened to most of my stories so often that they thought they belonged in print. Even my grandchildren thought so. They have experienced some of the events and have known some of the characters involved. And to my surprise, at least five professional writers volunteered their services.

The guy I picked is a gem. Actually, we hardly knew each other before this undertaking. Now we are almost pen pals. Every time my phone rings, I think it's Sam. He has taken on this project with a zeal and dedication that I shall always remember. And I am in his debt.

If this book manages to attract your interest or curiosity to any degree, all credit should go to Sam Carchidi. He works fulltime for *The Philadelphia Inquirer* and how he manages his hours I really do not want to know. But he and his family have my everlasting gratitude.

— *Bill Campbell*

This heartfelt project could not have been done without assistance from numerous people. Foremost, I'd like to thank my wife, JoAnn, who, as my unofficial editor-in-chief, gave this book guidance and direction, and somehow kept things running smoothly in our household while I was locked away in my office.

This project would not have been possible, of course, without Bill Campbell and his wonderful family: his wife, Jo, and his daughter, Chris. I want to sincerely thank them for allowing me to tell this inspiring story. Jo, you were a delight. And to think all I needed to get you talking about Bill was to bring my father-in-law's homegrown tomatoes! Chris, you have your father's gift for storytelling — and I feel so privileged that our paths crossed.

Bill, thanks for your patience and friendship — and for having an impeccable memory. You never ran out of stories and I feel badly that some of your tales didn't make it into print, simply because we ran out of room. Maybe we can use them in the sequel!

To Ray Didinger, a man who exudes class, thank you for writing your moving Foreward. Your words sing.

There are dozens of others who deserve thanks. I just hope that I don't inadvertently omit someone.

To Bill's sister, Julie Rooney, you are a remarkable and courageous woman and I thank you for your help.

To KYW's Bill Roswell, you are the best. Roswell unselfishly donated his time to put together the CD that includes some of Bill Campbell's most famous radio broadcasts. When you talk about the most professional people in the broadcasting business, Roswell is near the top of the list.

Also, a thank you to Bill's KYW coworkers Harry Donahue and Steve Butler, along with former KYW employees Mark Helms and Roy Shapiro.

A heartfelt "thank you" to former pro athletes Dick Allen, Johnny Callison, and Angelo Musi, and to those who work for some of the professional teams' varied offices, including club chairman Bill Giles, Larry Shenk, Marc Sigismondo, Dan Baker, Fred McKie, and Rob Brooks of the Phillies; Derek Boyko with the Eagles; and Harvey Pollack and Patti Butler with the 76ers.

To impressionist Joe Conklin of WPEN, you were, to borrow a Campbellism, UNBELIEVABLE. And a special thanks for spreading Bill's voice to another generation of listeners.

To Phillies broadcaster Harry Kalas, your graciousness will always be remembered. You are a Hall of Famer in more ways than one.

A "thank you" to numerous media types, especially WIP's Angelo Cataldi. I won't hold it against you, Ang, that you think Soupy is a lousy singer.

Two members of the University of Pennsylvania's sports-information department, Heather Palmer and Tim Flynn, were extremely helpful, as was Mark Lloyd, director of the university's archives.

A special thanks to Tom Brookshier — who, like Bill Campbell, is a Philadelphia icon — and to Dean O'Keefe of the Naismith Memorial Basketball Hall of Fame. I'd also like to thank Herbie Ashburn, Richard Ashburn, Karen Ashburn, Tom Lamaine, Art Camiolo, Mike Craven, Joe Weachter, Jim Gallagher, Merrill Reese, Jayson Stark, Frank Fitzpatrick, Bill Lyon, Stan Hochman, Jack Scheuer, Anthony Gargano, Harry Gamble, Steve Mix, Monsignor William Brennan, Dr. Boris Libster, Frank Riepl, Tom Dowd Jr., Joe Dowd Sr., Joe Dowd Jr., Freddy Massa, Rich Wescott, Larry Litwin, Jackie Miller, John Musciano, Kevin Brown, Dave Gross, Glenn Coates, Frank Catania, Steve McHugh, Tony Graham, Ed Grant, Tom Williams, and my bosses at *The Philadelphia Inquirer*. In one way or another, you all contributed to this book.

I am indebted to the folks at Middle Atlantic Press — Pat Koen, Barry Koen, Blake Koen, and Jim DiMiero — for their belief in this project.

And, last but not least, thanks to my parents for buying me a transistor radio when I was eight years old and helping me discover Bill Campbell.

— *Sam Carchidi*

PHOTO CREDITS

Page 18 . . . . .Photo courtesy of Bill Campbell.

Page 21 . . . . .Photo courtesy of Bill Campbell.

Page 28 . . . . .Photo courtesy of Bill Campbell.

Page 39 . . . . .Photo courtesy of Bill Campbell

Page 41 . . . . .Photo courtesy of Bill Campbell

Page 48 . . . . .Photo courtesy of Bill Campbell.

Page 52 . . . . .Photo courtesy of Bill Campbell.

Page 69 . . . . .Photo courtesy of the Associated Press.

Page 75 . . . . .Photo courtesy of the *Philadelphia Inquirer.*

Page 92 . . . . .Photo courtesy of Bill Campbell.

Page 94 . . . . .Photo courtesy of the *Philadelphia Inquirer.*

Page 105 . . . . .Photo courtesy of Bill Campbell.

Page 111 . . . . .Photo courtesy of Bill Campbell

Page 113 . . . . .Photo courtesy of Julie Campbell.

Page 116 . . . . .Photo courtesy of Bill Campbell.

Page 118 . . . . .Photo courtesy of the *Philadelphia Inquirer.*

Page 126 . . . . .Photo courtesy of Sam Carchidi.

Page 132 . . . . .Photo courtesy of Bill Campbell.

Page 146 . . . . .Photo courtesy of the Bill Campbell.

Page 157 . . . . .Photo courtesy of Bill Campbell.

Page 161 . . . . .Photo courtesy of Sam Carchidi.

Page 173 . . . . .Photo courtesy of Sam Carchidi.

Page 180 . . . . .Photo courtesy of the *Philadelphia Inquirer.*

Page 185 . . . . .Photo courtesy of Bill Campbell.

Page 193 . . . . .Photo courtesy of the Bill Campbell.

Page 196 . . . . .Photo courtesy of Bill Campbell.

Page 213 . . . . .Photo courtesy of Sam Carchidi.

Page 230 . . . . .Photo courtesy of Bill Campbell.

Page 233 . . . . .Photo courtesy of Bill Campbell.

Page 247 . . . . .Photo courtesy of Bill Campbell

AUDIO CREDITS

Special thanks to the following for allowing us to use their audio on the CD:

610 WIP

1210 WPHT

KYW 1060

The Philadelphia Phillies

The Philadelphia Eagles

NFL Films